THE OTHER FIRST WORLD WAR

ALSO BY DOUGLAS BOYD

HISTORIES

April Queen, Eleanor of Aquitaine
Voices from the Dark Years
The French Foreign Legion
The Kremlin Conspiracy
Blood in the Snow, Blood on the Grass
De Gaulle: The Man Who Defied Six US Presidents
Normandy in the Time of Darkness
Lionheart: The True Story of England's Crusader King

NOVELS

The Eagle and the Snake
The Honour and the Glory
The Truth and the Lies
The Virgin and the Fool
The Fiddler and the Ferret

THE OTHER FIRST WORLD WAR

THE BLOOD-SOAKED RUSSIAN FRONTS 1914–1922

DOUGLAS BOYD

First published 2014
by Spellmount, an imprint of

The History Press
The Mill, Brimscombe Port
Stroud, Gloucestershire, GL5 2QG
www.thehistorypress.co.uk

British Library Cataloguing in Publication Data.
A catalogue record for this book is available from the British Library.

ISBN 978 0 7524 9358 9

Typesetting and origination by The History Press
Printed in Great Britain

CONTENTS

ABBREVIATIONS

BSF	British Salonika Force
CP	Central Powers, German and Austro-Hungarian empires 1914–18
CSEF	Canadian Siberian Expeditionary Force
HID	Hungarian Reserve or Honved Infantry Divisions
IVF	*Imperatorskii Voyenno-Vozdushny Flot* – Imperial Russian Air Force
NKVD	People's Commissariat for Internal Affairs – Soviet law enforcement agency
OHL	*Oberste Heeresleitung* – German High Command
OAK	*Oberarmeekomando* – OHL counterpart in Vienna

INTRODUCTION

At the height of the Cold War 18-year-old men in Britain had to do two years' obligatory military service. My first year in RAF uniform was spent at Joint Services School for Linguists (JSSL), an extraordinary institution run by the three armed services but staffed by civilian instructors who turned out three 'intakes' a year of linguist/technicians capable of real-time eavesdropping on radio transmissions of Soviet ground, air and naval forces. In those pre-satellite days, the theory was that analysis at Government Communications Headquarters (GCHQ) of our handwritten logs would ensure NATO was prepared for any Warsaw pact invasion. Happily, it was never put to the test.

Our instructors at JSSL included a Red Army general, a Czech officer who had flown in the RAF during World War Two, an Estonian divorce lawyer, a Russian prince who became an Orthodox monk, a few rather nutty Russian ladies and Poles, Ukrainians and Balts – many of whom had survived terrible experiences during and after the October Revolution, the purges that followed, the Second World War and the Cold War. The ten months spent in daily contact with them taught us much more than just a language. Some students fell in love with Russian literature; others with the language; in me it inspired a fascination with Russian history, especially the bloody conflict between the Russian Empire and the Central Powers in Eastern Europe 1914–1918.

In contrast with the well-documented hostilities on the Western Front, this *other* First World War has been largely a mystery to the English-speaking public. Place names like Passchendaele, Ypres and Vimy Ridge were tragically well known to the general public after the Great War, as it was called, yet it would be hard for a Westerner to point on a map to Durrës, Przemyśl, Strij or Dvinsk, although names of some sites of appalling atrocity like Kosovo have sadly become familiar, and for the same reasons, much more recently. Researching sources in the combatant countries can be frustrating because even Russian military historians refer to this conflict as *zabytaya voyna* – the forgotten war. It is, for them, overshadowed by the Revolution that ended it and the bitter civil war that cost millions more lives immediately afterwards, followed by the famines of collectivisation that killed yet further millions and the Stalinist purges and the deaths of 30 million Soviet citizens in the Second World War.[1]

The conflict along the frontiers between the Russian Empire and the Central Powers – the German and Austro-Hungarian empires – was called by Westerners 'the eastern front'. For those millions who fought and died there, it was a war bitterly contested on three main fronts stretching for a thousand miles and named from the perspective of St Petersburg/Petrograd, the 'northern front', the 'western front' and the 'south-western front'. For clarity in this book, these names will be used for the Russian fronts and the hostilities in Western Europe will be called the 'Western Front'.

The conflicting priorities of the Russian army commanders seemed sometimes devoid of any common strategy. As far as the Western Allies were concerned, the role of Russia was to drain manpower away from the enemy forces on the Western Front at critical moments when the full force of the German armies might have broken through the Allied lines or blocked a new offensive.

Understanding of the Russian war is made difficult because many place names have changed and borders shifted: Lemberg in Austrian Galicia became Ukrainian Lviv, then Polish Lwów and is again Lviv in Ukraine; Memel, then in East Prussia, is now Klaipeda in Lithuania, and so on. But what's in a name? as Shakespeare asked. Nearly 9 million men marched off to fight 'for King and Country' in the First World War, and one in ten paid with his life, yet Britain's reigning monarch King George V bore the very German family name of Saxe-Coburg und Gotha until 25 April 1917, when it was thought more politic to change it to the very British 'House of Windsor'. For the same reasons his relatives the Battenburgs likewise changed their German name by translating it literally into English as Mountbatten.

The 'official' war in Eastern Europe ended eight months earlier than in the West after Berlin resorted to what is now called 'a deniable dirty trick', smuggling Vladimir I. Ulyanov, aka Lenin, out of neutral Switzerland and back to Russia, resulting in his country's premature exit from the war under the Treaty of Brest-Litovsk, signed on 3 March 1918. That allowed the Central Powers rapidly to move twenty-three divisions to the Western Front, to serve there in the final months of the war. It was a brilliant gamble that might have cost the Allies victory, had not sufficient American men and materiel arrived in Europe in the nick of time.

After the war in Europe, Britain and France slowly re-built themselves – although France was never the same country again – and the US was virtually unaffected. In the east, the war destroyed all four principal belligerents – the German, Austro-Hungarian, Ottoman and Russian empires – altering the course of world history. By the time of Brest-Litovsk, an estimated 3.7 million Russian soldiers lay dead beneath the battlefields and 3.9 million more were held as prisoners of war, in addition to all the wounded and with at least another million civilians also killed. The shattered empire of Tsar Nicholas II was reduced to anarchy, famine and a civil war where every weapon including massacre, torture and poison gas was used against combatants and civilians alike.

The Western Allies despatched expeditionary forces to Murmansk/Archangel, the Baltic, Ukraine, the Caspian Sea and Siberia. Thousands of UK troops, US servicemen, Canadians, French, Belgian and Japanese personnel were there tasked initially with safeguarding the vast accumulation of Allied materiel intended for the Imperial Russian war effort. After the Revolution they found themselves fighting Soviet forces for four years alongside some very dubious local allies.

During those years, what had been the Russian Empire was reduced to a closed world of terror where no one was safe, nothing worked, and only half the necessary minimum of food was produced for the starving population. The Finns, Poles, Ukrainians and the Baltic states took up arms to win independence from Russia. In Ukraine and Siberia, Churchill's interventionist force, the Czechs and Slovaks who had banded together in the Czech Legion and three separate White armies joined in a 'rainbow of death' with the Tambov Blue Army, the Polish Blue Army, the Ukrainian Green Army and the anarchist Black Army of anarchists fighting the Reds. The sequences in the film *Doctor Zhivago* showing armoured trains thundering along the Trans-Siberian railway, spreading death and destruction for thousands of miles across Central Asia, give some impression of the geographical extent of the terror.

Every war has its lunatic episodes. Unaware how little time he and his family had left to live, Tsar Nicholas II spent his days after replacing his uncle Nikolai as supreme commander of the Russian armies in visiting churches, kissing icons and honing his skill at the game of dominoes. His consort the Tsarina – like him a grandchild of Queen Victoria – was hated by the Russian people because she was German, and was known to be more grief-stricken over the assassination of her 'mad monk' Grigorii Rasputin than the suffering of the millions at the front, where her loyalties were never certain. Asked one day by a courtier why he looked miserable, the young *tsarevich* Alexei replied, 'When the Germans are beaten, Mama cries. When the Russians are beaten, Papa cries. When should I cry?'[2]

NOTES

1. Professor I.V. Narskii of Chelyabinsk State University on http://regiment/ ru./Lib/C/130.htm.
2. R.H. Lockhart *Memoirs of a British Agent* London, Putnam 1934, p. 104.

PART 1

SERBIA AND MACEDONIA

1

FIRST SHOTS

A good day to start weeping would have been 28 June 1914, in Sarajevo, the administrative capital of the province of Bosnia-Herzegovina, annexed by Austro-Hungary only five years earlier.[1] The *scheduled* big event of the day was the planned visit to the city of Archduke Franz Ferdinand of Austro-Hungary, accompanied by his wife, Countess Sophie Chotek von Chotkova und Wognin. Ironically, the archduke had been against the annexation of the province in view of the precarious domestic situation of the dual monarchy.[2]

A strange series of events was to relegate the actual visit to the sidelines – and that's where the weeping began.

Franz Ferdinand was paying a courtesy visit to the town because he had been nearby observing the annual manoeuvres of the imperial army in his capacity as *Generalinspekteur der gesamten bewaffneten Macht* or Inspector-General of all Austro-Hungarian armed forces. A nephew of the 84-year-old Emperor Franz Joseph, Franz Ferdinand had inherited a vast fortune at the age of 12 and gone on to fame and prospective fortune after his cousin Crown Prince Rudolf of Austro-Hungary shot his mistress, Baroness Vetsera, before committing suicide in the imperial hunting lodge at Mayerling on the night of 29 January 1889. Emperor Franz Joseph then named Franz Ferdinand's father heir presumptive of the dual monarchy. When he, in turn, died of typhoid fever, that honour came to Franz Ferdinand, who was groomed to become emperor one day. Despite all that, he became known as 'the loneliest man in Vienna' because he had fallen passionately in love with Countess Sophie and refused to marry any of the available ladies of more suitably elevated rank at the court. Finally given permission to marry Sophie by the ageing and extremely reluctant emperor, the couple produced three children who were debarred from the succession as offspring of a morganatic marriage.

Allowing Sophie, promoted to the rank of duchess, to accompany him into Sarajevo was a small compensation for the fact that she was not allowed to appear beside her husband at the court in Vienna, or even to ride in the same carriage there, because her social status placed her below all the archduchesses. Since the visit to Sarajevo was not a court function, Franz Ferdinand could choose for once to be seen in public with his beloved wife at his side. It was a lethal gesture of affection, respect and consideration for her current pregnancy.

The royal couple arrived in Sarajevo by train. With the army on manoeuvres nearby, it would have been easy for the archduke to have detached sufficient troops to line the route of the six-car motorcade through the city but he decided it would be more diplomatic in this restless and predominantly Slav province of the empire not to antagonise the local population. He also made a point of having the canvas roof of his car put down so that the crowds waiting along the route could get a good view of him and Sophie. For similar reasoning, both decisions would be echoed in the run-up to the assassination of US President John F. Kennedy at Dealey Plaza in the hostile city of Dallas on 22 November 1963. The confusion in the news media immediately following these two assassinations was because the major news organisations of the day had sent no reporters or correspondents to cover either visit, despite the hostility to Kennedy of many powerful people in Dallas and the insensitivity of Franz Ferdinand visiting Sarajevo on the 525th anniversary of the Battle of Kosovo, in which the army of neighbouring Serbia was defeated by a Turkish army, ending Serbian independence for more than four centuries.

Yet, should anyone have been thinking seriously of the archduke's security on that day in June 1914? The answer is yes, because this was the heyday of assassins. In peaceful Britain, Queen Victoria survived no fewer than seven known attempts on her life. In 1861 Russia's Tsar Aleksandr II was killed in the fifth attempt on his life. The French president had been assassinated in 1894, two prime ministers of Bulgaria in 1895 and 1907, Emperor Franz Joseph's wife Elizabeth in 1898, the king of Italy in 1900 and King George I of Greece only fifteen months before the fateful day in Sarajevo. Even closer to Sarajevo, the king and queen of Serbia had been murdered in their bedroom by a clique of their own officers in 1903. They were shot several times, hacked at by sabres and an axe and the queen's partly dismembered body was tossed over the balcony into the garden below. It was altogether a messy double murder for a gang of professional soldiers.

The list of European royalty, politicians, high officers of state and other public figures who succumbed to assassination in those years is long. The preferred weapon was a hand-gun; the second choice, because less reliable although more dramatic, was an 'infernal machine' or what we should today call an improvised explosive device — in other words, a bomb, often home-made, thrown by hand in a public place.

There was another reason to be especially prudent that summer day, which was the first anniversary of the defeat of 1389 since the liberation of Kosovo in the Second Balkan War only one year previously. Nor was that the last Balkan war: in June 1914 Muslim Albania was invaded by Orthodox Bulgaria and its main port Durrës was besieged. A local Croatian notable had indeed warned Countess Sophie that an official visit on such a date invited trouble, but she had brushed off his warning because all the people she had previously met on her visit to Bosnia-Herzegovina had shown 'so much cordiality and unsimulated warmth'.[3]

Shortly after ten o'clock on that warm, sunny morning, to the plaudits of the crowds, the motorcade was slowly proceeding along the embankment of the River Miljacka, known as the Appel Quay, towards Sarajevo's city hall. On their left were the warrens of the bazaar, unchanged since the Middle Ages, and where the imperial couple had strolled as tourists a few days before, unmolested by anyone. From the hillsides above Sarajevo, villas set in gardens and orchards looked down on the scene: a peaceful town whose European architecture was repeatedly interrupted by the minarets of mosques, a reminder that this had until recently been Ottoman territory. Indeed the mayor who greeted Franz Ferdinand at the station was Fehim Effendi Čurčić, still wearing a fez with his European suit.

The archduke and his wife were in the second car, a 1911 Gräf und Stift double phaeton luxury limousine owned by Lt Colonel Count Franz von Harrach, who was in the front passenger seat. At the wheel was Harrach's best driver, Leopold Lojka. Seated in the jump seat facing the imperial couple was General Oskar Potiorek, military governor of the province.

As the car drew level with the first of five Serbian terrorists spread out along the route, he lost his nerve and failed to throw his bomb. Each member of the team had a two-and-a-half pound bomb made in the Serbian state armoury in Kragojevac. Four of them also had a revolver from the same source and all were carrying poison, with which they were supposed to commit suicide, if captured.[4] A little further along the quay, a second terrorist named Nedjelko Čabrinović did throw his bomb at the car just opposite the main police station, but his timing was faulty and it bounced off the folded roof,[5] to explode beneath the following vehicle, injuring about a dozen passengers and bystanders, some seriously.

In the target car, the only damage was a small cut from a shard of metal on Sophie's cheek. The archduke was unharmed. Lojka attempted to accelerate away, only to stall the engine because the throttle was set to a sedate processional speed. Managing to re-start the motor, he continued with the remaining undamaged cars to the city hall, passing three other conspirators, none of whom took any action. They mingled with the now restive crowds, uncertain what to do next. Čabrinović swallowed his poison – which burned his throat but failed to kill him – and leapt over the balustrade, hoping to escape by swimming across the river. Owing to the summer drought, the water was only a few inches deep, so he landed on the river-bed 26ft below the balustrade and was quickly seized and bundled away by two civilians and two policemen, after being relieved of his automatic pistol.

On arrival at the town hall, the archduke greeted the mayor with: 'I come on a friendly visit and someone throws a bomb at me.' However, in the rigidly protocol-ridden society of the time, the reception passed with an exchange of polite addresses, after which Franz Ferdinand and Sophie left within the hour. The archduke decided, with nineteenth-century courtesy, to visit and console the injured victims of the explosion in the hospital, but his wife was understandably frightened that another attempt might be made on their lives. Her fears were pooh-poohed by General Potiorek. Asking with barely concealed sarcasm whether the royal couple thought the city was full of assassins, he got back into the car with them, to make his point that there was nothing to fear.

Lojka was not told of a last-minute change of route because protocol dictated that an adjutant should have given him the instructions. Unfortunately, the adjutant was lying injured in the hospital and no one thought to defy protocol by talking to the lowly chauffeur. So, halfway along the route, Lojka followed the car ahead, which had made a wrong turn. Potiorek yelled at him to stay on the main street, but it was too late. The car, having no reverse gear, had to be pushed back around the corner with the gear stick in neutral.[6]

By sheer coincidence, the third terrorist was eating a snack on the pavement just 5ft away from where the royal car was briefly immobilised. Dropping his food, 19-year-old Gavrilo Princip whipped out his Belgian-made Browning FN 7.65mm automatic pistol and fired two shots at point-blank range, hitting the pregnant Countess Sophie in the abdomen and wounding Franz Ferdinand in the neck, severing his jugular artery. The time was 11.15 a.m. The archduke's plumed hat fell off, scattering green ostrich plumes all over the rear of the car. Either Count Harrach or Potiorek seized the stricken man by his uniform collar to support him in his seat. Franz Ferdinand could hardly speak, although Harrach afterwards said he had murmured to Sophie that she must live for the sake of their children. On the car's arrival at the governor's house, thought to be safer than a hospital, she was found to be already dead. Her husband died shortly afterwards.[7]

As the car headed away from the scene of the attack, Princip attempted to commit suicide by swallowing his poison, but was arrested and hustled away by police, to save him from angry people who had seen the attack and wanted to lynch him. After a commendably correct trial in Sarajevo, the Austrian judge commented: 'The young assassin was under-sized, emaciated, sallow, sharp-featured. It was difficult to imagine that so frail-looking an individual could have committed such a serious crime.'[8] Princip was sentenced to twenty years' imprisonment, which was the maximum legal penalty for murder committed by a person less than 20 years' old. By 25 July 1914 all the other conspirators were also in custody, except one who escaped. Only one of the prisoners, aged 23, was hanged after trial because the youth of the others – all less than 20 years old – forbade their legal execution. Princip died of complications after amputation of an arm because of tuberculosis four years later in a hospital near his prison.

News of the assassinations spread rapidly in Sarajevo, leading to violent anti-Serb demonstrations that evening and the following day. Croats and Muslims looted Serb-owned shops and attacked Serbian schools, churches and newspaper offices. The violence rapidly spread to other parts of the Austro-Hungarian Empire.

Princip, Čabrinović and the others were not acting on their own initiative. They were members of a team of six terrorists handpicked by Colonel Dragutin Dimitrijević, head of Serbian military intelligence, who was also the leader of the terrorist organisation *Ujedinjenje ili Smrt* – meaning Union or Death. Under the *nom de guerre* of the Black Hand, this undercover organisation whose founders had conspired with the officers who murdered the king and queen of Serbia in 1903, was formed in 1911 and dedicated to uniting all Serbian-speaking people of the Balkans by violent means in a Greater Serbia. Black Hand recruits were inducted in a ceremony copied from the Freemasons, held in a dark room before a mysterious hooded figure, where they swore an oath of absolute obedience on pain of death:

> I swear by the sun that warms me, the earth that nourishes me, before God, by the blood of my ancestors, on my honour and on my life, that I will execute all missions and commands without question and take the secrets of this organisation to the grave with me. May God and my comrades in this organisation be my judges if, knowingly or not, I should ever violate this oath.[9]

By 1914 the Black Hand had several thousand adherents, all male, young and living in Serbia, Bosnia-Herzegovina, Macedonia and Bulgaria. It ran courses in firearms, explosives, sabotage and espionage. Although a 'secret organisation', its existence was common knowledge in the gossipy café society of Belgrade, where many army officers were recruited into its ranks. Serbian frontier guards included many sympathisers, which made travel into and out of the country easy for the members on clandestine missions. It was a sergeant in the frontier troops who smuggled across the frontier a suitcase containing the bombs and firearms used in the Sarajevo assassinations.[10] In the province of Bosnia-Herzegovina a number of separate underground societies grouped under the banner of *Mlada Bosna* – young Bosnia – associated themselves with the Black Hand.[11]

When Serbian Prime Minister Nikola Pašić had first learned that this terrorist organisation was plotting to assassinate Franz Ferdinand in Sarajevo, he did try to warn the imperial government in Vienna through Austro-Hungarian Finance Minister Leon Bilínski on 21 June, because Bilínski was responsible for the administration of Bosnia-Herzegovina. Yet, the warning was couched in language so diplomatic and circumlocutory that it was not acted upon.[12] Never has diplomatic ambiguity led to greater loss of life.

News of the double murder reached newsrooms in London – then usually quiet at midday on a Sunday – a couple of hours later in a telegraph message from Reuters news agency:

> Two shots. Sarajevo, Sunday. As the archduke Francis Ferdinand and his wife the Countess of Hohenberg [*sic*] were driving through the streets here today a young man, stated to be a student, fired two revolver shots at their motor car. Both were mortally wounded and died from their injuries within a few minutes.[13]

The news must also have reached newspaper offices in Vienna from Reuters at the same time, but the job of passing it on to the elderly Emperor Franz Joseph was long delayed because the strict etiquette of his court dictated that only certain people could speak to certain other people, who could speak to someone who could address the emperor, and not all the links in this chain of protocol were immediately available on a Sunday afternoon.

On 3 July at an official requiem mass for the victims in Belgrade, Prime Minister Pašić assured the Austrian minister that his government would 'treat the matter as if it concerned one of our own rulers'. As historian Christopher Clark comments: 'The words were doubtless well meant, but in a country with such a vibrant and recent history of regicide, they were bound to strike (the Austrian diplomat) as tasteless, if not macabre.'[14]

Two days later, on Sunday 5 July an official of the Austrian Foreign Office was assured by Kaiser Wilhelm II in Berlin that Germany would support Austria in dealing with Serbia, even if it led to war. Wilhelm was in the habit of uttering unwise remarks and making snap judgements that were the despair of diplomats. In a celebrated interview during his 1909 holiday on the Isle of Wight, reported by his host Sir Montague Stuart-Wortley, he had used the phrase, 'You English are as mad, mad, mad as March hares,' which hardly increased his popularity in Britain. Yet, his off-the-cuff undertaking to Austria must be his most regrettable and unstatesmanlike assertion.

A sense of unease pervaded those in the know in Vienna. On 15 July *The Times* printed a report from its correspondent in Vienna which gave the first hint to the British public that the assassinations were to have serious repercussions:

> A feeling of uncertainty which is affecting the public, is affecting the Vienna Bourse most adversely. Very heavy falls of prices were noted all round yesterday and, although during the early part of today a recovery took place, it is apprehended that it will not prove lasting.[15]

One week later, the *Times* correspondent in Vienna was reporting:

> There is a general feeling today that the end of the period of uncertainty as to what Austria-Hungary will officially demand of Serbia is approaching, if not impending.

Yet the *Manchester Guardian*'s correspondent was calm:

> Vienna is notoriously the most jumpy capital in Europe, and the talk about war between Austria and Serbia is surely not to be taken seriously.

He was wrong. An *Observer* leader told a different story:

> Experienced critics of foreign affairs have long been convinced that the Great War, if it ever came at all, would come with utter unexpectedness. Suddenly, in the Near East, a cloud that seemed no bigger than a man's hand threatens the blackness of tempest that overwhelms nations.

The British government was seemingly not yet worried that yet another assassination in the Tumultuous Balkans would embroil it. Yet *The Times* was one step ahead:

> War fever in Vienna. French pessimism. Germany the key to the situation. British naval manoeuvres. Orders to First and Second Fleet.[16]

On the reasonable assumption that the principal assassins had been recruited and trained for their mission in Belgrade, the Austro-Hungarian Foreign Minister drafted a harsh ultimatum to Serbia, relying on the assurance of the Auswärtiges Amt, or German Foreign Ministry, that it would prevent Russia from stepping in to protect its Serbian ally, should the argument escalate. The possibility of escalation was clearly considered because, although the terms of the ultimatum were approved internally on 19 July, it was not delivered in Belgrade until the evening of 23 July, nearly four weeks after the assassinations.[17] The day was deliberately chosen because the French president and prime minister were travelling home from an official visit to Russia and thus in no position to concert any immediate reaction with the Tsar's government in St Petersburg under the Franco-Russian mutual defence pact.[18]

Kaiser Wilhelm II was a grandson of Queen Victoria and cousin of Tsar Nicholas II, as was Britain's King George V. His complicated attitude to his British cousin was epitomised by his publicly expressed hurt that the British people did not love him, yet a number of paintings of great British victories at sea decorated his royal yacht, aboard which he departed for his habitual *Nordreise* – a summer cruise of the Norwegian fjords with a clique of all-male friends, none of whom displayed any great alarm at the turn events were taking.

There was a treaty dating from 1879 between Berlin and Vienna, under which each partner undertook to support the other in the event it was attacked by Russia. Yet, Austro-Hungary had not been attacked, so the Kaiser instructed his Foreign Office to inform Vienna that the double assassination possibly merited a temporary occupation of the Serbian capital Belgrade, but not a full-blown war. Unfortunately, Germany's Acting Foreign Minister Arthur Zimmermann[19] had already encouraged Emperor Franz Joseph in Vienna to avenge the death of his adopted heir with a declaration of war on Serbia.

In a gesture of pan-Slav solidarity for 'poor little Serbia', on 24 July Tsar Nicholas II initiated the 'Period preparatory to War' – so-called in the hope that Vienna and Berlin would not consider it a mobilisation as such. Repairs were put in hand on the inadequate railways in the west of the country; reservists were recalled; troops on manoeuvres hurried back to base; the garrisons of all fortresses in the Warsaw, Vilnius and St Petersburg military districts were put on a war footing; all leave was cancelled; millions of horses were re-shod; the imperial navy recalled all ships to harbour, there to be manned and provisioned for combat; potential enemy aliens were arrested; the Imperial Russian Air Force – which was the second largest in Europe, after France – was ordered to the west.[20] The list was endless and its meaning clear, not least in Berlin where, on 29 July the government warned St Petersburg that continuing mobilisation of Russian forces, under whatever title, would lead to German mobilisation.

Having Russia on-side, Belgrade replied to the Austrian ultimatum the following day, accepting all but two of the conditions but refusing to dismiss any allegedly compromised officials before further investigation and also withholding permission for Austro-Hungarian officials to conduct their own investigation in Serbia. Although Pašić did offer to submit these two issues to international arbitration, in the absence of an unconditional acceptance of the ultimatum Austro-Hungary promptly severed diplomatic relations. Franz Joseph signed a declaration of war in the morning of 28 July and a partial mobilisation of armed forces took place. In Belgrade those foreign residents still present made hasty plans to leave, as did many well-to-do families with second homes in the country or relatives who could accommodate them further away from the frontier. That they were right to do so was demonstrated that very day when two Serbian steamships carrying military materiel on the Danube were boarded by Austrian troops and seized as prizes. Serbian engineers blew up bridges to impede an invasion. On the following day, Austro-Hungarian artillery bombarded the Serbian capital.[21]

In the Balkan wars of 1912 and 1913, Serbia nearly doubled its size, acquiring territory by force of arms from its Ottoman-governed neighbours. Mass rapes and massacres of non-Serbs in the annexed territory were witnessed by Greek, Turkish, Bulgarian and Albanian diplomats as well as French and British consulate staff.[22] Yet Britain and France had managed to restrain Tsar Nicholas II from getting involved in those wars and Germany had similarly restrained Austro-Hungary. The Kaiser had therefore been hoping to keep this new dispute on the level of a yet another local Balkan conflict. He was certain that Serbia would back down, that Britain would refuse to get involved and that France and Russia did not want war.[23] Yet he now found himself trapped by the mutual defence treaty with Vienna into authorising a 24-hour ultimatum on 31 July, requiring the Russians to stand down their forces on the border and cease mobilisation. At the same time, an 18-hour ultimatum was sent to the French Foreign Office at the Quai d'Orsay in Paris, demanding an undertaking that France would remain neutral in the event of war between Russia and Germany. On the same day, Austro-Hungarian Commander-in-Chief Count Franz Conrad von Hötzendorf had cold feet at the way things were getting out of control after receiving messages from the Kaiser, German Chancellor Bethmann-Hollweg and Foreign Minister von Jagow and urging Vienna not to waste, by invading Serbia at this juncture, forces that would be needed in the coming war with Russia.

In all this chaos of preparation for war, most of the British media remained calm. The *Manchester Guardian* declared that its readers cared nothing for the problems of Belgrade. The *Daily News* saw no reason why British lives should be lost in a quarrel that was none of our business, as did the *Yorkshire Post*. *The Times* alone argued in favour of intervention. The British Foreign Secretary Sir Edward Grey – a man who preferred bird-watching and hill-walking to the cares of the high post he occupied – voiced his opinion that the French government was allowing itself to be drawn into a Balkan war, which Britain had always avoided, and would continue to do so.

Neither ultimatum evoking a reply within the time limits, on 1 August Germany ordered general mobilisation and declared war against Russia, prompting France, in turn, to order a general mobilisation.

On 3 August Germany declared war on France, having demanded the right to move troops across neutral Belgium, to whose defence Britain was committed. That night German forces crossed the Belgian frontier, prompting Sir Edward Grey to say: 'One by one, the lamps are going out all over Europe.' On 4 August Britain declared war. On the following day, German troops entered Luxembourg. A flurry of last-minute diplomatic moves attempted to prevent the escalation but by 12 August – less than seven weeks after the assassinations in Sarajevo – Europe was divided into two armed camps. The Western Allies – Britain, Belgium, France – with Russia, Serbia and Montenegro were able to call on about 9.5 million men against 8 million men in the armies of the German and Austro-Hungarian empires.[24] As far as artillery was concerned, there was rough parity at 8,000 guns each. However, although Russian guns were not inferior, calibre for calibre, the tsarist armies had a significant insufficiency of shell at the outset of the war.

On the other side, the Triple Alliance of 1882, confirmed as recently as 1912, made Italy a treaty partner of Germany and Austro-Hungary although the country was a signatory also to conflicting treaties with France and Russia, in part because it viewed Vienna's activities in the Balkans as hostile. On 2 August 1914 the Italian prime minister announced that his country would remain neutral, since neither of the two other partners in the Alliance had been attacked by Russia or France. Italy took the next step eight months later at an unheralded meeting in London on 26 April 1915. In return for an immediate loan of £50 million and on the understanding that Britain would support Italian annexation of Austro-Hungarian territory after the end of the war, representatives of the Italian government undertook to declare for the Allies. The following month saw General Luigi Cadorna's armies launching massive attacks on Austro-Hungary that cost 60,000 casualties in the first two weeks. By the end of the year Italian casualties had risen to 300,000 men. In the meantime, on 2 September 1914 Russia's old enemy Turkey had declared for the Central Powers in the hope of recovering territory lost to Russia in nineteenth-century wars. By then, the German navy was blockading the Baltic, hemming in the Russian Baltic Fleet and capturing the Aland Islands. In the Black Sea that November German and Turkish warships shelled Russian ports, including Odessa and the important naval base at Sevastopol. Although one fairly large-scale naval battle took place off Sevastopol, the main purpose of the German and Turkish warships was to interdict Russian imports of war materiel and food by this southern route. Casualties included a British steamer sunk near Odessa by a German submarine in August 1915.

It has been said and written that the two shots fired by Princip were the first shots of the First World War, but history is never so simple. If indeed they were the spark that ignited the powder keg – a metaphor that is often used – why was it primed and ready to blow?

Throughout the nineteenth century the major Continental powers expanded economically thanks to new technology and also geographically by, like Britain, grabbing colonies across the world. At the Congress of Berlin in 1878 the African continent was literally carved up by European statesmen drawing straight lines on a map, many of which defied linguistic and ethnic groupings, and still cause wars and loss of life today. The rapidly increasing tax base made possible by industrialisation also enabled the Continental powers to afford large standing armies which were equipped with recoilless artillery using the newly invented smokeless powder. More powerful than the old black powder, this propellant also enabled rifles to be fitted with magazines that speeded up the rate of fire and the muzzle velocity of smaller-calibre bullets. Water-cooled machine guns – of which the gas-operated Maxim and its derivatives were the most efficient – had revolutionised colonial wars, enabling a small crew tending one machine gun to kill hundreds of spear-wielding natives.

Since Britain and France had already entered into what was called the Entente Cordiale, the Franco-Russian pact turned this into a three-way power block known as the Triple Entente. Although increasingly powerful since unification under Bismarck and Kaiser Wilhelm II's programme of ship-building to create a navy large enough to challenge Britannia's rule of the waves, Germany saw itself as surrounded by hostile powers. Every school in the country had wall maps showing the Fatherland encircled by arrows representing enemy threats. Even the Baltic Sea was shown with arrows representing the British and Russian navies threatening death from seaward. For geographical and linguistic reasons, Germany formed its alliance with Austro-Hungary in 1879 despite political differences: the newly unified Germany was ultra-nationalistic and the rulers of the Austro-Hungarian Empire had good reason to fear that the nineteenth-century wave of nationalism contained the seeds of its destruction.

When France, still smarting from the loss of Alsace and Lorraine to Germany in 1871, allied itself with Russia, this meant that Germany would find itself conducting a war on two fronts, should it invade either neighbouring state. The German General Staff therefore adopted Count Alfred von Schlieffen's plan, which was to allocate about 90 per cent of its armies to invade France, leaving only 10 per cent initially to hold the Russian front. Although modified and arguably flawed by Schlieffen's successor General Helmuth von Moltke, the plan predicted France's defeat in six weeks, during which time Russia would slowly mobilise. After France's capitulation, sufficient divisions were to be rushed from the Western Front to nip off the Russian salient of eastern Poland. Crucial to this was the German railway network, which had expanded rapidly since unification of the Reich. Now that it was possible to move whole armies across vast distances many times faster than the pace of a marching man, a general could afford to take these new risks, but they were still risks.

As agreed at the Congress of Berlin, Bosnia-Herzegovina, which had previously been part of the Ottoman Empire, became an Austrian protectorate, although not an integral province of the Austro-Hungarian Empire. Its population consisted of a majority of Orthodox Serbs, with significant minorities of Roman Catholic Croats and Balkan Muslims, whose families had converted to Islam to curry favour with their overlords during the years of Ottoman domination. Austro-Hungary knew that Serbia, which had gained territory from the Ottoman Empire in the recent wars, also had designs on its new protectorate, inhabited by fellow Slavs. Landlocked Serbia wanted union with Montenegro,[25] which had its own sea coast but had long been separated from it by the Ottoman *sanjak* of Novi Bazar, a buffer zone created to frustrate Serbian expansion in this direction. The majority of Bosnians and Montenegrins spoke dialects of the Serbian language, so there were strong ethnic and linguistic links.

Serbia and neighbouring states in 1914.

From 1893 until his murder in 1903, King Alexander of Serbia trod what turned out to be a personally fatal path of compromise with the government in Vienna in the hope of not provoking Austria-Hungary into invading, while at the same time relying on the pan-Slav sympathies of tsarist Russia as the best insurance against such an invasion. After his assassination, no one in Belgrade dared to defy the Serbian extremists' claims to Bosnia-Herzegovina.

However, the chaos produced in Turkey by the Young Turks' revolt in 1908 against the autocratic rule of Sultan Abdul Hamid II left the Ottoman Empire unable to resist Austro-Hungary annexing Bosnia-Herzegovina into the empire as a fully integrated province on 6–7 October 1908. So, when the Ottomans lost their Balkan provinces in the wars of 1912 and 1913, Serbia, Montenegro and Bosnia-Herzegovina made an ethnic and linguistic bloc that was divided by political frontiers. When Vienna decided to hold the June 1914 manoeuvres near Sarajevo as a show of strength to pan-Serb extremists, this was taken by them as a challenge which led directly to the murders of Franz Ferdinand and Sophie on 28 June.

The above history-in-a-nutshell is a very simplified account of all the pressures in the region that culminated in the mobilisations of summer 1914.

NOTES

1. This was actually accomplished with Russian approval, in return for Vienna supporting Russian access to the Bosphorus.
2. C. Clark, *The Sleepwalkers: How Europe Went to War in 1914* (London: Allen Lane, 2012), p. 109.
3. Clark, p. 370, quoting V. Dedijer, *The Road to Sarajevo* (London: Simon & Schuster, 1967), p. 10.
4. Clark, p. 54.
5. Some accounts aver that Franz Ferdinand batted the bomb out of the way so that it fell behind his car.
6. Alternatively, if there was a reverse gear, the chauffeur stalled the car in engaging it.
7. There is an excellent animated reconstruction of the events on www.youtube.com googleable under *Film of Sarajevo Assassination*.
8. Clark, p. 381, quoting J. Remak, *Sarajevo* (New York: Criterion, 1957), pp. 194–6, 198.
9. Clark, p. 39 (abridged).
10. Ibid, p. 57.
11. Ibid, pp. 39–41.
12. Ibid, p. 60.
13. Newspaper quotations from John Simpson, *Unreliable Sources*, (Macmillan Digital Audio, 2010), disc 1.
14. Clark, p. 390.
15. Ibid.
16. Simpson, *Unreliable Sources*, disc 1 (abridged).
17. *Manchester Guardian* of 24 July 1914.
18. The Triple Entente was the product of the Franco-Russian alliance file://localhost/ebcid/com.britannica.oec2.identifier.IndexEntryContentIdentifier%3FidxStructId=172569&library=EBof 1894, the Anglo-French Entente Cordiale of file://localhost/ebcid/com.britannica.oec2.identifier.IndexEntryContentIdentifier%3FidxStructId=188822&library=EB1904 and an agreement between Britain and Russia in 1907.
19. Foreign Minister Gottlieb von Jagow was absent on honeymoon.
20. Clark, pp. 275, 478–9.
21. *Manchester Guardian* 29 July 1914.
22. Clark, pp. 44, 113.

23. Various sources quoted in Clark, p. 515.
24. Including reservists.
25. This is the old Venetian name, a direct translation of the Serbian *Crna Gora*, both meaning 'black mountain', and will be used in this book to avoid confusion.

2

POOR LITTLE SERBIA!

There are many more modern claimants to have originated the saying 'in war, the first casualty is truth', but it seems the honour must go to the Greek dramatist Aeschylus, who put the thought into words 2,500 years ago. One of the first things a government does after declaring war is to demonise the enemy and paint itself and its allies whiter than white, so the rallying cry among the Entente powers in 1914 was 'Poor Little Serbia', evoking the image of Germany and Austro-Hungary as big, bad bullies. Reinforcing that image, German-language newspapers in those countries carried a cartoon of a large mailed fist crushing the upstart neighbour, with the caption *Serbien muss sterbien* – a jolly play on words, meaning 'Serbia must die!'

The Serbian armies were so ill equipped that Austro-Hungary considered it could invade and occupy the whole country in less than four weeks. The timing was vital: that victory had to be achieved before Russia could transport reinforcements to Serbia and reach the front. It was also hoped in Vienna that diplomatic channels could be used to synchronise a Bulgarian attack on Serbia from the east with the Austro-Hungarian invasion from the north and west.

Vienna therefore made the July ultimatum deliberately unacceptable to Serbia. After Belgrade accepted eight of the ten demands, Austro-Hungary declared war in a telegram sent on 28 July 1914 and began bombarding Belgrade the following day by land-based artillery and monitors on the River Danube. At this stage, some 270,000 men in three out of the six Austro-Hungarian armies were stationed on the Serbian frontier under Plan B – for Balkan war – but 2nd Army was only available until the end of August, when it was due to disengage and be sent to the Russian front in Galicia under Plan R for Russland.[1]

The expression 'Austro-Hungarian armies' implies some degree of homogeneity, but they were drawn from a number of mutually antipathetic races; the late

Franz Ferdinand had often protested when Hungarian officers insisted on speaking incomprehensible Magyar among themselves in his presence. Many officers and the majority of 'other ranks' drawn from the eleven nationalities of the empire spoke neither German nor Hungarian, using no fewer than fifteen different mother tongues. This meant that, after the first wave of hostilities when junior officers had a high casualty rate, the command chain was to be complicated by many of their replacements having no common language with their troops. The majority of these newcomers in the officers' messes were university-educated middle-class German-speakers who mocked the accents, customs and cultures of Hungarian, Czech and other officers – and their own men.

As to the rank-and-file, wearing a variety of comic opera uniforms, soldiers of the vassal races included assorted Czechs, Slovaks, Croats, Poles, Italians and others more desirous of throwing off the Austro-Hungarian yoke than fighting for the dual monarchy, had they been given any choice. Many of them also had linguistic links with 'the enemy'. The Bosnian Serbs fighting in Austro-Hungarian uniforms spoke the same language as the Serbian troops confronting them and the Catholic Croatian soldiers, who were traditional enemies of the Orthodox Serbs for religious reasons, spoke a language very similar to Serbian and mutually intelligible with it.

With a population one-twelfth as large as that of the Austro-Hungarian Empire, the Serbs could muster some 450,000 soldiers upon full mobilisation, but roughly one in three had no weapon or even a proper uniform, which was seized upon by their Austro-Hungarian captors as justification for executing them as guerrillas, unprotected by the rules of war. Conventionally it was thought, all other things being equal, that an attacking force needed to be three times larger than the defenders, so it seemed at first that Serbia might be able to hold out, fighting as it was on familiar ground and 'for home and family'. However, one-third of the Serbian forces had to be deployed in the east of the country in case Bulgaria seized the chance to invade and re-occupy territory lost in the recent wars. The 1st, 2nd, 3rd and Užice armies, totalling around 180,000 men, were deployed in defensive positions near Belgrade, their capital which sat uncomfortably adjacent to the Croatian border. Fighting with them were Serbia's only initial allies – between 40,000 and 50,000 Montenegrin militia fighters.

Serbia did hold two trumps. Its officers and men had recent campaign experience in the Balkan wars, whereas the Austro-Hungarian officers up to general headquarters level lacked actual experience of combat. Conrad was hardly the warrior type, but a shy and reclusive man whose love-life was a masochistic relationship with a powerful married woman. Respected as a theoretician and teacher, he had never held a command under war conditions. Yet at the time of the annexation of Bosnia-Herzegovina he had stated that Serbia was a breeding ground of disaffection in the southern Slav areas of the empire, and argued publicly for a pre-emptive strike against Serbia no fewer than twenty-five times in 1913. It was all to no avail: Emperor Franz Joseph declared that he was a man of peace and refused to listen to this kind of talk.[2] Partly because of the emperor's pacifism and partly due to the permanent disarray that characterised Austro-Hungarian government, the empire spent on military preparations about half of what Russia, France or Germany did.[3]

Secondly, Serbia knew in detail the Austrian invasion plan, which had been betrayed by Colonel Alfred Redl. Having by drive and persistence risen from humble origins to become head of Austrian counter-intelligence, he had been blackmailed as a homosexual and bribed by Russian agents from 1903 to 1913 into feeding all Austria's military secrets, including its order of battle and mobilisation plans, to St Petersburg. The Russians, in turn, passed on to Belgrade anything that concerned it. He also betrayed his own agents to Russian counter-intelligence and discredited any Russian citizens offering to spy for Austro-Hungary. Due to a mix-up in the German and Austrian postal services, a letter containing money that was addressed to him under an alias in Vienna was opened. German counter-intelligence then informed Redl's own service, which staked out the main post office. When Redl appeared to claim his letter, he managed to escape, but was later arrested and left alone with a loaded revolver – the traditional way of allowing an officer to 'do the decent thing'. He did, committing suicide and depriving his former subordinates of any chance to interrogate him in detail.

Spying had traditionally been regarded as a dirty business, best left to the lower classes, who could be shot without compunction when caught, but the late nineteenth and early twentieth centuries were the age of the gentleman spy. Even more extraordinary than Redl's case was that of Wilhelm Stieber. Born in 1818 to a Lutheran pastor whose wife, Daisy Cromwell, came from the English nobility, Stieber refused to follow his father into the Church and was cut off without money after deciding to study law. This led to a career in the criminal police and eventually to setting up for unified Germany's first chancellor Otto von Bismarck a pan-German counter-espionage and military intelligence organisation. Yet, for fifteen years 1859–74 Stieber worked in Russia – Germany's traditional enemy – where he was instrumental in founding the Okhrana or tsarist secret police, charged with tracking down, among others, German spies.

Despite Austro-Hungary's Plan B invasion of Serbia being compromised by Redl, for a combination of geography and logistics they remained largely unchanged. The nominal commander-in-chief of all Serbian forces was Prince Regent Alexander, but Serbia's best military brain was Marshal Vojvoda Radomir Putnik, who was both elderly and in poor health. So much so that, on the fateful day when the declaration telegram arrived in Belgrade, he was receiving hospital treatment in Budapest. Briefly arrested as an enemy alien, he was freed and allowed to return home on the personal order of Conrad von Hötzendorf, although whether this was an act of nineteenth-century courtesy to a gallant opponent or to ensure that Serbian forces were commanded by a sick man, is unknown. In the event, Putnik did a good staff job, working from a hospital bed in Belgrade.

On 12 August 5th and 6th Austro-Hungarian armies commanded by General Potiorek crossed the Croatian border and moved into Serbian territory. Wanting a rapid victory as a birthday present for Emperor Franz Joseph, Potiorek attacked prematurely when only half his forces were in position in the hilly country of western Serbia, to fight what was known as the Battle of Mount Cir. Cir was actually a range of mountains dividing Potiorek's two armies, which needed to capture the fiercely defended crests in order to support each other. Back in Belgrade, Putnik had been expecting a more logical attack into the rolling plains of the north but, once he realised Potiorek's move was the main attack, he ordered Serbian 2nd Army to link up with the smaller 3rd Army to drive the invaders back across the border. After four days of combat, the Austro-Hungarians were forced to retreat. For such a small-scale and short campaign, casualties were relatively heavy: 18,500 for the Austro-Hungarians, plus 4,500 men taken prisoner, and 16,500 on the Serbian side. Even more unpleasantly, Austrian troops under General Lothar von Hortstein took civilian hostages in and around the town of Šabac, where as many as 4,000 of them were massacred according to reports that are difficult to verify.

First Austrian invasion of Serbia. Contemporary map with anglicised place-names, e.g. C Šabac is spelled Shabatz.

Under pressure from its allies, Serbia next sent its 1st Army into Syrmia – a county of the Croatian Vojvodina lying to the north-west of Belgrade – with the aim of delaying the movement of the Austro-Hungarian 2nd Army to the Galician front as planned. Meanwhile the Timok division of the Serbian 2nd Army conducted a diversionary attack. But the move was too late, the Timok division suffered a further 6,000 casualties and Potiorek seized the opportunity to re-invade western Serbia from Bosnia with his 5th and 6th armies on 7 September.

Despite fierce resistance by Serbian 2nd and 3rd armies, the Austro-Hungarian 5th Army gained a bridgehead on the Serbian bank of the River Drina. To counter this, Putnik brought his 1st Army back from Syrmia but, although initially successful, it rapidly became enmired in fighting for Mačkov Kamen mountain, where both sides suffered horrendous casualties in successive frontal attacks and counter-attacks. As on the Western Front, the two sides then settled into trench warfare, in which the Serbs were at a disadvantage, having no proper boots – but only *opanci* or woven leather peasant shoes, quite unsuitable for waterlogged trenches – because there was no factory in Serbia capable of mass-producing water-resistant army boots. More importantly, there was only one munitions factory in the country capable of producing artillery shells – at the rate of 100 per day – so the Serbian guns soon fell silent, while Austro-Hungarian logistics kept the invaders' artillery firing in this campaign. To compensate for this, Serbian sappers dug tunnels beneath the Austro-Hungarian trenches in a stretch of the line where only a few yards separated them, so that they were as close as on Vimy ridge in Flanders. Hearing enemy soldiers discussing an imminent infantry attack, the Serbians blew their mine just in time, gaining a brief respite.

However, superior equipment and logistics enabled the Austro-Hungarians to launch another massive attack on 5 November. This time, the Serbs withdrew in good order, but with no artillery cover, owing to the lack of shells for their guns. After 1st Army lost its commander from wounds, the new general defied Marshal Putnik by ordering a mass retreat to shorten the front, which meant abandoning Belgrade to the enemy, who entered the capital on 2 December. Potiorek then took the risk of moving his entire 5th Army into the Belgrade area, to wipe out the Serbian right flank, leaving 6th Army alone to hold the main Serbian force. If he had been lucky, as Napoleon called it, that could have ended the war with a Serbian surrender. It was perhaps unfortunate for Serbia that a consignment of long-promised artillery shells arrived from France at this critical juncture, enabling Marshal Putnik to gamble on a massive counter-attack which shattered the Austro-Hungarian 6th Army on 3 December. Wrongly positioned, 5th Army could give no assistance and also broke and ran when attacked by the 2nd and 3rd Serbian armies, causing Potiorek to order a general withdrawal across the Croatian border, which allowed Serbian forces to march triumphantly back into Belgrade on 15 December.

It was a return to the *status quo ante*, but after enormous casualties, which were to set the pattern for this theatre of the war. No accurate records exist, but Serbian killed, wounded and missing in action totalled about 170,000 men at this stage, against a figure of some 215,000 casualties and missing in action among the invading forces. Potiorek was sacked by Franz Joseph and replaced by Archduke Eugen of Austria, who attempted to rebuild his shattered armies while the Serbians fought an even more lethal enemy. An epidemic of typhus claimed 150,000 civilian lives during the winter of 1914–15, news of which deterred an Austro-Hungarian return. Medical services being at best rudimentary in the main towns and non-existent for most of the Serbian population, aid from forty-four foreign individuals and governments was required to halt the epidemic by the end of the year. Among others, the self-made British tea millionaire and philanthropist Sir Thomas Lipton transported a volunteer medical team in his private steam yacht *Erin* to Salonika (modern Thessalonika) on the Adriatic coast of Greece to set up hospitals in Serbia.

Early in the New Year, pressure from German High Command – *Oberste Heeresleitung* (OHL) – obliged Conrad von Hötzendorf to launch a new offensive against Serbia with the aim of re-opening the Berlin-Constantinople railway, which passed through Serbia. The Ottoman Empire had allied itself with the Central Powers at the end of October because it was reliably believed that a victory for Russia would result in it grabbing the Bosphorus and Dardanelles at the end of the war. This had been an aim of Russian imperial policy for several centuries, since the reign of Catherine the Great. After several defeats, the Turkish armies urgently needed replacement materiel that could only be supplied along the railway. Supporting Turkey was not exactly in Austro-Hungarian long-term interests, but after Italy declared for the Triple Entente in May 1915 Conrad von Hötzendorf opted to settle 'poor little Serbia' for good before he found himself fighting a war on two fronts.

Serbian troops also invaded Albania and captured the capital, Tirana. Allied diplomats having failed to bring it on-side, Bulgaria declared for the Central Powers in September, after being promised a part of Greece and the return of a vast stretch of territory lost to Serbia in 1885 and 1913. In geological terms, the Balkan countries constituted a zone of constant tectonic activity, in which it was hard to see where the next earthquake would happen because so many states wanted to expand, and could only do so at the expense of neighbours. This was not an easy decision for the self-styled 'Tsar' Ferdinand of Bulgaria but, after the failure of the Entente forces at Gallipoli and a major Russian defeat at Gorlice, it did seem to him that the Central Powers must eventually win the war. An unlikely leader even in time of peace, Ferdinand was yet another scion of the house of Saxe-Coburg und Gotha, whose second cousin Queen Victoria had considered him too effeminate to be ruler of a country. She was not alone in this. His tactless cousin Kaiser Wilhelm II once infuriated Ferdinand by patting him knowingly on what he called 'your postern gate', i.e. the seat of Ferdinand's pants – as a result of which Bulgaria ordered its armaments not from Germany, but from France.

During all these months the Serbs had also been attempting to rebuild their armies and replace the materiel expended in the fighting of 1914. The first Czech volunteers arrived in Serbia; eventually there would be 50,000 of them and two Russian 'special brigades' in-country. Together, they faced Bulgarian 1st Army on its eastern border and the German 11th Army and Austro-Hungarian 3rd Army on Serbia's northern and western frontiers. There was also a British presence. On 30 July 1914, when Britain was not yet at war with Germany, First Lord of the Admiralty Winston Churchill ordered the Royal Navy's Mediterranean Fleet to protect French transports carrying colonial troops from North Africa to France 'without engaging superior forces'. As a result of this, Rear Admiral Ernest Troubridge, commanding a squadron of four cruisers and eight destroyers, was shadowing the German battle cruiser SMS *Goeben* and the light cruiser *Breslau*. Troubridge's cruisers were slower than *Goeben*, which meant that the German commander could dictate the when-and-where of engagement. *Goeben* also had 11in guns as against the 9.2in British guns. In addition, it had 11in armour plate at critical places, against the British cruisers' armour plate only half that thick.

Troubridge was thus both outranged by the German guns and unlikely to be able to inflict any critical damage. He nevertheless intended to engage if this was possible at short range, but was persuaded by his flag captain that there was no point in so doing. The two German warships escaped into Turkish waters, where they were inducted into the Turkish navy to avoid internment, Turkey being neutral at that time. Foreseeing the havoc that these two ships could cause in the Black Sea, Churchill was furious and refused to accept that his ambiguous wording was at the root of Troubridge's decision. Accused at court martial of failing to engage the *Breslau*, Troubridge was acquitted because of that wording. He was, however, not forgiven by their Lordships of the Admiralty for failing to 'go down with his ship, all guns blazing' – which is what probably would have happened. With Churchill and their Lordships against him, Troubridge was never to be given another sea-going command. Instead, their Lordships appointed him Admiral of the Danube, where he commanded a force of men in the Royal Naval Brigade and soldiers manning artillery along the Danube frontier of Serbia. This force managed to sink two Austrian gunboats and also hammered away at the forces massing on the northern bank of the Danube, delaying their crossing by one whole day.

Of the first 3,000 men who crossed, 2,500 were wounded, killed or taken prisoner. A French battery nearby was located by Austrian aircraft, and heavily shelled, but continued firing until it was surrounded and its ammunition exhausted. Wrecking . their guns, the French artillerymen fought their way through the Austrian encirclement and headed south. Troubridge managed to save both his men and their guns, getting them all the way to Salonika, where, between 5 and 10 October the 10th (Irish) Division and French 156th Division and 17th Colonial Division plus some Foreign Legion elements had been landed. This strategically important port had been wrested by Greece from the Turks in the war of 1912–13 – a war in which Athens had doubled its territory and population at the expense of the Ottoman Empire, narrowly beating a Bulgarian column in the race for Salonika. Troubridge's achievement was barely recognised and public ridicule was later to attend him when his second wife, the sculptor Margaret Gertrude Taylor, left him for her lesbian lover, the author Marguerite Radcliffe-Hall.

The Greeks in 1915 had mixed political sympathies, with King Constantine I pro-German and Prime Minister Eleftherios Venizelos pro-Allied.[4] At least, that was what people in the West believed. The truth was that Constantine was an advocate of the *megáli idéa* – the 'great idea' of uniting under his rule all the Greek-speaking peoples of the eastern Mediterranean basin and winning back the prestige, the territory and the power that Greece had enjoyed in classical times. He had spent several years in Germany and even been given the courtesy title of field marshal by Kaiser Wilhelm II, but nevertheless refused the Kaiser's invitation to join the Central Powers because he believed that neutrality was the best position for his country in the current war.

On 7 October in coordinated attacks on the northern and western borders of Serbia, Austro-Hungarian and German troops invaded on several axes under the cover of a sustained artillery barrage, heading again for Belgrade, where a spirited resistance saw street fighting lasting several days before the city capitulated on 9 October. By this time, much of the city was a field of ruins, even the royal palace and the hospitals being shelled.[5] Less than a week later, the Bulgarian 1st and 2nd armies crossed Serbia's eastern frontier on two axes: in the north towards Niš and in the south towards Skopje. Both were successful, forcing the defenders to retreat – at which point, assailed on two fronts, Serbia was done for.

With the main Serbian forces about to be surrounded near Belgrade, there was no option but to retreat southwards. The Battle of Kosovo – a name to become sadly familiar to Western Europeans during the ethnic cleansing in the former Yugoslavia in 1998–99 – began on 10 November 1915. By 21 November virtually all Serbia was under enemy occupation although a Franco-British column was still facing off Bulgarian 2nd Army in the south of the country. By 4 December the last Serbian units were on the run in a desperate attempt to fight their way through to the Allied enclave around Salonika, where 13,000 officers and men in three French divisions and five British divisions had landed, too late to intervene seriously in Serbia itself. The progress of the retreating Serbs was hampered by tens of thousands of refugees attempting to keep up with them, driven from their homes terrified by reports of atrocities committed by the invaders.

The British Salonika Force (BSF), commanded by Lieutenant General George Milne, was surprised by the cruel Macedonian winter, which put 23 officers and 1,663 men out of the line with frostbite and exposure. Pte Reg Bailey of the 7th Royal Berkshires with the BSF kept a diary in which he wrote:

We were served out with woolly skin coats that made us look like a polar expedition. We had to scramble marches [sic] over the mountains where the snow lay feet thick. Rum was served out and extra blankets and anti-frostbite ointment for the feet and when you dressed in the morning boots and puttees were frozen stiff and water-bottles solid.[6]

There was a wide variety of dress among even the British troops at Salonika, contemporary photographs showing men even in the base area wearing sleeveless leather jerkins over their uniforms and Balaklava helmets under their steel helmets and puttees wound around legs from ankle to knee, to keep trouser bottoms out of the ubiquitous mud.

A week after the Bulgarians attacked on 7 December, all the British troops retreated back into Greece, where the area around Salonika was transformed into one huge military camp with a wired perimeter 90 miles long,[7] sarcastically dubbed by German observers 'the greatest internment camp in the world'.[8] This did not mean that all the men lived in barracks. Those on the perimeter had to camp as best they could in the sub-zero wind, taking shelter in caves or under canvas in gullies and ravines whose stony ground defied picks and shovels for digging in. The depression that was setting in as time dragged by can be sensed by reading between the lines the Christmas Day diary entry of Lt Colonel H. Jourdain of 5th Connaught Rangers:

The country was covered with frost and looked quite white at 7 a.m. I distributed cigarettes and some parcels of comforts and gave the men an issue of rum and some beer. They behaved very quietly and well and there was never anything that could be classed as undue hilarity.[9]

No, indeed. Nor was King's George V's Christmas message any comfort to Tommy Atkins shivering in Macedonia, with the monarch's talk of 'upholding the honour of the British name'. What, the average Tommy must have wondered, had become of the famous promise to 'bring the boys home' by Christmas 1914?

Salonika at Christmas 1915 was at the end of a long supply line that was vulnerable to German and Austro-Hungarian U-boats which caused losses of shipping bringing materiel, food and, most importantly for morale, mail from home. On land, the mixed Allied force was not 'a happy ship'. In the Crimean war, British commander Lord Raglan failed to get on with the successive

French commanders, and was in the habit of referring to the Russian enemy as 'those Frenchies'. So, in Salonika the command of the Anglo-French forces was frequently a battle of wills between General Milne, as senior British officer, and French commander General Maurice Sarrail, who outranked him. Milne agreed with his masters in London that an offensive over difficult terrain against well-prepared enemy positions in Bulgaria would be costly and unlikely to succeed. Politically well-connected, but with a reputation for squandering his men's lives, Sarrail was an up-and-at-'em soldier. His troops at Salonika, although rather grandly designated Le Regiment de Marche d'Afrique, consisted of four battalions of Tunisian Zouaves and one battalion of the Foreign Legion, which had been badly mauled at Cape Hellas in support of the Gallipoli beachhead. Among the legionnaires was at least one American volunteer, whose letters to sister or girlfriend Miss Florence House, living at 420 West 117 Street in New York City, turned up on eBay in 2012.

The Serbian retreat turned into a headlong rout southward into friendly Montenegro and eastward into Albania, which was not friendly. En route, three new enemies presented themselves to the long columns of soldiers and the tens of thousands of civilian refugees fleeing with them. The onset of winter was perhaps neutral. It made progress along bad roads and roadless tracts of mountainous country arduous work for famished refugees, but it also delayed the logistics train of their pursuers, who gradually dropped further and further behind and eventually abandoned the pursuit. A new element in the equation was the aerial reconnaissance carried out by German Fliegertruppen pilots, whose photographs and reports convinced the commanding German General August von Mackensen and through him OHL that it was unnecessary to pursue the beaten Serbs any further in worsening weather conditions.[10]

Nevertheless, exposure claimed many victims, especially among the children and old people. The second enemy, from which there was no escape, was starvation which, allied with hypothermia, claimed increasing numbers of lives so that the route they had followed was littered with emaciated corpses. And primitive Albania was no safe haven, but the home of the third enemy. In revenge for the depredations of Serbian occupying forces in the autumn of 1912 after the creation of the kingdom of Albania, which left half the Albanian-speakers on the wrong side of the new frontiers, irregular forces attacked the long column of mostly unarmed Serbian men with their women and children, to steal whatever remained of value. They took even the last reserves of food.[11] Finally, about 150,000 Serbs – for the most part adult males who had once been fit soldiers – limped, staggered and crawled as far as the Adriatic coast, where they were embarked on Allied ships, evacuating them to the Greek islands and Salonika. The privations they had endured caused thousands more to succumb, including Marshal Putnik, who died in a French hospital.

Austro-Hungary's second invasion of Serbia did succeed in re-opening the Berlin–Constantinople railway at a cost of some 67,000 casualties. The Serbs suffered 90,000 killed in combat and 174,000 taken prisoner. Overall, including civilians, 850,000 people had died from a pre-war population of 4.5 million – a death rate of one in five.

An account of the arrival of enemy troops in Priština, the capital of Kosovo, on 10 or 11 November 1915 was given to the Swiss forensic expert Dr R.A. Reiss of the University of Lausanne by a Greek doctor, named Atanasiades, who remained in the city, trusting to his then neutral Greek nationality.[12] He reported that the Bulgarian cavalry arrived about 2 p.m., followed by Austrian and German infantry. Shops staying closed the following day, the soldiery broke in and looted everything that took their fancy. In private houses, they plundered food stores and stole furniture to burn for heating and cooking. Requisitioning food, at first against vouchers of doubtful validity, but later without any receipt, the German commandant named Hartmann imprisoned members of the city council and threatened to shoot them if supplies were not forthcoming in increasing quantity. Depredations went so far as to include all the beds from the hospitals, causing injured Serbs to be thrown out into the street. According to the doctor's report, which is not verifiable, Turkish residents of Priština had not fled because the Ottoman Empire was allied to the Central Powers. After some Turkish women had been raped, several German officers and NCOs were murdered.

Dr Atanasiades then travelled to Belgrade, relying on his neutral status, and witnessed wholesale looting of private houses, factories and public buildings with entire trainloads of booty being despatched to Austro-Hungary and Germany. When Greece declared for the Allies, he was arrested, taken to Niš and from there forcibly conscripted to serve in Bulgarian hospitals for fifteen months. Sent back to Niš, he was imprisoned again and learned from Serbian civilian prisoners that they had been arrested to extort money from them, failing payment of which they risked execution or deportation. Dr Reiss' account is accompanied by photographs of men being taken to execution by Bulgarian soldiers and men rounded up for deportation to Bulgaria. In one photograph, smiling officers and men of 11th Prussian Grenadiers stand beside gallows at Jagodina, south-east of Belgrade, on which are hanging the bodies of eight Serbian victims. Other photographs show similar executions of civilians of both sexes at Kruševac and Aftovac.[13]

Incredibly, against all the odds, in the Bulgarian zone of occupied Serbia a resistance fighter named Kosta Vojinović raised an underground army which briefly 'liberated' Toplica near Niš until his uprising was savagely repressed at the end of March 1917 by combined Austrian and Bulgarian forces.

NOTES

1.   There was also Plan I for Italy. In German: *Balkan, Russland und Italien*.
2.   Clark, pp. 104–5.
3.   Ibid, p. 217.
4.   A. Wakefield, *Christmas in the Trenches* (Thrupp: Sutton, 2006), p. 58.
5.   *The History of the Great War*, ed. N. Fowler (London: Waverley Book Co.), vol. 7, pp. 1253–5.
6.   Wakefield, p. 59.
7.   Ibid.
8.   M. Chappell, *The British Army in World War 1 (3) The Eastern Fronts* (Botley: Osprey, 2007), p. 24.
9.   Wakefield, p. 62.
10. R.L. DiNardo, *Air and Space Power* article on www.airpower.au.af.mil/chronicles/cc/dinardo.html.
11. Clark, pp. 282–3, 357.
12. R.A. Reiss, *The Kingdom of Serbia – Infringements of the Rules and Laws of War Committed by the Austro-Bulgaro-Germans* (London: Allen & Unwin, 1919 (facsimile edition 2012 by Forgotten Books)), pp. 67–9.
13. Ibid, pp. 88–9. Although Aftovac is not to be found on modern maps, it is possible that the name has been changed.

3

MAYHEM AND MASSACRE IN MACEDONIA

Serbia, as a belligerent power, was out of the war, but the war was not out of Serbia. After the country was completely occupied, civilian deaths rose sharply in a campaign of ethnic cleansing. Prominent civilians, politicians, thinkers and teachers were rounded up and force-marched into the east of the country, occupied by Bulgarian forces. Many ended up at the town of Surdulica, a day's walk from the Bulgarian frontier, where mass executions took place every day, claiming an unverifiable 9,000 civilian lives in that place alone. The few eyewitnesses who survived testified that killing was at first by shooting, then by bayonet to conserve ammunition, and finally by clubbing with blunt objects and rifle butts. Rape was commonplace. Serbian villages and towns were looted and burned to the ground, livestock driven off, orchards cut down and wells poisoned, to discourage any survivors from returning. Adult males not killed in the massacres were forcibly drafted into the Bulgarian army in blatant contravention of the Rules of War as laid out in the 1899 Hague Convention, to which both Serbia and Bulgaria were signatories.[1] It stipulated that POWs should be removed from danger and not be required to contribute to their captors' war effort.

Winston Churchill, who had briefly been a prisoner during the Boer War, once defined a POW as 'a man who asks you not to kill him just after he has failed to kill you', and it is to be expected that some one-on-one violence occurs in that situation. However the systematic maltreatment of POWs in this campaign was revenge for well-documented Serbian atrocities in the Balkan wars of 1912–13, when whole villages of Albanians and Bulgarians were exterminated, with male inhabitants driven into prepared killing zones at night and there clubbed to death in order not to alarm their families with the noise of rifle shots, after which the houses were fired, to flush out the women and children, who were bayonetted and bludgeoned to death. Soldiers refusing to take part in the massacres were threatened with court martial.[2] The Austro-Hungarian minister in Belgrade commented at the time in an internal memorandum that Serbia was a state where 'murder and killing have been raised to a system'.[3]

The New Year of 1916 saw the Salonika enclave reinforced with four more Allied divisions, additional Serbian and Italian units and two brigades of the Russian Expeditionary Force – of which, more later. Many of the Tommies and their comrades-in-arms were unclear whether the 90-mile-long wired perimeter was to protect them from the Bulgarians or the anti-Allied Greeks on the other side of the wire. It was, of course, useless against the next threat which literally hung over them at the end of January. A dark-painted Zeppelin based 400 miles away in Hungary – a long journey at roughly 70mph – flew over the Allied base on the last night of the month, dropping several tonnes of bombs on the town of Salonika. Retiring unscathed, it returned on 17 March with equal success. A dawn air raid by several enemy aircraft in March was driven off after three of them[4] had been shot down. On the night of 4–5 May, after being awoken by the sound of bombs falling, Lieutenant George Collen wrote down a record[5] of the Zepp's third sortie. He and other officers left their tents to see it coned by searchlights in the night sky. An immense flash that briefly lit up their camp 15 miles inland marked its end after crash-landing on the foreshore. Several units claimed the credit for bringing down the monster, although the crash of the airship is usually attributed to the guns of HMS *Agamemnon*, moored in the harbour. The eleven-man Zeppelin crew survived the crash-landing and set fire to their highly flammable dirigible before being taken prisoner by French and Serbian cavalry while half-naked after stripping off their soaking uniforms in an attempt to dry off in the feeble sunshine.

On 12 March hundreds of Allied guns opened fire on the Bulgarian positions on high ground along the west of the line. In twenty-four hours more than 200,000 shells were fired at the enemy trenches and fortifications in Sarrail's bid to 'break the line'. However, enemy casualties were low because the defenders took shelter in deep concrete bunkers constructed on the reverse slopes of the mountains, where they were hidden from the Allied gunners. On 14 March there began a six-day struggle for the heights dominating the city of Monastir (modern Bitola), where Sarrail's men suffered heavy casualties. At the mountain called Chervenata Stena or Red Wall five French divisions took ground and were repulsed several times in a slaughter that alternated heavy artillery bombardments with bayonet attacks into machine gun fire so sustained that the Bulgarian defenders ran out of ammunition and took to rolling tree trunks and throwing rocks down on the French soldiers scrambling uphill towards them. Even transport up to the lines was difficult, with the spring rains turning flat land into seas of mud, through which everything had to be pulled by draught mules and oxen, with sledges more practical than wheeled vehicles in the malarial swamps of the Struma valley, where wheels sank into the morass.

Not until early May was the peak finally taken, after the Bulgarians withdrew to neighbouring high ground. On 18 May a new Bulgarian offensive equipped with German hand grenades and flamethrowers – newly introduced to this theatre – and supported by well-sited artillery, caused casualties as high as 75 per cent in the two French regiments on Red Wall, whose survivors made no further move against the enemy. Not until 19 November was a mixed Franco-Serbian force able to capture Monastir, the Serbs having suffered 27,000 casualties, representing one-fifth of their total force. Although Sarrail claimed the 'liberation' of the city as a victory, and assigned French, Serbian and other troops to occupy sectors of it, the city was overlooked by Bulgarian artillery on Mount Baba, which bombarded it daily for the rest of the war. Together with damage by bombs dropped from aircraft, this progressively destroyed just about every building until Monastir, once an important Ottoman administrative centre, was flattened. Among the incoming rounds were incendiary shells that set whole streets on fire. According to Swiss investigator Rodolphe Reiss, civilian casualties exceeded 1,500 and the 20,000-plus surviving civilians took shelter in the cellars, which, being below the level of the much damaged sewerage system, swiftly became foul and insanitary, leading in turn to the rapid propagation of infectious diseases including tuberculosis.[6] Knowing the inhabitants were spending the nights in the cellars, the Bulgarians took to bombarding the city with gas shells during the night. The gas, being heavier than air, sank into the cellars, causing death after up to half an hour of suffering.[7]

Another enemy was also causing casualties among the Allied troops – and presumably the Germans and Bulgarians on the other side of the lines. If not actually killing many, it certainly put hundreds of men *hors de combat*. The Allied front in Macedonia included some of the worst malarial land in Europe. To combat the pestilential mosquito, daytime patrols during periods of low activity became fatigue parties, hacking down undergrowth and long grass and pouring diluted creosote into puddles and ponds to kill the larvae. Before going out on a night patrol, each man had to smear his face and neck with mosquito repellent that smelled like almonds and looked like boot polish – and wrap a muslin veil around his head with the ends tucked into his collar.

The major engagement of British troops on the right of the line in 1916 was the first Battle of Lake Dojran at the beginning of August, theoretically in support of General Sarrail's attempt to break the enemy line west of the River Vardar – a major watercourse that roughly bisects Macedonia north-west to south-east. Various stretches of the river are known by its Greek name of Axios and a Slavonic name, Cerna – meaning black, from the colour of its waters. East of the river at Lake Dojran, which straddled the Greek-Bulgarian border in the centre of the British line, one British division and three French, totalling 45,000 men with 400 artillery pieces in support, launched an offensive against the excellently prepared Bulgarian fortifications around the lake, which were occupied by the 2nd Thracian Infantry Division. The attack went in on 9 August with a heavy artillery barrage, but was repulsed, with heavy losses. Four more attacks on this very hostile rocky terrain, where all the advantages lay with the defenders, followed on 10, 15, 16 and 18 August. All were repulsed by the Bulgarians, who drove the surviving Allied forces back to their start lines, causing a total of 5,024 pointless casualties. Many small wounds were caused by the shirtsleeve order and baggy shorts necessitated by the heat, with steel helmets replaced by soft felt hats, the wide brim turned up at one side.

At the inter-Allied strategy conference held at Chantilly, France, in November 1916 it was agreed that offensives planned for spring of the following year should include an attempt to knock Bulgaria right out of the war using the hotch-potch collection of British, French, Italian, Romanian, Russian and Greek forces in the Salonika enclave. The Allied plan called for attacks to be concerted right along the Macedonian front as soon as the winter weather abated. In anticipation of an Allied attack in the spring, the Bulgarian high command requested six further German divisions, so that it could go over to the offensive in Macedonia, but this request was refused by OHL and the joint German-Bulgarian defenders therefore settled in and consolidated their positions.

The main enemy for the Tommies on the right of the line that winter was the damp and cold. Pte Christopher Hennessy of 2/15th Londons wrote home:

> As the bivvies (tents) were open-ended, there was no protection from the Arctic blast. The state of the weather was such that men began volunteering for guard duty. The reason for this was that the guard kept a big fire going all night. On the whole it was a pleasant way to spend a cold night, except that the heat stirred the lice into a frenzy of activity.[8]

In between the few actual battles, men of the BSF came to appreciate the live-and-let-live attitude of 'Johnny Bulgar' in the line opposite their positions, who celebrated the Orthodox Christmas on 7 January. Since he had left the British alone on 25 December, the BSF reciprocated on that day.[9] They were still there twelve months later, when King George V sent them a message with the usual 'hearty good wishes' and wished them 'a restful Christmastide and brighter days to come'.

Sarrail's plan for 1917 looked good on paper, but failed to take into account the fractured command chain and disparate qualities of his heterogeneous forces. It called for Serbian 2nd Army, such as it now was, to attack west of the River Vardar at the same time as British troops advanced east of the river, while a mixed French-Italian force moved against a loop in the river known as the Cerna Bend and a French-Greek force also attacked west of the river. General Milne still regarded the role of the Allied forces in Macedonia as being to hold the

German and Bulgarian forces so that they could not be transferred elsewhere, but Sarrail pulled rank and 'borrowed' some British units. After many postponements because this or that national contingent was not ready, the British launched the Second Battle of Dojran on 24 April, to find that the defenders had not been idle during the winter, but had improved their positions considerably.

After seven days and nights of pointless losses, it became obvious to Milne that, since none of the other Allied attacks in this theatre was ready, the advantage of simultaneity had been lost. At the Cerna Bend the French-Italian force, whose commanders thought Sarrail's plan totally unworkable, were strengthened by the arrival of a Russian infantry brigade. What Sarrail thought they would achieve, except being able to exchange intelligible insults with the Bulgarians opposing them, is unknown. The 11th German-Bulgarian army, under German command, had prepared its defensive positions here well, with its best troops in the forward lines and adequate reserves in the rear to deal with any Allied breakthrough. Although out-gunned and out-manned by the Allies opposing them, they had the advantage of the terrain.

The Bulgarian front line consisted of concrete strongpoints and a complicated system of trenches and dugouts for the infantry, protected by wire entanglements up to 15m deep. Allied forces confronting them included sixty-nine Serbian, Italian, French colonial and Russian battalions with more than 500 machine guns and 412 artillery pieces. On 5 May, in the Second Battle of Lake Dojran, ninety-one Italian and French batteries blasted everything in sight opposite them, causing casualties among the Bulgarians occupying the flat terrain, but little damage to the German gunners on the strategically important hills overlooking the plain. The barrage was interrupted by the arrival of German fighter aircraft and the approach of dusk saw firing die down, which enabled the defenders to evacuate casualties and make good breaks in the wire entanglements. The following day was much the same, except that counter-battery fire from the German positions grew more effective thanks to aerial reconnaissance and probing attacks by Allied troops were repulsed without difficulty. On Day 3 of the offensive, the Allied barrage was renewed with thousands of shells raining down on the Bulgarian lines. They responded to probing attacks with probes of their own to ascertain the imminence of the main Allied move.

In fact, the main attack had been put on hold until 9 May because so little had been achieved by all the thousands of shells expended. The use of four observers in baskets slung beneath tethered balloons increased somewhat the accuracy of the fourth day's Allied barrage but damage to enemy artillery positions was still negligible, with only ten gunners killed or wounded and few guns put out of action. In addition, the enemy was able, by analysing the varying intensity of the Allied barrage along the 23km line to make a very fair guess where the main attack would be coming in.

The attack on an 11km front, involving French, Italian and Russian infantry, went in at 0630hrs on 9 May. The Italians took a stretch of the Bulgarian front lines whose coordinates were well known to the German gunners on the heights, who laid down a barrage that pushed the Italians back to their start lines. A similar story was enacted elsewhere, with heavy losses for the attackers, in several cases because troops of another contingent failed to secure the flanks – and this despite the expenditure of 32,000 shells on that day alone. A desultory series of attacks continued throughout the afternoon. The only significantly successful attack of the day was by the Russian 4th Infantry Regiment at Dabica, where prisoners included four German officers and seventy-plus other ranks. Even this gain could not be held, however. The Russians were pushed back by mid-evening, at which time no Allied gains had been made, for a reported loss of 5,450 casualties, counting dead and wounded, against 1,626 casualties among the Bulgarians and an unknown number of losses among the German troops. Sarrail was a never-give-up type, who followed up with fresh attacks in this sector on 11 and 17 May – all to no avail. On 21 May even he had to admit there was no point in further losses.

The year had seen long periods of boredom for the BSF, which had lost over 5,000 casualties to little gain. As the front sank into stalemate, increasing numbers of BSF were posted to Mesopotamia for General Allenby's drive against another Johnny – Johnny Turk. Their depleted numbers were made up by local troops, Greece having declared for the Allies on 29 June.

Officers could sometimes get into Salonika and see women in the streets but the men in the depopulated battle zone lived in an all-male world of desolation and discomfort, except for the wounded, who were treated in the base area by Canadian and Australian female nurses and male orderlies. The nurses could on exceptional occasions be enticed to dinner at an officers' mess, as at Christmas 1917 when Captain Alfred Bundy of Middlesex Regt described in a letter home how he and his brother officers entertained in their mess some of them from the Australian hospital. Rather ungallantly, he described the ladies as so unattractive that only an officer who had had too much to drink would have been likely to make any improper advances. Nursing uniform of ankle-length skirt, long jacket, collar and tie, with leather gloves when off-duty, did little for a girl's looks. All the same, Bundy had to admit that the female company added to the gaiety of the meal. When a space was cleared for dancing, some officers did their duty while others flirted surreptitiously under the beady eye of the matron, who was chaperoning her girls.[10] It was all very well for him to be picky, but the officers' entertainment contrasts with the Christmas of the men on the front line around Lake Dorjan, whose only relaxation was taking turns to visit an improvised concert party pantomime in Kalinova, where Robinsoe Crusoe was stranded in Muckidonia with Mrs Crusoe, played for laughs by a most unfeminine soldier in drag.

The memorable event of 1918 – indeed the last memory for many Tommies – was the Third Battle of Lake Dojran, which pitted British 12th Corps, supported by the Seres Division of the Greek army and some of Sarrail's colonial forces from North Africa, against the Bulgarian 9th Pleven Division that had used its time well to dig in and fortify the opposite bank of the lake under German instructors. During fierce fighting that peaked on 18 and 19 September 1918, every available weapon was employed by both sides, from spotter planes and observation balloons to artillery firing gas shells. On the ground, the dug-in improved Vickers–Maxim machine guns were attacked by men wielding bayonets, sharpened spades and cudgels, useful at close quarters if one survived the approach. A rolling barrage using British 8in howitzers did not greatly facilitate the attackers' task because they had to advance uphill over broken ground against the enemy positions, scrambling from cover to cover into a hail of fire from German-manufactured Spandau machine guns while wearing cumbersome, primitive respirators – or else risk succumbing to the heavier-than-air gas, probably from British shells, that lingered in the hollows and ravines.

Sweating under a pitiless sun, trying to see the terrain ahead through misted-up goggles, never mind spot the well dug-in enemy machine gun positions, the men were also cut down from above by shrapnel shells fired by more than 100 enemy guns. Above them circled Allied aircraft whose observers, tasked with correcting artillery fire, were unable to make out the situation on the ground through the heat-haze, the gun-smoke and the dust from explosions, or to drop orders to men cut off in the confusion of rocks and ravines below. There were some 200 Allied spotter planes and bombers deployed in the theatre, compared with only thirty or so Taube and Fokker aircraft on the other side.

The Bulgarian front line was overrun and some Greeks reached the second line before being driven back with heavy casualties. The 7th South Wales Borderers were especially hard hit. By the end of the morning, most of the attacking force lay dead or wounded on the slopes, as did its officers, including both colonels. The 12th Cheshire Regiment, 9th South Lancs Regiment and 8th King's Shropshire Light Infantry lost up to 67 per cent of officers and men after being ordered to advance into interlocking fields of machine gun fire. No Allied gains had been made by the end of the day. Tormented by thirst and wounds, the fallen of both sides wept and called throughout that night for help which did not come.

On Day 2, artillery support was ill coordinated as the Cretans advanced in a dawn attack and took some Bulgarian trenches before being repulsed with heavy losses. Fresh British units and some French colonials again suffered about 50 per cent casualties with no territorial gains in the hopeless assault, echoing the senseless slaughter on the Western Front. Of the British troops, Scots fusiliers and Highlanders of the 77th Brigade advanced with the same difficulty as the Welshmen who lay in their path, dead or dying from the first day's fighting.

The Scots, in turn, left half their number dead or wounded in the futile engagement. By the end of the second day's fighting, Allied losses were estimated at nearly 8,000 men against less than 3,000 Bulgarian casualties.

All that to occupy a few Bulgarian trenches and the strategically useless ruins of Dojran town, but Milne was hailed as a victorious commander on the grounds that the Dojran action had tied down the Bulgarian reserves and allowed the French–Italian attack to the west of the Vardar to break through the enemy line.[11] Some days later, probing patrols reported a strange silence in the Bulgarian positions around Lake Dojran and found them abandoned. To avoid being taken in the rear by the Allied breakthrough west of the river, the defenders had retreated in good order, leaving rearguards to delay any pursuit.

One hostilities-only officer on the staff of British 28th Division described chasing the enemy up through the Rupell Pass and into Serbia. The way was strewn with cast-off clothing, dead horses, wrecked machine guns, discarded ammunition, deliberately damaged rifles and bayonets with the locking ring torn off. The British were impressed by the way that the German officers had planted gardens to grow chilli and tomatoes in front of Swiss-style chalets they had built along the ravines. Most impressive was a bath-house constructed over a natural hot spring, where officers and men enjoyed a swim in the mineral waters. He considered that the conduct of the Tommies was exemplary, compared with that of the Serbian soldiery who had arrived first, as witness 'the grim evidence … in the shape of blackened Bulgar corpses at an abandoned hospital … sitting up in their beds and rotting.' Back in Macedonia, living in tents beside the muddy mule lines, they heard and saw on the night of 10–11 November rockets and flares sent up the Greeks camped nearby. A bugle sounded a call none of the enlisted men recognised, until an old sweat, walking back from a boozy evening in the sergeants' mess, said, 'Don't you know the Cease Fire when you hear it?'[12]

As the Austro-Hungarian and Bulgarian occupation forces withdrew from Serbian soil in the last months of 1918, what remained of the Serbian army, supported by British and French troops, pushed into the power vacuum and reached their old borders two weeks before the Armistice. Serbian deaths in combat alone were the highest of all the Allied belligerents, at around 26 per cent of all men mobilised.

The total cost of the war to 'poor little Serbia'? Although awarded some reparations and a little formerly Bulgarian territory under the Treaty of Neuilly in November 1919, and temporarily occupying territory as far north as Pecs in Hungary and Timisoara in Romania, this did little to compensate the material damage to tens of thousands of homes, factories, schools and hospitals which, in today's terms, would amount to many billions of dollars. And how could this landlocked country get back on its feet with more than half its adult males killed in combat, massacred or dead from disease? In addition, by the end of hostilities, war-crippled Serbia had 114,000 disabled veterans to care for and a half-million orphaned children to support.

The unification of the region by the creation of the Kingdom of Serbs, Croats and Slovenes, which in 1929 became Yugoslavia – or land of the southern Slavs – did nothing to eradicate the legacy of hatred from the events of 1912–13 and 1914–18 that was to spawn another round of genocide during the Second World War and yet again after the break-up of Tito's Yugoslav Federation following his death in 1980 – conflicting accounts of which still echo in hearings of the International Criminal Tribunal for the Former Yugoslavia in The Hague.

It was, of course, impossible for the repatriation and demobilisation of all the Allied forces on the eastern fronts to follow swiftly on the Armistice of 11 November. Most of the officers and virtually all the 'other ranks' were still there at Christmas, when General Allenby's Order of the Day dated seven weeks after the Armistice ordered the men restlessly awaiting return to civilian life to resist the temptations of wine and women! Back home, there were mutinies in Calais and Folkestone and 3,000 soldiers marched through London in protest at their delayed demobilisation. The mood was similar in Macedonia, where Captain Bundy was confronted with a complete breakdown of military discipline among men quite rightly angry that they had been given no indication of when they would be sent home:

> I had to talk to a whole company that were disgracefully abusive to their officers. I realised that any show of military authority would be fatal, so I reasoned with them. My remarks were greeted by catcalls and rude noises, but I knew the men were anxious to return to England, so I announced that if there was (insubordination) I should have the offenders arrested and kept back till last.[13]

Some of the BSF boarded ships thinking they were homeward-bound, but ended up at Baku in Azerbaijan, where half the world's petroleum had been produced before the war from wells owned by the Nobel brothers, better known for smokeless gunpowder and the annual awards. Since Russia's exit from the war after the Treaty of Brest-Litovsk, all was not 'peace on earth and goodwill towards men' on Christmas Day 1918 there, either. The 'other ranks' were confined inside barracks doubly guarded, to avoid clashes with armed patrols of Red Guards who had cut off the power supply. Even the wounded in hospital who were fit enough to use a rifle were placed on standby. A task force of Royal Engineers, protected by armoured cars, managed to get the power station running again on the day after Boxing Day, but a Bolshevik attack was expected at any moment.[14] Some men were also posted to Sevastopol on the Crimean peninsula and stationed in what had been the tsarist navy's barracks. Even there, the Allied command imposed a curfew and provost patrols shot on sight anyone found in the streets after 9 p.m.

It was not just the 'other ranks' who resented the long wait to go home. There is a telling photograph taken at Christmas 1918 of four officers clustered around a stove in the tented mess of 95th Russel's Infantry in Macedonia, looking distinctly glum and miserably cold in their foul weather clothing. Officers and men alike resented the apparently random early selection of men for demob, which was theoretically based on their usefulness in re-starting commerce and industry back home. It took the appointment of Winston Churchill as Secretary of State for War in January 1919 to institute a demob programme based on the principle of first-in, first-out that rewarded a man's age, length of service and wounds suffered.

Ich hatt' einen Kamerad / 'nen bessern findst Du nicht, the German soldiers sang: I had a comrade, as good as you can find. Soldiers' songs were never so important for the British armed forces as they were in European armies, inured to marching long distances in Continental conflicts, but something of the same hopeless sadness must have been in the minds of the Tommies who eventually packed up to leave Salonika in 1919, thinking of all their comrades who lay in the extensive war cemeteries all over Macedonia. There were even three men who had been executed by firing squad for unspecified offences, and another executed in Serbia.[15] Generals, who can afford to take the strategic view, would say that they had successfully tied down Central Powers' forces which could have been used elsewhere, but it would be impossible to justify all the British and other Allied deaths in Macedonia by any in-theatre gains.

NOTES

1. Although they did not sign the 1907 Convention.
2. K. Boeckh, *Von den Balkankriegen zum ersten Weltkrieg- Kleinstaaten Politik und ethnische Selbstbestimmung auf dem Balkan* (Munich: Oldenbourg, 1996), pp. 167–8.
3. Clark, p. 113.
4. Or possibly four – sources differ.
5. *The Outlook*, 26 July 1916, pp. 749–50.
6. Reiss, p. 34.
7. Ibid, pp. 30–1.
8. Wakefield, p. 106 (abridged).
9. Ibid, p. 110.
10. Ibid, pp. 145–6.
11. Interesting personal accounts may be found on www.1914–1918.net/salonika. htm and http://canalblog.com/archives/2007/11/23/6989822.html.
12. Issue 46 of *I Was There* (published 1938–89) on www.1914/1918.net/Salonika. htm (abridged).

13. Wakefield, p. 164 (abridged).
14. Ibid, pp. 190–1 (abridged).
15. A. Babington, *For the Sake of Example* (London: Paladin, 1985), pp. 244–5.

PART 2

THE CLASH OF GIANTS

4

ON THE GROUND

The Russian folk song *Dva Velikana* – meaning, two giants – tells of Napoleon's Grande Armée confronting the armies of Tsar Aleksandr I, climaxing at the Battle of Borodino, outside Moscow. The clash on what Westerners call the 'eastern front' 1914–17 was another conflict of giants, with millions of men on both sides confronting each other with all the weapons of twentieth-century warfare, despite which most generals of the Russian high command still considered the bayonet charge the best way of winning a battle, no matter how high the casualties. They were not alone. Certainly, Conrad von Hötzendorf considered that the morale of his men in uniform was more important than training, equipment and armament. In his widely read book *Zum Studium der Taktik*, he warned that digging in was bad for the fighting spirit and could cost an army dearly.[1] With men exposed to the rapid fire of improved machine guns and high-explosive shelling, as well as anti-personnel air-burst shells invented by Lieutenant Shrapnel and improved by Captain Boxer, both of the Royal Artillery, it was a criminal dereliction of duty on the part of their officers not to order them to dig in.

With commanders whose brains were still in the eighteenth century sending their subordinates en masse against the terrifying power of twentieth-century weaponry, it was inevitable that war on the Russian fronts was to cause millions of casualties, a considerable number of them unnecessary in strictly military terms. Researchers have criticised uneducated Russian peasant conscripts for trying to describe the horrors of being marched forward into a barrage by using such similes as 'thunder', 'earthquake', 'hell' and so on,[2] but is this so different from images used by educated Westerners – like Wilfred Owen's 'monstrous anger of the guns', 'the stuttering rifles' rapid rattle' and 'shrill, demented choirs of wailing shells'?[3]

Because of the vast distances over which combat ranged in this war of movement, individual one-on-one physical violence was more important than in the

West. When the artillery had yet to arrive, or had no shells to fire, and infantrymen had no cartridges for their rifles, killing was often face-to-face with bayonet, sword, lance, sharpened spades and blunt instruments. Paradoxically, because this kind of confrontation was between men and not by remote-control shelling as in the West, there were also many episodes where an enemy soldier was allowed to surrender because he did not assume a threatening posture or on occasion groups of enemy soldiers walked forward with shouldered arms to surrender en masse.

One foreign observer of the Russian front hostilities was a British officer, Colonel Alfred Knox,[4] referred to by Winston Churchill as 'an agent of singular discernment, whose luminous and pitiless despatches' had been of great use to the British government in following developments there.[5] Having been military attaché at the St Petersburg embassy, Knox knew Russia. He spoke German, Russian and French – the second language of the Russian educated classes – and was personally acquainted with Tsar Nicholas, Commander-in-Chief Grand Duke Nikolai and many of the senior officers of the Russian armies. After the war, he published a book entitled *With the Russian Army 1914–1917, Being Chiefly Extracts from the Diary of a Military Attaché*. It starts with a modest observation: 'The writer can at any rate claim to have enjoyed greater opportunities for observation of the Russian army than any other foreign observer, both previous to the war as Military Attaché to the British Embassy at Petrograd, and during the war as liaison officer at the front.'[6] It is a claim well borne out by his many eye-witness accounts. That other eye witness, Robert Bruce Lockhart, wrote of Knox, '… no man took a saner view of the military situation on the Eastern [sic] front and no foreign observer supplied his government with more reliable information'.[7]

Although not an eye witness, Winston Churchill summarised from afar the conflict in the east: 'In the west, the armies were too big for the land; in the east, the land was too big for the armies.' Indeed, a greater contrast with the largely static trench warfare of the Western Front would be hard to imagine, so it is necessary to comprehend the enormous distances over which the slaughter of the Russian fronts was perpetrated in order to understand the logistical problems facing both sides in order to move men and materiel to the front lines. In this war of movement, simply ensuring that food, clothing and ammunition reached the millions of men with fodder for millions of horses was an insoluble headache – let alone organising the *polevaya pochta* – the field postal services that provided that essential morale-booster, a letter from home.

From the start of the war until March 1918 saw the signing of the Treaty of Brest-Litovsk, 2 million Austro-Hungarian troops and about a quarter of all the German armies were tied up on the Russian fronts, where a million Austro-Hungarian soldiers and three-quarters of a million Germans, plus nearly 4 million Russians died and were buried or had their bodies scavenged by animals if no one

The Polish salient. Contemporary map with anglicised place-names.

had time or inclination to dig a grave. And then there were the uncounted civilian casualties of all ages …

At the Congress of Vienna in 1814–15, a huge slice of modern Poland was occupied by tsarist Russia and referred to as 'Congress Poland', with the greater part of Napoleon's Duchy of Warsaw as a huge salient reaching westwards almost to Germany. Between it and the Baltic coast lay the German province called East Prussia. To the south of the Polish salient down to the Romanian border was Austro-Hungarian territory.

To *Stavka Verkhovnovo Glavnokomanduyuschevo* – the Russian General Staff, usually abbreviated to 'Stavka' – the Polish salient under Russian occupation was a double-edged weapon. Its western extremity lay just over 200 miles from Berlin and, from its northern border, it offered the possibility of a swift drive to the Baltic coast lying less than 50 miles away – which would cut the German garrisons of East Prussia off from reinforcement by land. Yet, the salient was itself vulnerable to a pincer movement by the German forces in East Prussia to the north and Austro-Hungarian forces in Galicia to the south. This would trap all the Russian garrisons in the salient and many thousands of other troops deployed there. Thus, on the maps in Berlin, Vienna and St Petersburg, the salient represented a threat that needed to be dealt with at the outset of hostilities.

The original Russian strategy was to station defensive forces along the East Prussian border to contain the German garrisons there while first concentrating on destroying the weaker Austro-Hungarian forces south of the salient, both less efficient and worse equipped than the Germans as well as being largely composed of men from vassal states who had no love for Emperor Franz Joseph, no loyalty to his government, no sense of identity with the army in which they were forced to serve – and often no common language with their officers. One of them was a Czech named Joseph Bumby. He had enlisted on 2 August in the Bohemian town of Kroměříž, been transported in a cattle wagon to a position south of the salient and there, on 21 August, witnessed the total solar eclipse that left the world briefly 'dark with a greenish-blue tinge'.[8] With his European education, he knew what was happening, but one wonders what the illiterate, superstitious Russian soldiers on the other side of the lines made of that phenomenon. Bumby describes the confusion of arriving in the night and trying to find the regiment's designated position, which turned out to be just a few hovels to accommodate several hundred men. All was chaos:

At Kielce, midway between Warsaw and Kraków, the regiment was dug in when attacked by Cossack (cavalry) and we had to assault a burning town and run the gauntlet in crossing a bridge 150 feet long over the river under intensive shrapnel bursts. The bridge was blown up. Men died around me. In the woods we saw an observer in a high tree, and shot him. We slept that night on the ground under a cold rain. After lunch we had to retreat to a village with three churches. [From a number of such descriptions it is apparent that Bumby and his comrades had no clear idea where they were.]

We asked the peasants for wood to make a fire and dry our clothes, but they wouldn't give it, so we broke down their fence and burned that. Half an hour away, we bought some milk and eggs, so that was okay. One night we slept in a school, on the benches or under them. Alcohol was forbidden us in Russia, but we found vodka the Cossacks had left in the cellar, and drank that. But we didn't have any bread, nor did the local people. There was no field kitchen, so we killed some geese with sabres, for which the peasants wanted us to pay. When we tried to deepen our trenches, the sandy soil just slid down into them.[9]

Stavka believed that the hundreds of thousands of Slavic soldiers in Franz Joseph's armies – the Poles, Czechs, Slovaks, Croatians and others – would rather surrender to their brother Slavs in Russian uniform than fight them in the service of their Austrian and Magyar overlords. In many cases, this proved to be correct, with whole units surrendering at the first contact. After Austro-Hungary had been knocked out of the war – or so the thinking went at Stavka – there would be time to deal with the German armies in East Prussia, whose strength would have been drained by the higher priority of the battles on the Western Front.

Unfortunately for Russian interests, since 1911 there had been secret meetings between Stavka and the French high command, at which it had been agreed that, when war came, Russia would launch diversionary operations when the Western Allies were under pressure. This inverted the previous Russian strategy, with Grand Duke Nikolai considering himself honour-bound after the German invasion of Belgium to launch his first offensive against East Prussia, obliging OHL to keep there whole divisions that could otherwise be moved to the Western Front.

On the other side, the complication in OHL's plan for nipping off the salient was that it required detailed coordination and synchronisation with its counterpart in Vienna, *Oberarmeekomando* (OAK), to attack the salient simultaneously from the south. In East Prussia the German garrisons and frontier forces were all well trained, disciplined and equipped. However, Berlin had low expectations of the performance of the disparate Austro-Hungarian forces south of the salient – which dropped even lower after the commencement of hostilities. OHL therefore gambled on being able to use the vast majority of its armies in the west under the Schlieffen Plan, as modified by von Moltke, to surround Paris and force a French surrender within a few weeks, as had been done in the Franco-Prussian war of 1870. Anticipating that Russian mobilisation would be slow, due to the vastness of the country and the poor communications, OHL planned, after taking Paris, to switch sufficient divisions to the Russian front before the Tsar's armies were ready to take the offensive. On paper in Berlin, this plan looked possible but, as von Clausewitz had remarked a century earlier, 'No campaign plan survives first contact with the enemy's main force.'

Russia had theoretically universal military conscription, calling up 1.3 million men each year before the war, which rose to 1.7 million in 1917. In the infantry and field artillery, conscripts served three and a quarter years; in the mounted and technical troops, twelve months longer. After this, they were in the reserves, liable to call-up in time of need. Already by 0600hrs on 1 August, at each of the ninety-four police stations in St Petersburg – a city of 2 million inhabitants – between 2,000 and 3,000 reservists were waiting to enlist. As soon as their discharge papers had been checked, they were marched off under police guard to their barracks.

There were thirty-seven army corps comprising seventy infantry divisions and eighteen rifle brigades, twenty-four regular cavalry and eleven independent cavalry and Cossack cavalry brigades. Each army corps had two 6-gun batteries of light howitzers and a battalion of three sapper and two telegraph companies. Infantry divisions normally consisted of four 4-battalion regiments and a field artillery brigade of six 8-gun batteries. The rifle brigade contained four 2-battalion rifle regiments and an artillery division of three 8-gun field batteries. The regular cavalry division contained four regiments, each of six squadrons. These were grouped in two brigades, of which the first contained the dragoon and lancer regiments and the second the hussars and Cossacks.

Russia commenced the war with the equivalent of 114 infantry and about 36 cavalry divisions – which, in Knox's words, 'represented a poor effort compared with that of Germany and France, for the adult male population liable to military service in the vast Russian Empire on January 1st, 1910, was 74,262,600 men.'[10] Thanks to corruption and privilege, many men simply did not serve. He also remarked that 75 per cent of recruits were drawn from the peasant class, and that the Tartar domination and subsequent serfdom – which had only been abolished a half-century before – had robbed them 'of all natural initiative, leaving only a wonderful capacity for patient endurance'. As to their training, he wrote:

> Since 1911, when I was appointed in St Petersburg, I had always attended the annual manoeuvres of the Military District, where accredited foreign officers were always invited as guests of the Tsar. We lunched and dined at his table, used his motor-cars, rode his horses, and attended with him nightly performances at the local theatre. We saw much martial spectacle, but very little serious training for modern war.[11]

Within the Polish salient and to the east of the front lines the Russian conscripts looked like the peasants most of them really were in civilian life, wearing baggy drawstring trousers under a short, belted smock with soft uniform cap. In summer, to save carrying a greatcoat, the soldier's blanket was rolled up with ends tied together and worn bandolier-style over the left shoulder, leaving the right arm free for the rifle – if he had one! In some units 30 per cent of men trained with a broomstick or wooden stave and were ordered into battle with a pocketful of bullets and instructions to pick up and use the rifle of the first dead man they stumbled over. In retreat, Russian officers tended to sacrifice men to save artillery, which was considered more valuable than peasant lives.

Most of the issued rifles were *vintovka Mosina* – a version of the 1891 Mosin-Nagant repeater – the so-called 'three-line rifle', with its magazine holding five rounds, made by the Nagant company in Belgium.[12] Although an adequate weapon in the hands of veterans, it was wildly inaccurate when used by raw recruits. There were also single-shot black-powder Berdan II rifles dating from 1870 that had been re-machined in Belgium to use smokeless ammunition of the same calibre as the Mosin-Nagants and accept the same bayonets. The re-machining was not a simple or cheap job because black powder ignited at lower pressure than the new smokeless propellant, so a new bolt with locking lug had to be invented. Losses in battle also obliged the Tsar's ordnance department to purchase from yesterday's enemy nearly 800,000 Arisaka rifles – the weapon that had played a significant part in the Japanese defeat of tsarist forces in the far eastern war of 1904–5. Desperate to keep Russian troops in the war, France also delivered 450,000 obsolete single-shot black-powder 1874 Gras rifles and 100,000 Austrian-made black-powder repeaters. For the same reason, Italy supplied 400,000 1870/87 Vetterli-Vitali 3-shot repeating rifles. Although going some way to making good the deficit numerically, such a wide variety of different bores and variable reliability and accuracy predictably caused problems.

The various Russian armies disposed of approximately 4 million Mosins in various models[13] principally the full-length infantry rifle and the short-barrelled Cossack and dragoon models for use by mounted troops. To cope with inadequate manufacturing capacity at the three main government arsenals, the Russian ordnance department had ordered a half-million M1891s from the Manufacture Nationale in Chatellerault, France – all of which delivered before the outbreak of war. It also belatedly ordered 3.5 million rifles from Remington and Westinghouse and 300,000 model 1895 Winchester repeaters from the USA – of which total some 1.6 million were delivered before the Treaty of Brest-Litovsk.[14] After the Russian defeat by the Japanese in the war of 1904–5, Vladimir Sukhomlinov, as War Minister 1909–15, had worked hard with French and British help to modernise the Russian armies, purchasing Krupp 120mm quick-firing light howitzers and 150mm quick-firing Schneider-Creuset howitzers, on which Russia's seven divisions of heavy artillery – twenty-one batteries of heavy guns in each army – were in the middle of retraining when the war began. Each infantry division was allotted six 8-gun batteries of the M1902 model howitzers which fired a 76.2mm shell up to 6km, and each rifle brigade had two 6-gun batteries of 1909 Krupp 121.9mm howitzers.

Sukhomlinov did succeed in integrating machine gun crews, sappers and field batteries into infantry regiments. He also ended the custom of making up numbers in units that had suffered heavy casualties by withdrawing those units from the line and permitting the exhausted survivors a period of rest and recuperation. Russian cavalry had only two divisions of artillery, shared with the infantry and rather heavy for fast-moving cavalry warfare. Sukhomlinov also made the mobilisation system more efficient, as was proven when the Central Powers were surprised by its speed in 1914.

Most Russian machine guns were the water-cooled 1910 improved Vickers–Maxim model, some with a filling funnel on the top to allow snow to be used as coolant in freezing conditions. Sukhomlinov set up a factory to produce these in Russia, but at the outset of hostilities all the tsarist armies had to share just over 4,000 machine guns, many of them without carriages for rapid movement in advance or retreat. Talking of rapid movement, when it came to moving large bodies of men, the 150,000-men-strong 2nd Army, for example, disposed of just ten cars and four motorcycles in the summer of 1914. Altogether, the several armies shared 418 modern trucks. In movement by rail, Russia was similarly disadvantaged. For every 100km^2 of the Russian fronts the tsarist forces had available 1.6km of track, on which to move men and supplies, against 32km for every 100km^2 on the German side of the lines. To compound the inequality, Russian rolling stock moved at half the speed of German trains.[15] That shrewd and cool observer of the Russian war machine Colonel Knox reported: 'For a long war, Russia was outclassed in every factor of success except in the number of her fighting men and their mollusc-like quality of recovery after severe defeat.'[16]

Despite his best efforts, undermined by vested interests and the Russian tradition that an officer's nobility of birth took precedence over his military competence or lack of same, Sukhomlinov had been unable to free much of the available artillery from its static role in the frontier fortresses – which he wished to eliminate entirely as being irrelevant to a mobile modern war. In 1915 he would be proven right, as Warsaw, Kovno, Przemyśl, Grodno and even Brest-Litovsk either surrendered or were abandoned to the enemy, with the loss of most of their guns and millions of rounds of ammunition.[17] Although his political and professional detractors later criticised his refusal to accept criticism, his inefficient administration and especially his failure to modernise the corrupt and inefficient Russian armaments industry, it is probable that no other man could have achieved much more than Sukhomlinov in the time available. Although having the appearance of a twentieth-century society in some of its largest cities, much of Russia was strangled by inefficiency and corruption – it was customary for factory owners to pay kickbacks of 5 or 6 per cent to state officials who placed orders with them. Its industrial installations were choked with outdated technology and its ruling classes as blindly resistant to change as medieval monarchs. At enormous cost in his subjects' lives, Peter the Great had dragged his country into the Enlightenment of its Western neighbours, but the subsequent centuries of Romanov rule had failed drastically to keep step with industrial development in Europe.

Each German division on the Russian fronts boasted two heavy guns of 150mm, nine 12-gun batteries of 87.5mm guns, three howitzers and twelve machine guns. Austro-Hungarian artillery had the benefit of excellent guns produced in the Skoda Iron Works in Bohemia, like the 149mm Model 14 howitzer – the drawback of which was its sheer weight that required breaking down into two pieces for separate transportation.[18] Artillery allocated to the Russian front consisted of forty-two regiments of field guns, fourteen regiments of field howitzers and eight divisions of cavalry artillery. A Russian army corps was slightly larger than a Hapsburg corps and also had more field guns: 108 to 96, but the Germans, with 144 field guns, had a significant advantage.[19]

In 1914, although OHL had issued 3,000 shells per gun, Russian ordnance provided only 1,000 shells per gun at the declaration of war and could manufacture only 1.5 shells per gun per day after the onset of hostilities – a grotesquely inadequate situation when artillery bombardments prior to a major offensive could run to 700 rounds per gun per day, or more. Colonel Knox was reliably told that national daily production of shells peaked at 1,300 per day while the armies were consuming around 45,000 per day. Even more scandalously, given the scale of arms production, the daily output of the state rifle factory at Tula in 1914 was five – repeat, *five* – rifles a month although it was tooled up to produce 5,000. As historian Timothy Dowling points out in a very comprehensive examination of the situation, two out of every three shells emerging from the barrel of a Russian gun were imported – as were two-thirds of the bullets fired by Russian small arms. Both Colonel Knox and French Ambassador Maurice Paléologue commented that the 5 million men mobilised were equipped with only 1.2 million rifles in the front lines and 700,000 in reserve.[20] The shortage of armaments was echoed in the insufficiency of just about every kind of ancillary equipment. General Aleksandr Samsonov's 2nd Army possessed only twenty-five telephones; for the first months of the war artillery brigades had no telephones; Morse operators and their transmitting sets were in short supply.

On the German side of the lines, because of the priority given by OHL to the invasion of France, only General Maximilian von Prittwitz's 8th Army was allotted for the defence of East Prussia. Yet two-fifths of Russia's peacetime army was located around Warsaw in Russian-occupied Poland, making the salient a huge reservoir of men and materiel poised for action at short notice, of which roughly half was allocated for an attack on Austro-Hungarian forces to the south. In July and August 1914 Russian mobilisation was faster than the Germans had reckoned possible because of the clandestine call-up during the diplomatically termed 'Period Preparatory to War'. By the end of the year, 5 million men were in uniform, of which 2.2 million were front-line troops.

Although the Tsar's uncle Grand Duke Nikolai reluctantly accepted the position of commander-in-chief on the approach of war, he had formerly been inspector-general of cavalry and commander of the St Petersburg military district – and thus had no prior knowledge of Stavka's plans, which had been made two or three years earlier. He was in any case somewhat of a figurehead, surrounded by his own court and usually preferring 'not to get in the generals' way'.[21] On Saturday 15 August, Colonel Knox was on board the Grand Duke's train and noted its good but simple cooking with a glass of vodka or wine and cognac with the coffee.[22] His host occupied himself on the journey in rubber-stamping Plan 19A. It was an ambitious pincer movement by two armies invading East Prussia from south and east in the hope of trapping vast numbers of German forces in a pocket from which they could not escape[23] and thus forcing OHL urgently to bring reinforcements from the Western Front.

It is worth mentioning here an obstacle to any mechanised Central Powers advance into Russian territory, or of a similar Russian advance into East Prussia or Galicia. In 1891, the Russian government had opted for a railway gauge that was not Robert Stephenson's standard 4ft 8½in gauge adopted in all other European countries[24] and equivalent to 1440mm, but a gauge of 1524mm. It seems that Russian paranoia decided on this to make things difficult for any invader, whose rolling stock would not run on Russian rails, but there is another explanation. An elderly railway engineer who had been around at the time of the construction of Russia's very first railways told an engineering student that high officials went for instructions to Emperor Nikolai I.

They told him that, all over the world, the gauge normally used was 1440mm. And they asked him, 'Should we do the same, or make ours bigger?' And the answer they got was: 'By the cock, bigger.'

When the officials left the Emperor, they thought it over. How were they to understand the words of His Highness? If he were speaking metaphorically, then these words would mean *why bigger* and then they should make the gauge at 1440mm. But what if he had had in mind exactly what he said?

None of the high officials would risk returning to the emperor to ask him what he had meant. They decided to enlist help from Nikolai's personal physician and asked him to tell them how big was the organ that the Emperor had mentioned. The doctor told them: 'Eighty-four millimetres.' So they added that to 1440mm and from that time on, the gauge of our railroads has been 1524mm. Nowhere else in the world will you find this gauge.[25]

After learning how many far more important decisions of Tsar Nicholas II were never questioned for reasons of protocol, although costing thousands of lives, the reader may choose which explanation to believe.

It was possible to re-lay the narrower gauge European rails on Russian sleepers – with a problem on the bends – but not always possible to re-lay wider Russian track on the shorter European sleepers. Unless undamaged German rolling stock could be captured, it was not immediately possible for a Russian advance to exploit the enemy's excellent railway system. For the Germans and Austrians, invading Russia was complicated by the extremely ill-maintained dirt roads in the frontier areas, many of them impassable during the spring and autumn rains, when they turned into rivers of mud.

NOTES

1. T.C.Dowling, *The Brusilov Offensive* (Bloomington: Indiana University Press, 2008), p. 9.
2. Narskii.
3. W. Owen, *Anthem for Doomed Youth* (published 1920 privately by S. Sassoon in *Poems of Wilfred Owen*).
4. Although, in other books, he is referred to throughout as 'General Knox', he was at this time a colonel. See, e.g. Lockhart, p. 80.
5. M. Egremont, *Forgotten Land: Journeys among the Ghosts of East Prussia* (New York: Farrar, Straus & Giroux, 2011), p. 157.
6. Published London: Hutchinson, 1921, of which vol. 1 may be downloaded from http://www.archive.org/details/withtherussianarmy101knoxuoft.
7. Lockhart, p. 137.
8. Bumby mistakes the date. His account is downloadable from *Dostupné z Metodického portálu* on www.rvp.cz.
9. Bumby account (abridged).
10. A.W.F. Knox, *With the Russian Army 1914–1917* (London: Hutchinson, 1921), vol. 1, pp. xx, xxi.
11. Ibid. and p. 37 (abridged).
12. Because calibres in Russia were than measured in *linii* and not millimetres or inches. This corresponded to 0.31in or 7.62mm.
13. Some estimates put the figure as low as 3.8 million. Knox was informed the true figure on mobilisation was 4.3 million.
14. More detailed information is available on www.worldaffairsboard.com/world-wars/arming-ivan-russian-small-arms-wwi/htm.
15. Dowling, pp. 7–8.
16. Knox, vol. 1, p. xxxiv (digitised version made available by University of Toronto).
17. Dowling, p. 5; also N. Stone, *The Eastern Front 1914–1917* (London: Penguin, 1998), p. 32.
18. M.S.Neiberg and D. Jordan, *The Eastern Front 1914–1920* (London: Amber Books, 2008), p. 53.
19. Dowling, pp. 5–6.

20. Ibid, pp. 6–7.
21. Stone, p. 52.
22. Knox, p. 45 (abridged).
23. Plan 20 was due to come into force in September, and might have made a difference.
24. Itself copying the gauge of industrial wagon-ways.
25. F.V. Muchulsky, *Gulag Boss*, tr. D. Kaple (Oxford: OUP, 2011), p. 139.

5

IN THE AIR AND AT SEA

For a country so backward in just about every other branch of technology, it is surprising that Russia had the second largest air force in Europe, after France. The Imperial Russian Air Force – *Imperatorskii Voyenno-Vozdushny Flot* (IVF), to give it its correct name – was even able to claim the credit for the first enemy aircraft ever destroyed in flight. Piloting a Nieuport IV monoplane, the aerobatic pioneer Staff Captain Pyotr Nesterov was the first man to fly a loop. On 25 August 1914[1] he repeatedly fired his pistol at an Austrian Albatros BII on a reconnaissance mission, then deliberately flew his Morane-Saulnier Type G monoplane into the Albatros. His specific intent is unknown because, in addition to causing the Austrian aircraft to crash, killing pilot and observer, his own plane was so damaged by the collision that it also crashed, killing him when he fell out on the way down.[2] There were no parachutes at the time, except for observer officers in tethered balloons, because it was thought that this would cause nervous pilots to bail out before they needed to, instead of flying their valuable craft back to base for the necessary repairs.

Formed in 1910, IVF traced its beginnings back to earlier experimental flights by pioneers like Konstantin Tsiolkovsky and Igor Sikorsky, who emigrated to the United States in 1919 after the Revolution. Before the war, he built a four-engine airliner named after the Russian folk hero Ilya Murometz, but commonly called 'the big 'un', at his Russo-Baltic Wagon Company factory in Riga. Powered by French-built Salmson air-cooled engines, the civilian version had panoramic windows lining the large and comfortable insulated cabin, heated by the exhaust pipes, with wicker armchairs for up to sixteen passengers, a table, bunk, electric lighting – and the first airborne toilet! Hatches on either side of the cabin allowed the flight engineer to scramble out onto the lower wing to service the engines in flight. For the time, it was an extraordinary piece of engineering and set a world record by flying from St Petersburg to Kiev in Ukraine, a return trip of 2,400km, in under twenty-eight hours' flying time with only one refuelling stop in each direction.

The several military versions designed for service as heavy bombers had a gun position equipped with an 8mm machine gun and a 37mm cannon set in the middle of the upper wing, where the gunner had 180-degree vision at the cost of being completely exposed to the elements. Up to eight other machine guns could be fitted in various positions, including a tail gunner pod, making this an early Flying Fortress. All this armament and the armour-plating that protected the motors made the Ilya Murometz the least favourite target for CP fighters, which also found the powerful prop wash dangerously destabilising if they got too close when attacking from the rear. Navigation instruments were still primitive but did include a drift indicator and simple bombsight. Bomb racks could accommodate up to 800kg of bombs. Seventy-three of these amazing machines were built in all, flying over 400 sorties and leading the way in squadron-strength raids, night bombing, photographic damage assessment and the dropping of safe-conducts to encourage enemy ground troops to desert.[3]

The total of 5,000 aircraft of all types built in Russia between 1914 and the end of hostilities included 'flying boats' as float-planes were then called, constructed for the Imperial Russian Navy. Construction of all aircraft was limited by the need to depend heavily on foreign aero engines – mainly from France. Austro-Hungary did not do much better, but Germany allegedly produced over 45,000 aircraft during the war. Spare parts were also a big problem for Russia, given the wide variety of makes and models, for many of which spares were not available locally. Ground crews therefore tried to fit non-standard parts, which caused additional unreliability so that, as the war ground on, many aircraft in front-line squadrons would not have been considered airworthy at any other place or time.[4]

For all the undoubted skills of Russian aircraft constructors and fliers, in the first months of hostilities IVF aircraft were confined to reconnaissance and artillery observation roles because the military applications of flying machines had yet to be fully appreciated. In December 1914 an *otryad* or squadron[5] of Ilya Murometz aircraft was tasked with bombing missions against both German and Austro-Hungarian armies in the first step towards the carpet bombing of cities forty years later.

Among the other aircraft in IVF was the Anatra DS, built in Artur Anatra's factory at Odessa in the Ukraine. This was a two-seater reconnaissance biplane with 150hp Salmson Canton-Unne water-cooled radial engine that necessitated an ugly cooling radiator mounted on the centre of the upper wing. The DSS model had radiators mounted on the plywood sides of the fuselage or under the nose. It had a maximum speed of 144kph and ceiling of 4,300m. The pilot had a forward-firing machine gun and the observer used a second machine gun firing in a wide arc. Also made in the Anatra factory was the oddest-looking aircraft of the war. The Anadwa VKh was a twin-boom three-seater biplane light bomber composed of two Anatra D fuselages, of which the left one was occupied by the pilot, and the right by his observer. The machine gunner was seated in a nacelle mounted on the centre of the upper wing, providing excellent all-round vision and field of fire. Powered by twin 9-cylinder air-cooled Gnome rotary engines, it could carry a bomb-load of 600kg at a maximum speed of 140kph and service ceiling of 4,000m.

The Moskva MB 2-bis single-seater fighter was powered by a single Rhône air-cooled rotary engine that gave it a maximum speed of 130kph and ceiling of 3,200m. The single machine gun was not synchronised, on some models firing above the propeller arc. Other models had bullet deflectors on the propeller blades, which seems a bizarre idea today. In 1916 two Russian engineers collaborated to produce the Savelyev Quadruplane. The four wings were in a strut-braced box tilted forward with a Morane-G fuselage fitted between. Underpowered when first flown in April 1916, it went into production with a more powerful Gnome-Monosoupape or Clerget 9-cylinder air-cooled rotary engine, giving it a maximum speed of 132kph and a ceiling somewhere above 2,000m, sufficient for reconnaissance work.

The Voisin-Ivanov was another biplane made in the Anatra factory, primarily for ground attack roles. Fitted with a Salmson P9 water-cooled radial engine, it carried a crew of two with one machine gun and a bomb-load of less than 100kg. Its design was based on the French Voisin LAS pusher biplane, which enabled the observer sitting in the front seat to have a clear field of fire to the front and sides. Maximum speed was 150kph with a ceiling of 3,500m. More than 100 were produced and some continued in use after the Revolution until lack of spares eventually grounded most aircraft in Russia.

At the start of the war, Germany had 200-plus aircraft in a corps designated *Die Fliegertruppen*, or flying troops. For the first months of hostilities their main activity was reconnaissance, often performed by pilots flying the reliable Rumpler-Taube monoplane which had been in production since 1912 and was instrumental in causing many casualties among Allied troops in Macedonia. As the combat potential of aircraft was realised, in late 1916 the German air force was renamed *Die Luftstreitkräfte*.

The Fokker MV was an unarmed single-seater monoplane, first produced in 1913. With its single wing above the cabin, it afforded excellent visibility of the ground below and was widely used in early months of hostilities. It was also the platform from which the more successful Fokker EI was developed. Marks II and III were also single-seater fighters, which first appeared on the Russian front in 1915. The EIII had a more powerful engine than the earlier models and one 7.92mm machine gun. At end of 1915 this was superseded by the Mark IV with an up-rated engine and two machine guns. The Mark V, with its Gnome-Lamda 7-cylinder rotary engine had a tubular metal construction that made it light and strong. Some modified Mark VIII models were designated AI and AIII, and fitted with a single 7.92mm parabellum machine gun. The Fokker DVI was an all-metal biplane with a speed of 200kph that could reach a ceiling of 6,000m. However, it only arrived on the Russian fronts in April 1918, at the time of the Armistice.

The Albatros DIII biplane was feared by Russian pilots as the most dangerous German aircraft of the war, with its speed of 165kph and a ceiling of 5,000m. Its successor the Albatros DV biplane was reputed to be able to out-fly most Allied aircraft with the exception of the Bleriot-SPAD 7. The Roland CII appeared on the Russian fronts early in 1916, and was used for local and long-range recce, correction of artillery fire and precision bombing until mid-1917. The Fokker Dreidecker triplane was inspired by the British-built Sopwith triplane. With the fuselage between the two lower wings, early models had structural problems but the Mark V and later models stood every test on the Russian fronts starting in February 1917. Because of its inherent instability, the aircraft was loved by fighter aces for its ability to take immediate evading action and was the machine of choice for the German ace Manfred von Richtofen. It was in one of these that he was shot down and killed in April 1918.

The AEG GIII was the first German long-distance bomber – and range was imperative on the widespread Russian fronts. It was produced from mid-1915 onwards and was in service from the end of that year. It had two machine guns and could carry a 300kg bomb-load. The Zeppelin-Staaken RVI was another long-distance heavy bomber. Armed with four machine guns, it could carry eighteen 100kg bombs. The four powerful Maybach engines were mounted in two pods on either side of the fuselage that each had one pusher and one puller propeller. Between the two motors in each pod was a space for the flight mechanic to sit when carrying out in-flight maintenance.[6] Although built in Germany, the Hansa-Brandenburg C1 biplane was passed on to Austro-Hungarian fliers as being not quite good enough for use as a fighter, although adequate for reconnaissance roles. Surprisingly, twelve Austro-Hungarian airmen scored sufficient kills with it to be labelled aces.[7]

Although a side-show to the main conflict on land, the Baltic was itself a theatre of war. Here, Russia was at a great disadvantage because, during the Russo-Japanese war, Admiral Zinovi Rozhdestvensky had led the Russian Baltic Fleet from the Latvian port of Libau (modern Liepaja) to relieve the blockade of Port Arthur by the Japanese – a task well beyond the capacity of the Russian Pacific Fleet. On 14 May 1905 this fleet belatedly set course from Vietnam's Cam Ranh Bay for the surviving Russian naval base at Vladivostok, Port Arthur having already surrendered during the long voyage. Admiral Togo Heihachiro's more modern and better armed warships were waiting in ambush in the Tsushima

Strait between Japan and Korea. In the long and bloody Battle of Tsushima 27–29 May the Russian fleet lost over 200,000 tons of shipping, against Heihachiro's losses of 300 tons. Casualties were similarly disparate, with 4,830 Russian sailors killed and 6,000 taken prisoner, including the admiral, while Japanese casualties totalled less than 200.

Nine years later, with the Russian Baltic Fleet still well below strength, by 26 August 1914 both German and Russian submersibles patrolled the Baltic.[8] In October 1914 a German submersible sank the Russian cruiser *Palladia* in October 1914 and a Royal Navy submarine sank the German heavy cruiser *Adalbert*. When the German cruiser *Magdeburg* went aground while mine-laying off the Gulf of Riga, its crew was evacuated by an escorting destroyer but left behind their code books, which greatly helped to break encrypted German radio traffic when forwarded to the British Admiralty. In the Baltic both sides laid thousands of mines, claiming several ships, and also shelled coastal towns held by the enemy.

In late August and early September 1914 Polish-born IVF pilot Jan Nagórski was the first man to fly over the Arctic, making five search missions in his Farman MFII biplane in the hope of finding the lost Russian polar explorer Georgi Sedov. It was an incredibly brave undertaking, given the state of low-temperature engineering knowledge and the fact that the only lubricant was castor oil. Nagórski's subsequent war service included flying as eyes-in-the-sky for the Baltic Fleet from a base at Turku, Finland, where he was the first man to loop the loop in a float-plane, in September 1916. In 1917 his aircraft was damaged far out over the Baltic and Nagórski declared missing in action when he did not return to base. After several hours in very cold water, he was picked up by a Russian submarine and recovered from exposure in a military hospital in Riga. Because the report of his rescue and recovery never reached his HQ, he was declared dead – and stayed that way for thirty-eight years! In 1955 he attended a lecture in Warsaw where he was referred to as 'a dead Russian aviator' and announced to the amazed audience that he was neither Russian nor dead.[9]

NOTES

1. According to the Old Style calendar then used in Russia.
2. More details on http://en.wikipedia.org/wiki/Pyotr_Nesterov.
3. See also http://en.wikipedia.org/wiki/Sikorsky_Ilya_Muromets.
4. Much interesting information on Russian aviation and aircraft construction of the time to be found on
   http://www.alexanderpalace.org/aerialrussia/flyingmen.html.
5. Literally, a group, but since that has a specific aeronautical meaning 'squadron' seems a better translation.

6. More details about contemporary German aircraft on http:vakul.ru/istoriya-aviacii/aviaciya-germani-vo-vremya-pervoj-mirovoy-vojny.
7. Neiberg and Jordan, p. 97.
8. A submarine is a vessel that can travel reasonable distances under water; these early craft travelled on the surface and submerged for action – hence the term 'submersible'.
9. More on http://en/wikipedia.org/wiki/Jan_Nag.

6

SIGNALS FAILURE ON THE LINE TO TANNENBERG

On 15 August Russian 1st Army, based in Vilna under General Pavel von Rennenkampf, drove into northern East Prussia from the east. The other arm of the pincer, Russian 2nd (or Warsaw) Army under General Aleksandr Samsonov had originally been intended for a strike southwards into Galicia, but moved instead northward across the border into East Prussia on 20 August. Between the two prongs of the Russian attack, there was no coordination, partly because of inadequate logistics; partly due to the difficult terrain of the Augustovo Forest and the Masurian Lakes which lay between them; but mostly because the two army commanders were known for refusing to speak to each other, even when face-to-face. Rennenkampf also refused to speak to his own chief of staff or to read any communication addressed to the chief of staff and not to himself. So inadequate were his communications with his front commander, General Yakov Zhilinski at northern front HQ in Bialystok that Zhilinski was reduced to pleading with Stavka for assistance. Five messages were sent from Stavka to Rennenkampf, who did not deign to reply, or to receive an emissary from Grand Duke Nikolai. It says a lot about the senior officers of 1st Army that its cavalry commander, the elderly Khan of Nackichevan was unable to mount a horse because he suffered from piles – and ended by having a nervous breakdown.[1]

The two Russian armies tasked with the adventure into East Prussia totalled 208 battalions and 228 squadrons of cavalry against less than 100 battalions in German 8th Army opposing them. In terms of military planning, the staff of 2nd Army had arranged for 10,145 hospital beds to be available for casualties from the campaign, a number sufficient only for the victims of syphilis undergoing treatment.[2] Fortunately for the enemy, Russian intelligence was generally appalling: on one occasion General Nikolai Russki commanding 3rd Army on the south-western front acted on a war-game assumption that he was outnumbered while actually facing nine Austro-Hungarian divisions with twenty-two of his own.

All sides were already intercepting and/or jamming each other's diplomatic radio traffic, but military signals interception was in its infancy, although the Germans were sufficiently technically advanced for them regularly to decipher coded communications between the Western Allies in Flanders. Russian military radio communications were transmitted *en clair*, and thus easily intercepted by front-line German signals intercept units, which were so efficient that Marshal Joffre's Order of the Day for the Battle of the Marne in September 1914 was deciphered and read by the German High Command before it had reached the French front line.[3]

After Rennenkampf's initial victories at Stallupönen (modern Nesterov) on 17 August and Gumbinnen (modern Gusev),[4] on 20 August, Prittwitz learned of the approach of Samsonov's army, and panicked, ordering a strategic retreat all the way back to the River Vistula – which meant evacuating most of East Prussia. On reflection, he amended this order to a retreat to the River Passarge,[5] which still left the 50 × 20 mile German enclave of the Königsberg peninsula cut off and relying on re-supply by sea. As head of OHL, Helmuth von Moltke immediately decided to sack Prittwitz and telegraphed on 22 August to 66-year-old retiree General Paul von Hindenburg, calling him back to the colours. Hindenburg's soldierly reply was a 2-word telegram: *Bin bereit* – am ready – after which he got on the next train to Hannover and a return to military life. Moltke also sent a letter by courier to Major General Erich Ludendorff, appointing him chief of staff to Hindenburg and ending: 'There is no one I trust more than you. Perhaps you can save the situation in the East.' That *perhaps* is a measure of the alarm engendered in Berlin by Prittwitz's panic.

After retirement, Hindenburg lived on his estate in East Prussia, where his wife had wanted to plant apple trees, until he remarked dryly that it would be pointless because, by the time they were mature, the area would be occupied by Russians. In fact, it was occupied by Poles, but the apples would not have filled German bellies either way. Hindenburg devoted three years in walking tours of the province, during which he familiarised himself with the topography, noting probable avenues of invasion by Russia and the best ways of frustrating any such incursions. After the defeat in 1918, Hindenburg became the great apostle of the *Dolchstosslegende* – the stab-in-the-back fantasy that Germany's defeat on the battlefield had little to do with Allied superiority in arms and manpower, even after the arrival in Europe of US troops and materiel, but was mainly due to treachery by the civilian population, by mutineers and Communists – and eventually, of course, the Jews. So it was that he, as president of the Weimar Republic, summoned Adolf Hitler to become chancellor of the first Nazi government, although privately referring to him as 'the Austrian corporal'. Ludendorff, who had been

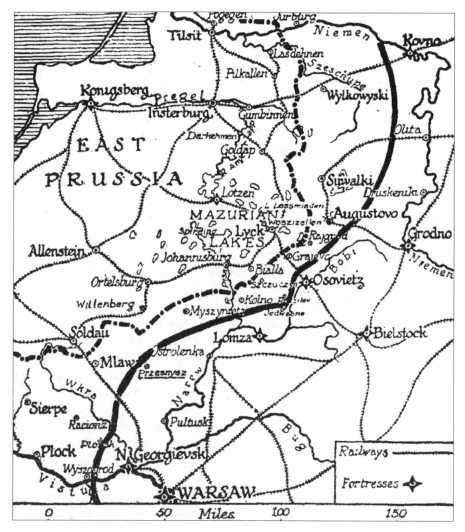

East Prussia – the area invaded by Rennenkampf and Samsonov. Contemporary map with anglicised place names.

one of the co-accused at the 1924 trial of Hitler's cabal, had by then changed sides and wrote scathingly to his old commander about Hitler's rise to power. But all that was a long way in the future.

Inspecting the south-western front a long way south at Rovno, where he met General Nikolai Ivanov, the genial 55-year-old front commander, Colonel Knox described his new host as being 'simple and unpretentious in his manner', having worked his way up the ladder from humble beginnings. This was reflected in the fare at table. Russian peasants used to say, '*Shchi da kasha, pishcha nasha*' – cabbage soup and gruel of buckwheat, that's all we ever get to eat. It was also what Knox got to eat at Ivanov's table, where no wine was to be served until the war was ended. It amused the English observer to see Princes Dolgoruki and Karakin imbibing lemonade instead.

After the meal, the officers went outside to talk to the troops and Knox spoke to one 'fine fellow, over six feet tall, belonging to the 4th Heavy Artillery Division.' This reservist told him that he had left a wife and five children at home. When assured by the officers that he would survive, the artilleryman shook his head sadly. 'It is a wide road that leads to the war,' he said, 'and a narrow path that leads home again.' Knox had heard General Samsonov complaining about the problems of launching an offensive in these regions, purposely left roadless by the Russian government to delay any enemy incursions. Heading towards the town of Dubno – on horseback, of course – Knox recorded passing a column of the 127th Infantry Regiment plodding along through the deep mud under torrential rain at a pace little faster than marking time, and with a look of unreasoning misery on their faces. He summed them up as unlikely to win their imminent contact with the enemy.[6]

The new command team taking over German 8th Army 400 miles to the north-west in East Prussia decided to adopt a plan by Prittwitz's deputy operations officer Colonel Maximilian Hoffmann – a baby-faced officer with full lips and pince-nez spectacles that belied a shrewd military mind. Like Knox a fluent Russian-speaker who had spent several years in Russia, Hoffmann had witnessed the mutual recriminations of Samsonov and Rennenkampf after the defeat of Mukden[7] during the Russo-Japanese war of 1904, and was certain that it would be possible to surround Samsonov's army long before Rennenkampf came to its rescue – and trap it in what they called *eine Kesselschlacht* or 'killing cauldron'. Accordingly, General Hermann von Francois' I Corps was transported by the efficient German rail network to confront the left flank of Samsonov's army, where some inconsequential skirmishes had already taken place, while XVII Corps and I Reserve Corps, commanded by Generals Mackensen and von Below, were held ready to march south and tackle Samsonov's right wing. The inherent risk in Hoffmann's plan was that the outer defences in the south of the Königsberg enclave would be substantially depleted in manpower until German 1st Cavalry Division was redeployed to screen them, and that Rennenkampf's 1st Army *could* swing south to threaten the German left flank in order to take the pressure off Samsonov.

Taking command on 23 August, Hindenburg and Ludendorff immediately approved Hoffmann's plan. Still advancing north-westwards on the following day, Samsonov was having logistics problems and understood from General Zhilinski in Byalistok that all was going according to Plan 19A in the north. He had no idea that Rennenkampf had paused to regroup after Gumbinnen instead of pressing on in a south-westerly direction to effect the planned link-up of the two armies. Lindendorff ordered General von François' I Corps to begin its attack on Samsonov's left flank on 25 August but François held back for two further days, protesting to Ludendorff and Hoffmann, who travelled in person to put pressure on him, that his artillery was still in transit. François' correct assessment of the situation, and his failure to attack prematurely, nevertheless earned his superiors' lasting hatred and effectively stunted his military career after Hindenburg and Ludendorff were subsequently given command of all the German armies.

Back in Berlin, Chief of Staff Helmuth von Moltke was uneasy about the situation in East Prussia, surprising Ludendorff by telephoning him to say that he was detaching a cavalry division and three army corps from France and sending them to the Russian front. Knowing that Schlieffen's dying words had been, 'Keep the right flank strong', Hindenburg and Ludendorff both considered that the promised reinforcements could be far better used in France, where the drive to surround Paris was already slowing down because the right flank was *not* sufficiently strong. Although they protested that they did not need reinforcements in East Prussia, these were sent anyway, proving Schlieffen's dying fears prophetic as the weakened right flank was brought to a halt well short of its objective.

Shortly after the conference with François, on 25 August Hoffmann received two clear-language signals intercepts of Russian transmissions. The one from Rennenkampf's HQ revealed not only the exact distance then separating the two Russian armies but also gave away the compass bearing on which 1st Army was advancing. The intercept from Samsonov's HQ revealed how he believed erroneously that the German forces ahead of him were withdrawing northwards. In fact, by pursuing them, he was leading his army further into a trap. Ludendorff wondered whether the intercepted signals could have been a ruse because it seemed incredible that neither would be in code, but Hindenburg supported Hoffmann's assessment that they were genuine. Accordingly, German XX Corps was moved into position between Allenstein and Tannenberg.

There, German XVII Corps attacked Samsonov's right flank near Seeburg and Bischofstein on 26 August. The battle is rather confusingly referred to in German war history as the Battle of Tannenberg although geographically at some distance from there. This was a later idea of Hoffmann's, to expunge the memory of the humiliating defeat of the Teutonic Knights in that area by a Polish-Lithuanian army in 1410. German XX Corps was able to hold a line near Tannenberg, while the Russian 13th Corps drove unopposed on Allenstein. In twenty-four hours, German I Corps under François had neutralised Samsonov's left flank. For whatever reason, he disregarded this and obstinately drove his five centre divisions onwards to their doom after German XVII Corps turned his right flank. The next day, General François used his artillery and now adequate stock of shells to break through Russian 1st Corps. Colonel Knox commented that one Russian regiment had nine out of sixteen company commanders killed; a company that began the action 190-strong lost all its officers, had 120 other ranks killed and most survivors wounded.[8] But worse was to come. Russia still had vast reserves of men, permitting the replacement of a quarter-million men taken prisoner or killed at Tannenberg and the First Battle of the Masurian Lakes. What it did not have was an endless supply of rifles, from which to replace the quarter-million rifles lost with these men.

Hoffmann received another uncoded intercept, from Zhilinksii to Rennenkampf, which indicated clearly that Russian 1st Army had *not* been ordered to march to Samsonov's support with all possible speed. On the strength of this, Ludendorff despatched von Below from Bischofsburg to strengthen the German centre, with Mackensen ordered south to close the ring around Russian 2nd Army.

Hoping to save the bulk of his army, Samsonov withdrew Russian 13th Corps from the drive on Allenstein, to redeploy it against the German line east of Tannenberg. On 28 August, as German forces squeezed both Russian flanks, Samsonov at last panicked, with his forces dispersed and reinforcements unable to reach him from the rear. That evening, he ordered a general withdrawal. Even had Rennenkampf been ordered to come to his aid, it was now too late, as the way was blocked by fast-moving German cavalry. Ordering 2nd Army to fall back to the southwest and regroup, Samsonov was wrong-footed by another refusal of François to mindlessly obey orders – in this case, to move north in case Rennenkampf, by forced marches, did come to Samsonov's support. Instead, François ordered I Corps to drive eastwards to the south of Samsonov's centre and block its retreat to safety in the Polish salient. This insubordination contributed greatly to the German victory, but did not restore him to Hindenburg's favour.

Samsonov's situation became completely unsustainable after German XVII Corps joined up with I Corps on 29 August. Something of the confusion and chaos can be gleaned from Knox's diary. His entry for that day was a pious hope that Samsonov had not underestimated the strength of the German forces advancing towards him from the west and north-west. Chatting to a French pilot named Poiret, who had been flying dangerous low-level reconnaissance missions for the Russians north-west of Neidenburg (modern Nidzica), where his observer had been wounded that morning by shrapnel in the leg, Knox was told that the pilot's assessment, based on observation, was that Samsonov was about to be hit by three entire army corps. Visiting the field hospital to enquire after Poiret's wounded observer, he found little sign of preparation for casualties. With no beds provided, the wounded were lying haphazardly on the floor, the lucky ones having at best some straw to lie on.

During the visit, the sound of nearby rifle fire caused Knox to run outside and look up. An enormous Zeppelin was hovering overhead at a height of 900 to 1,000m. It dropped four bombs in quick succession, killing six men and wounding fourteen others. Rifle fire being totally useless against such a target, a nearby battery was brought into action, damaging the airship and forcing it to land. The crew was taken prisoner, to everyone's great relief.

There were few women to be seen in this scene of desolation. Watching the survivors of two army corps straggle into the town of Ostrolenka, Knox learned that General Martos of 15th Corps had been injured when a German shell landed on his car. With him at the time was a German-speaking officer's wife called Aleksandra Aleksandrovna, who had been acting as his interpreter. Apparently uninjured, she panicked, jumping out of the car after the explosion and ran off into the forest, never to be seen again.

Realising too late that his army was surrounded and trapped, Samsonov continued the hopeless fight for two further days until surrendering at a cost of 92,000 officers and men taken prisoner, another 50,000 killed and wounded and the loss of more than 400 guns.[9] By then, Knox was back in Warsaw, which had been bombed several times by German aircraft and airships. More alarmingly, he found that the massive Poniatovski bridge over the Vistula was being wired for demolition. The families of government officials were already leaving for the safety of Mother Russia, with their menfolk preparing to follow them at a moment's notice. A member of the State Duma, or Russian parliament, told him that Stavka envisaged losses of about 300,000 men in the defence of the city. Meeting the Frenchman Poiret again, he found him pessimistically saying to all and sundry that, if the Russians allowed Warsaw to be taken, it showed they were beaten.

So much Russian equipment had been abandoned on the field of battle by Samsonov's men – including all their guns and transport – that more than fifty freight trains were required to transport it all back to Germany for further use. German casualties totalled less than half the Russian losses.

Like Rennenkampf, Samsonov had made his reputation as a cavalry commander. This, as Knox commented, was of no value in preparing the two generals to command large numbers of troops against their German opponents who were ruthless professional soldiers trained in the efficient, modern deployment of infantry and artillery, as well as the cavalry, and also knew the terrain of East Prussia intimately.[10]

In the early hours of 28 August Samsonov made what Knox called a 'mad decision', cutting himself off from his base and half his forces and sending much equipment, including all the wireless transmitters and receivers back to Russia.[11] Knox found the general and his staff sitting on the ground, poring over their maps. Samsonov stood up and ordered eight men of the *sotnya*[12] of Cossacks that acted as his bodyguard to hand over their mounts. Privately, he told Knox that the position was very critical, and advised him to head for the rear while there was still time. Samsonov then rode off to see how things were going at the front with his own eyes, as he had been accustomed to doing in Manchuria during the Russo-Japanese war of 1904–5. The eight officers and the rest of the *sotnya* rode off to the north-west on the Cossack ponies, while Knox was driven slowly back to Neidenburg, wondering whether the town with its Teutonic castle was still in friendly hands. In the town, badly damaged by the Russian artillery in Samsonov's attack, everything was quiet, although shells were bursting 2 or 3 miles to the north-west. Walking wounded and stragglers were wandering aimlessly about among the ruins. One soldier, who had been caught looting, was screaming in agony as he was flogged with a *knout* by Cossacks outside the commandant's house. His ordeal ended when a single shot was fired as the officers drove out of town.[13]

Although able at the last possible moment to escape from the pocket with about 10,000 officers and men, Samsonov and his staff had no contact or communication with the outside world after the evening of 29 August and were finally accompanied only by the remnant of their Cossack escort. From various survivors' accounts, the story of their final hours was gradually pieced together. After being out of communication for three whole days, Samsonov and his staff officers became lost after he told the Cossack escort, who had suffered severely in charging a machine gun position, to shift for themselves. On the night of 29–30 August the small group of officers was stumbling on foot through the forest north of the railway line from Neidenburg to Willenberg. Holding hands to avoid losing one another in the darkness, they had one compass, but no maps. As Knox commented, Russian maps were in any case inaccurate and badly printed, but to have no maps at all defies imagination. Finally the matches they were striking to consult the compass gave out. Samsonov kept saying, 'The Tsar trusted me. How can I face him after such a disaster?' He went off into the darkness and the other officers heard a shot. After searching unsuccessfully for his body, they managed to reach Russian-held territory, having covered 40 miles on foot. Samsonov's corpse was later recovered by German troops and given a respectful military funeral.[14]

The capital named St Petersburg by Peter the Great – the name was now thought to be too Germanic – was rechristened on 31 August with the Slavic name Petrograd. To the north of the great Russian defeat at Allenstein/Tannenberg, Rennenkampf still had fourteen divisions, a rifle brigade and five cavalry divisions, with Russian 10th Army on its way to join him with six more combat-ready divisions. Hoffmann immediately set in motion the mammoth manoeuvre of moving German 8th Army, hampered by the need to guard and feed all those prisoners, north-east to tackle Rennenkampf. His plan was classically simple: splitting forces so that the right wing could swing to the north-east through the Masurian Lakes to cut the Russian lines of communication and interdict the arrival of 10th Army, while the main force engaged Russian 1st Army. Underestimating the speed at which well-trained German troops could be redeployed on their home ground by a railway system that enabled large numbers of men to be transported long distances very rapidly, Rennenkampf failed to secure his position while this was still possible.

Observing the chaos all around him, Knox noted that Army Orders reached local commanders sometimes as late as 10 a.m., so that troops being redeployed could only set off on foot at noon. Communication between the various corps had to be maintained by wireless but, as many staffs had not a single officer who could encipher or decipher, the messages were sent in clear, allowing the German intercept stations to prepare for every move. Reaching Allenstein on 27 August, many of Rennenkampf's soldiers believed it to be Berlin.[15] The sight of a modern, neat, tidy German city defied the imagination of a Siberian peasant conscript, used to mud roads and primitive housing unchanged since the Middle Ages. How could the enemy possess two such prosperous cities? he must have wondered. The conscript would have had as little idea of European geography as a Briton would know of Omsk or Tomsk. Four decades later, in 1958 when an RAF linguist colleague of the author asked a sentry at the small Soviet war memorial in West Berlin in Russian how he liked being stationed in Berlin, the sentry replied, '*Chto eto takoye, Berlin?*' 'What's Berlin?'

Colonel Knox rightly considered it his duty to pass back to London the gist of his observations of the disastrous East Prussia campaign. Asking permission of front commander General Zhilinski to return to the renamed capital, from where he could send his despatches, he was informed that protocol demanded he must first obtain permission from Grand Duke Nikolai. Stavka was ignorant of the enemy's movements and corps commanders were informed only of the immediate objectives of neighbouring units, but told nothing of what had happened to Samsonov's army. So this was an excuse to keep him waiting in Bialystok for three days because Zhilinski feared the consequences of the only foreign officer to observe the debacle talking about it in Petrograd, where he was trying to cover his own inadequacy by accusing Rennenkampf of failing to move to Samsonov's assistance and turning a personal profit from supplies contracts. However, Rennenkampf turned to his friends in the cavalry establishment, who persuaded the Grand Duke that the whole debacle was all Zhilinski's fault. Nikolai believed them and told the Tsar, who dismissed Zhilinski, leaving Rennenkampf to fight badly another day.[16] During his enforced wait at Stavka that ended on 6 September, Knox noted that the nerves of all ranks were so shaky that troops fired at every aircraft appearing in the skies and occasionally even at their own officers' automobiles.

Within a week of the German victory at Tannenberg/Allenstein, eight German divisions confronted Rennenkampf with seven more, including two of cavalry, threatening his exposed left flank. Analysts have interpreted this to mean that Hindenburg and Ludendorff were not so much trying to annihilate Russian 1st Army as to force it to retreat back towards its start line at the border. If that was the plan, it worked even better than could have been expected. On 7 September, three German divisions attacked the Russian left flank in the First Battle of the Masurian Lakes, meeting sustained Russian resistance.

On 10 September Rennenkampf sacrificed two divisions to gain the time to disengage his main force in a strategic retreat. Slowed down by the need to march eastwards through their own chaotic, horse-drawn supply trains still heading for the abandoned front line, his men nevertheless managed to make 20 miles a day, travelling faster than their pursuers, who made no serious attempt to block their retreat to the frontier. Whether this was a retreat or a rout, is debatable. Certainly it was a costly manoeuvre that left a further 200 artillery pieces behind and the better part of two whole armies – totalling around a quarter-million officers and men – in East Prussia as casualties or prisoners by the time the German spear-heads reached the border on 13 September and the front stabilised.

The Russian attack on East Prussia did arguably disrupt OHL's execution of the modified Schlieffen Plan in France and play a part in preventing the fall of Paris, but its failure was a high price to pay for helping the Western Allies because it lowered morale at all ranks in the Russian armies and triggered a number of retreats over the next twelve months.

NOTES

1. Stone, pp. 58–9.
2. Ibid, p. 49.
3. G. Elliott and H. Shukman, *Secret Classrooms* (London: St Ermin's Press/Little, Brown, 2002), p. 173.
4. In Kaliningrad *oblast*.
5. Knox, p. 56.
6. Ibid, pp. 50–1, 61 (edited).
7. It was widely believed that they had actually come to blows.
8. Knox, pp. 64–5.
9. Stone, p. 66, although Russian casualties are approximate.
10. Knox, p. 85.
11. Ibid.
12. A squadron, nominally of 100 riders.
13. Knox, pp. 70–2 (edited).
14. Ibid, pp. 82, 86–7.
15. Ibid, p. 84 (edited).
16. Stone, footnote to p. 95.

7

THE GALICIAN GRAVEYARD

South of the Polish salient, the Russian front line ran for more than 300 miles through Galicia and the Bukovina (an Austrian duchy bounded on the north by Galicia and on the west by the Carpathian Mountains) to the Romanian frontier, skirting the Pogórze Karpatskie – the Carpathian foothills. Even in peacetime, it was an area of such depressing poverty that hundreds of thousands of Polish-, Lithuanian- and Yiddish-speaking peasants and villagers had fled from it in economic migration over the previous three or four decades in the hope of a more prosperous life elsewhere – the more fortunate ones settling in the New World.

The Russian forces south of the salient were the 3rd, 4th, 5th and 8th armies confronting Austro-Hungarian 1st, 3rd and 4th armies, with 2nd Army still engaged in Serbia. Conrad's essential problem was that his forces were ill coordinated. There were many incidents where ground forces shot at their own aircraft and this was only stopped when they were forbidden to fire on *any* aircraft. Nevertheless, Conrad took the offensive first, assuming that he would be able to strike a telling blow before Russian mobilisation was complete and thus interdict any rapid drive by the tsarist armies westward into Silesia, which was a stepping-stone into Germany itself. As in the Second World War, some of the distances in this theatre were immense, but the distance from the western edge of the salient to Berlin was less than 250 miles. Unless completely demolished in a German retreat, the excellent railway system would have made short work of that.

Concentrating his 1st and 4th armies on the southwest of the salient along the Vistula and Bug rivers, Conrad aimed to take the Polish towns of Lublin and Kholm. This now had little strategic point because Moltke's modified Schlieffen Plan had diverted to Alsace and Lorraine the two German armies originally allocated to drive south from East Prussia and link up with their Austro-Hungarian allies to nip off the Polish salient.

On 23 August Russian 4th Army advanced to attack the town of Kraśnik before being driven off by Austro-Hungarian 1st Army two days later. This minor defeat turned into the Battle of Komarów starting on 26 August, in which Russian 5th Army was only saved from total annihilation by the quick reactions of the confusingly named General Pavel Wenzel von Plehve. Most of the seven Russian generals of 1914 with German names came from the Baltic provinces, but Plehve was a Prussian who had chosen to serve in the tsarist army in the belief that promotion would be more rapid. Described by Colonel Knox as a wizened little rat of a man aged 65, Plehve was in poor health – and would be dead of natural causes before the end of 1916 – yet had a keen intelligence. He was unpopular with his troops, but not with his staff officers, who appreciated his quick grasp of a situation and the decisiveness that was to save the bulk of an army on this occasion.

At Komarów, neither side having had time to dig in or make permanent fortifications as in the static warfare on the Western Front, Plehve's right flank was vulnerable due to the defeat of 4th Army at Kraśnik. True to form, Plehve executed a strategic withdrawal northwards, albeit with the loss of 20,000 men and 100 artillery pieces. To support Plehve, south-western front commander General Nikolai Ivanov brought 3rd and 8th Russian armies into play, but the slowness with which the Russian reinforcements arrived at the front – many of them after marching 100 miles or more from the nearest railhead – meant that the arrival of General Nikolai Russki's 3rd Army was too late to block the Austrians' move. This, in turn, made Conrad von Hötzendorf over-confident. He attacked with two whole armies on 30 August, only to find that General Rudolf Ritter von Brudermann's 3rd Austrian Army was heavily outnumbered by Russian 3rd and 8th armies at the First Battle of Lemberg (modern Lviv). This time it was the Austro-Hungarians who had to retreat, with the loss of 20,000 men and seventy guns. In tennis terms, the score was fifteen-fifteen.

The loss of 20,000 men … As Stalin once remarked: 'A single death is a tragedy, a million deaths is a statistic.' A tiny insight into the misery and suffering is afforded by an episode in the life and death of the 27-year-old Austrian Expressionist poet Georg Trakl. Called up as a reservist and drafted at Innsbruck in August 1914, he was given the rank of lieutenant attached to the medical corps on the basis of having one year's experience as a trainee pharmacist. Three weeks later, after the Battle of Grodek near Lemberg, he found himself in charge of ninety wounded men in a filthy barn. Operations including amputations had to be carried out without anaesthetic and even 'successful' ones resulted frequently in death from shock and sepsis. One wounded man shot himself through the head in front of the ineffective Trakl. Outside the barn, the corpses of several hanged deserters swung from the branches of the trees. The horror of it all gave Trakl a nervous breakdown, for which the 'treatment' was to be locked in a cell with an officer suffering from delirium tremens. Transferred to a military hospital near Kraków,

The northern front at the end of August 1914.

he became so obsessed with the fear of being executed as a deserter that he committed suicide early in November.[1]

Between 3 and 11 September at the Battle of Rava-Russkaya — to be the site of an infamous German punishment camp for recalcitrant Allied POWs in the Second World War — General Moritz von Auffenberg commanding Austro-Hungarian 4th Army received an order from Conrad to wheel south and come to the aid of General Brudermann's 3rd Army. This opened up a gap between Auffenberg's 4th Army and General Viktor Dankl's 1st Army. When this was revealed to Ivanov by aerial reconnaissance, it was immediately exploited by cavalry from General Russki's 3rd Army, with nine divisions brought to bear on the weak point. Auffenberg's force was only able to avoid encirclement by accepting heavy casualties and abandoning men and equipment in a long retreat back to the foothills of the Carpathian Mountains. Although the error of judgement was Conrad's, the blame for this was placed on Auffenberg. It was neither the first nor the last time a junior commander carried the can for his superior's error, which was not corrected until 21 June 1915 when Rava-Russkaya was recaptured from the Russians.

After sending his despatches to London, Knox travelled from Petrograd to the south of the Polish salient, at Zlota near Lublin. There, on 23 September he was reminded why his Russian hosts called the period of spring and autumn rains *rasputitsa* – meaning, the time when you can't use the roads. Motor vehicles being immobilised by the rains and deep mud, he was riding on horseback over the most dreadful roads he had ever seen, even in Russia, wearing a *shuba*, or Russian officer's fur coat, against the keen wind. It was a garment he had taken to wearing because nervous sentries had more than once shot at him in his British greatcoat, mistaking him for an enemy officer.

With the whole area deliberately left a nearly roadless *glacis* – as he termed it – to impede the invading enemy, he observed the problem this caused when it came to transporting ammunition, food for the men and fodder for the horses forward to the front line, with the result that both men and horses were on short rations. The entire 5th Army had been six days without even bread to eat, and the men were exhausted. Its commander General Platon Lechitsky told Knox that the delay in launching an offensive on his sector of the front was entirely due to the impossibility of re-supply.

Despite being attacked by a band of 200 armed *sokoly*, or falcons as the Polish partisans called themselves, Knox was not the only officer to sympathise with the local civilians who, although powerless to resist the *sokoly*, were held responsible for their actions by the Russian troops. The elderly owner of one house where he was billeted told him that her grandfather had fought as a partisan against Russia in 1863. At another billet his hostess confessed to going out of the house only once since the Russian troops arrived because the habit of the infantrymen and Cossack cavalry of 'doing their business anywhere' made it impossible for her to walk about her own property. From her and other unwilling hosts, he learned the tragedy of the Polish men of military age, who were forcibly conscripted *by both sides* to fight against their brother Poles. In one billet, Knox watched a young lieutenant who spoke German interrogating a captured enemy NCO by the light of a single candle in a room crowded with Russian officers. Captured officers were not questioned because Russian etiquette held that an officer was a gentleman, whose honour should not be insulted by any invitation to give information against his own side.[2]

In Russian-occupied Poland there were also two embryo underground armies. One was organised by Jozef Pilsudski, who believed that only armed struggle against the tsarist hegemony would free his oppressed people – which made the Central Powers his allies. The other was headed by Roman Dmovski, who considered that Polish independence could be obtained as a reward for fighting alongside the Russian armies and relying on the Tsar's vague promises about Polish independence. By the end of 1917 three Polish army corps totalling 75,000 men were serving in the Russian armies.[3]

On 14 September 1914 Moltke was relieved of his duties by the Kaiser as a penalty for the failure of his modified Schlieffen plan and replaced as German chief of staff at OHL by Erich von Falkenhayn, who was to last two years in the job before being, in his turn, put out to grass. At OAK in Vienna the concern of the moment was disengaging Austro-Hungarian 2nd Army from the Serbian front. It arrived in Galicia too late to prevent the Austrian line being pushed back between Gorlice and Tarnow with its left flank on the Vistula River and the right in the Carpathian Mountains. This represented a retreat of 135 miles in places and left the whole of Austrian Galicia in Russian hands with the exception of the strategic fortress-city of Przemyśl, thought to be so impregnable that Conrad had installed his HQ there at the start of hostilities.

Even to call this a fortress-city is unhelpful to many Anglo-Saxon readers, who may not be familiar with the permanent strategic dispositions that Continental powers had to make near their land frontiers. The walled garrison town of Przemyśl was an important road, rail and river junction defended by a complex of twenty-five autonomous forts with a dozen batteries covering otherwise dead ground between them. The basic garrison troops numbered 50,000–60,000 men but, with all the outlying fortifications, more than double that number were cooped up within the Russian siege lines, which were effectively an inward-facing fortress enclosing the outward-facing Austrian fortifications, pummelled daily by Russian artillery.

The investment of so important a fortress as Przemyśl was a morale-boosting triumph for the Russian armies and may have played a part in Russian 8th Army under General Aleksei Brusilov reaching the Carpathian Mountains, having pushed back more than 100 miles the Austro-Hungarian forces opposing it. Since Conrad had lost 1.5 million men as casualties and POWs already in the war, increasing numbers of German officers and NCOs were now being embedded in Austro-Hungarian units to serve as *Korsettenstangen* – literally, the whalebone stays that kept a corset from wrinkling up. Without them, this latest Russian offensive could have spelled the end of Franz Joseph's armies.

On 24 September Russian 3rd Army under General Radko Dimitriev launched an attack on the Przemyśl complex without waiting for the arrival of sufficient siege artillery. In three days of hopeless attacks, Dimitriev lost 40,000 men, but

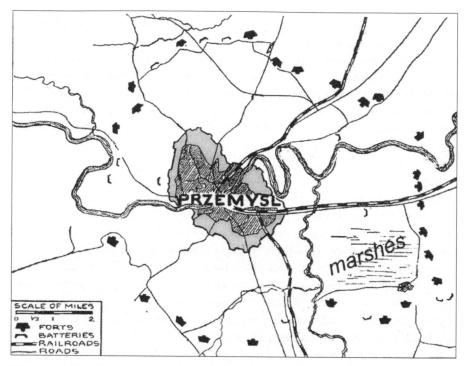

Sketch map of Przemysl fortress complex (after Knox), showing outlying forts and batteries.

failed to penetrate the Austrian defences. Simultaneously, Hindenburg launched an offensive targeting Warsaw and an Austrian relief column was known to be heading for Przemyśl with the aim of linking up with the garrison and taking the Russians in the rear. Dimitriev prudently withdrew across the San River. However, by the end of the month, the drive on Warsaw had been repulsed and the relief column had made little progress. Russian 11th Army under General Andrei Selivanov re-invested Przemyśl on 9 November, not to take it by storm, but to starve the garrison into submission. Sporadic contact with the outside world was maintained by airmail – miniaturised correspondence sent by pigeon post and baskets of ordinary mail transported by balloons, subject to the vagaries of the winds. Letters of no military significance that landed in Russian territory, including poems by Hungarian Corporal Géza Gyóni, were first forwarded to Petrograd to be censored before being forwarded by international post to the addressees.

OHL hastily transferred four German army corps 500 miles south from East Prussia to the Kraków area, just behind the Austrian lines. This force, designated 9th Army, was concentrated between Thorn and Posen and commanded by General Mackensen. So, when the Russian advance into the mineral-rich region of Silesia, south of the salient, began, Mackensen was well placed to attack the right flank. The Russians were again having re-supply problems.

On 19 November, Knox noted a critical shortage of ammunition for the 2nd Guards Division, which had used 2,150,000 rounds in three days of combat, and was down to a mere 180 rounds per rifle. Meeting a regimental ammunition train of empty carts, he was asked by the drivers where the ammunition dumps were, but could not tell them. For four long days, the ammunition was held up somewhere en route, so that men in the trenches in weather with temperatures well below zero were trying to fight off numerically superior attackers without any ammunition. Men froze to death in the trenches at night and tactical aerial reconnaissance was rendered impossible, owing to the intense cold. Once air-borne, an airman could cover only about 25 *versty* (16 miles) before returning to thaw out. Although the Russians in this sector had 'an overwhelming prepon-derance of guns' they were useless as no shells were available at the batteries.[4]

In the Battle for Łódź on 6 December Russian 5th Army counter-attacked but had to retreat and the danger to Silesia was removed. By the end of the year, German gains for the months of fighting included part of western Poland around Łódź and some inroads into the Russian Baltic provinces. In the south, Galicia remained in Russian hands, but the problem for all the Russian armies was shortage of ordnance, with the in-country munitions factories producing about one-third of the actual consumption of rifle ammunition at the front. A subsidiary problem Knox does not seem to have recorded was mentioned in the diary of Florence Farmborough, a young Englishwoman serving as a nurse in a dressing-station near the front lines. By chatting with the wounded men, she picked up the cares and preoccupations of the ordinary Russian soldier:

> Lately, ammunition had been sent in large quantities to our Front, but little of it has been of any use. Out of one consignment of 30,000 shells, fewer than 200 were found to be serviceable. Cartridges were sent in their hundreds of thousands and distributed among the men in their trenches, but they were of a foreign cast and would not fit the Russian rifle. Large stores of Japanese rifles had been despatched to neighbouring divisions, but the Russian cartridges failed to fit them.[5]

A conscientious observer, Knox wished to avoid the error of reporting local problems as being general. He spent a week at Stavka, where he was told that the shortage of rifles was due to losses of weapons with men who had been taken prisoner, plus those wounded and killed during retreats and even during advances. The need for care in the collection of discarded weapons after an engagement had been entirely overlooked because the first drafts arrived at the front fully armed, allowing lazy officers in the forward areas to suppose that the reserves of weaponry were inexhaustible. On several occasions, Knox had observed dis-carded rifles lying on a battlefield two and three days after the fighting ended.

One Guards commander told him that, when his men took over trenches from another unit in the line, they had found Russian rifles used as roof supports in the dugouts. Men were rarely punished for abandoning their weapons when fleeing an enemy attack. Even an offer of six roubles for each Russian rifle handed in and five roubles for each Austrian rifle failed to produce results. In Petrograd drafts of reinforcements were being entrained for the front with only one rifle between three men and the Assistant Minister of War stated that the impossibility of arming them with personal weapons was delaying the despatch of 2 million conscripts to the front.

Nor was artillery ordnance in any better shape. The theoretical initial stock of artillery ammunition had been 1,000 rounds per gun. With the daily expenditure of shell in the first hundred days of the war averaging 45,000 rounds, and Russian factories not having produced more than 3,000 3in shells per day, it was estimated on 3 December 1914 that Russia's reserves of artillery shells were down to less than 1 million rounds. The daily output of the armament factories was expected to rise to 20,000 a day by July 1915, which was still far from adequate for the 9 million conscripts, reservists and regulars. In this dire situation, contracts for the delivery of 8 million rounds by 15 November 1915 had been placed inside Russia and contracts for a further 4.5 million placed abroad, with the British company Vickers signing a contract to supply 2 million rounds. At the earliest, the foreign orders were not expected to be fulfilled before March 1915; in fact, most foreign deliveries were to arrive as much as a year later than that, after the ice in the White Sea had melted in 1916. The British government did not help by refusing to guarantee Russian payment although £8 million in gold had been sent to Britain on account in October 1914 and, for outstanding amounts, interest was charged at 5 per cent.

The cause of these problems was that, whereas Chief of Staff General Yanushkevich had recommended in the spring of 1914 that reserves of artillery shells be raised from 1,000 to 2,000 rounds per gun, the State Duma had still not voted the necessary credits before war broke out. In November, after the loss of so many guns in East Prussia, Stavka ordered that every 8-gun battery be slimmed down to six guns. In effect, this meant that an infantry division now had a complement of only thirty-six guns, instead of forty-eight. However, even with the reduced number of guns, shortage of shells had become the governing factor, although other shortages included 500,000 boots, sorely needed by men in waterlogged or snow-filled trenches during the harsh winter weather. As happened on the Western Front, the suffering men on both sides near Przemyśl arranged a truce on Christmas Day. As in Flanders, this infuriated both high commands.

On 16 December 1914 Grand Duke Nikolai had explained to a French liaison officer that, on all fronts, the Russian armies were retreating due to shortage of ammunition. On 26 December Knox heard him say at Stavka that, if Russia had to depend on its own resources, a large-scale offensive would be out of the question before August 1915. Any earlier attack would depend on supplies of ammunition from abroad. It was actually a great mercy that the Russian advance had been halted on the left bank of the Vistula, and not broken through into Silesia, where a sustained enemy counter-attack would have brought about a major disaster, with whole divisions running out of ammunition,[6] but there were already signs of great discontent in the ranks, with men commonly shooting themselves in the hand to provide an excuse to be invalided to the rear, helped by an unnecessarily large number of 'carers'.

The Kaiser, in his habitual indiscreet and over-optimistic manner, had prophesied at the outbreak of hostilities: 'We'll be in Warsaw by Christmas.' Even more prematurely, Emperor Franz Joseph had appointed an Austrian 'governor of Warsaw' before the first shots were fired. As the New Year dawned, their armies were no nearer capturing Warsaw. To increase pressure on the defenders, on 31 January, 18,000 shells containing xylyl bromide tear gas – not a forbidden weapon under the 1899 Hague Treaty – were fired on Russian troops along the Ravka River on the western edge of the salient, but this had little effect because the extreme cold froze the gas, which a change in the wind blew back on the German positions. Not so in the warmer weather of May and June, when more than 6,000 Russian casualties were caused by the release of an alleged 263 *tonnes* of chlorine gas, 13,000 cylinders of the gas being released on one day in June. The high number of fatalities was due to the stock of Russian gas masks being stored in Warsaw and never issued to troops in the line.

With the Allied blockade biting hard, Germans were short of basic food. Already that spring 9 million pigs were slaughtered in Germany because some bureaucrats believed they were being fed on bread that could otherwise be consumed by humans. There was a brief glut of pork and sausages at very low prices before the bureaucrats acknowledged that they had created a grave shortage of meat and fertiliser. The following year, they achieved the same 'economic miracle' with sauerkraut![7]

South of the Polish salient, the Austrians called for help and OHL responded to OAK's appeals by allocating artillery of 302 light field pieces, 146 heavy guns and ninety-six trench mortars of varying calibres to General Mackensen's 11th Army. He was tasked with preparing a massive counter-offensive on the axis Gorlice–Tarnow. What Conrad thought was going on in the new army's assembly area behind the Austrian lines, is anyone's guess because the Germans mistrusted Austrian security to the point of not telling him. Since this was on his sector of the front, Conrad made an unsuccessful attempt to exert his control over Mackensen, which was predictably rejected by OHL.

Colonel Knox did not confine his diary notes to matters purely military. He noticed that the local Poles did not flee before an Austrian advance but, when the Germans were attacking, the roads were blocked by long columns of Polish farm carts transporting families and their few moveable possessions to the east, away from the fighting. Old men, women and children, including tiny babies, huddled together on top of their pitiful bundles, shivering in the cold and rain. Visiting another field hospital, he was told by a Polish surgeon that he had only ten doctors to care for 600 wounded men and that the hospital hygiene and sanitation were totally inadequate. In the middle of a typhoid epidemic, the town of Zvolen had given over its church to serve as a stinking holding station for Austro-Hungarian wounded – mostly Magyars who could not speak much German to communicate with Knox. They were dying because there was no medical care and they had been without anything to eat for several days. Knox accompanied a Russian officer of 9th Army to the local station to see why no mail was being received. There, they were shown enormous piles of mail bags weighing about 2,000 *pudy*, or 32 tons, but the chief *chinovnik* – the station master – simply said that the regional governor had not provided carts, on which to distribute the mail. Knox commented: 'A man like this should be hung [*sic*] when one remembers how poor fellows at the front long for news from home.'[8]

Fortunately, many letters from Siberian conscripts have been collected and preserved at Omsk, where *gorodskii duma* – the town council – was thanked many hundreds of times for sending parcels of what were called in England 'soldier's comforts' to its men fighting 2,000 miles away at the front. The contents included stationery on which the literate could write home, or write letters for their illiterate comrades. The *duma* was thanked for sending vests and underpants, tobacco and cigarette paper, needles and thread. Soap was especially appreciated because there was nowhere to buy it at the front with every town laid waste and villages burned to the ground. Spoons were another important item 'without which one can starve here', as one soldier wrote. Pre-printed cards for the illiterate read: 'I am well/wounded. I hope you are well. Please send', followed by a long wish-list.

On 14 December 1914, machine gunner S. Gordienko wrote home: 'Intensive battles. We were sent into action ten times and could not even get a smoke for several days.' Early in 1915 another man wrote to plead with the council to send to his field post address a 14-row button accordion 'because it is spring here and all nature rejoices and we wish to cheer our souls also'. Sentiments were simply, often frigidly, expressed, perhaps because dictated to a literate comrade: 'Hallo, dear wife, receive my Easter greetings. This is to tell you that I received the parcel you sent last December.' On 28 March 1915 rifleman Mikhail Nikiforov wrote: 'Thank you, dear father, mother, brothers and sisters for your valuable gifts. We wish you good health and long life.' Pyotr Dopgayev of 43rd Siberian Infantry Regiment wrote to the council in Omsk at Easter 1915: 'Thank you for the parcel with shirts and cigarettes. We have been at the front for nine months.' A comrade added: 'We are willing to spend our lives for the Motherland and the Tsar and we do not forget you at home.' Viktor Zhanzharov wrote on 29 March 1915: 'Received your gifts. Thank you for not forgetting us. We have now pushed the enemy back 142 *versty*.'[9] That was roughly 100 miles.

Literate soldiers could write at greater length, as in this exchange:

Hallo, dear comrade Fedya!
I write in reply to yours of 14 January. Has Misha been killed? I was in a battle where bullets cut down my comrades, in front, behind, to right and left. The ranks of my friends and comrades are continually thinning, until there comes that second when a bullet or piece of shrapnel … Samin has been wounded by shrapnel in the leg and is in hospital in Petrograd. I do not know if he has broken a bone. In battle, bullets punctured my mess-tin and my kit-bag. I had taken cover with kit-bag and mess-tin on my back. My spine is okay but I was wounded in two places. Our old commander was killed at Soldau.

The reply, written on 25 February 1915 from the northern front was:

Hallo, friend of Fedya!
Best wishes for Easter. I wish all of you can spend this holiday in good health, but must inform you that I have been wounded on 18 February in a battle between Przasnysz and Mlave. In seven battles I was okay, but had to pay the price in the eighth. From 1 February to 18 February we were in action all the time. The big battle was on 2 February, when we lost ninety out of 240 men. On 11 February we attacked a village nine miles from Przasnysz and gave the Germans hell, but I was wounded by grenade fragments in right side of body – ear, temple, cheek, upper lip, shoulder and bones of middle finger on right hand broken. Small splinters the size of a pinhead got in left eyebrow and right eyelid. If you are writing home at Easter, pass on the news of what has happened to me. I am temporarily in hospital at Vitebsk.[10]

On 18 January Knox was lunching at Plehve's HQ when a German biplane flew over and dropped a dozen bombs. It was a trifling matter compared with the enormous artillery bombardments that softened up a position before a major attack, but this new form of warfare was considered an unsporting breach of the customs of war, so that Plehve swore, if the airman were brought down, he would immediately hang him from the highest tree in the village.[11]

The first offensive of 1915 was launched by the Austro-Hungarians on 23 January, to drive the Russians back from the Carpathians. As historian Norman Stone commented:

The offensive maybe looked sensible on a map. On the ground … mountains had to be scaled in mid-winter; supply lines were either an ice-rink or a marsh, depending on freeze or thaw; clouds hung low and obscured the visibility of artillery targets; shells either bounced off ice or were smothered in mud; whole bivouacs would be found frozen to death in the morning. A Croatian regiment that had to spend the night in the snow lost 28 officers and 1,800 men from frostbite. Rifles had to be held over a fire before they could be used … but Conrad's staff, comfortably installed in their villas in Teschen with their wives in attendance, waved protests aside.[12]

Hindenburg ordered Mackensen to sever the strategic railway between Łódź and Warsaw – a battle with all the horrors of Flanders, including artillery firing gas shells, at the same time as the two 10th armies locked horns in the Second Battle of the Masurian Lakes 7–22 February. With one Russian army corps there having to be sacrificed to save the other three, tsarist losses totalled 100,000 men taken prisoner and half as many again lost as casualties. Before the winter gave way to spring, Russian troops had finally been driven out of East Prussia. The Kaiser, who had come to observe this pseudo victory, rewarded Falkenhayn with the order *Pour le Mérite* – Germany's highest decoration.

Throughout January and February 1915 Conrad was obsessed with the relief of Przemyśl before the garrison's supplies ran out in mid-March. On paper, he had twenty divisions for this counter-offensive, but on the ground ice and snow prevented movement, although his artillery continued an ineffective bombardment of the Russian positions. In the second half of February a number of local attacks went in – often by men who could not understand their officers' orders – to no great effect. The wounded froze where they lay and men who were strong and healthy in the evening were dead from exposure in the morning. It has been calculated that Conrad's casualties in this operation totalled 800,000 men, or nearly eight times the number of comrades in Przemyśl, whom they were supposed to be relieving.

In Galicia, Knox heard of one Russian gunner officer being threatened with a court martial if he fired more than three shells per gun per day without special orders. Yet German forces in Mackensen's advance that spring found large stocks of Russian shells that had never been issued. Another problem for the Russian gunners was the steadily increasing wear on the recoil mechanism of their guns, which affected their accuracy. 'It was cruel,' Knox wrote: 'to see our batteries standing idle while the enemy threw some 1,200 heavy shell into our trenches. At length a couple of our guns opened up, but their efforts had not the slightest effect on the enemy batteries.'[13]

Yet, Conrad's armies were facing disaster too, despite Mackensen's German troops stiffening the line in the Gorlice–Tarnow sector, south of the Vistula

River. In late February 1915 Conrad calculated that no relief of Przemyśl was possible and informed its commander General Kusmanek von Burgneustädten that the garrison had been written off. Further north on 1 March Russians drove back the German lines near Przasnysz but a week later were defeated at Grodno.

The siege of Przemyśl was nearing its end. Given sufficient siege artillery, General Andrei Selivanov's troops successfully stormed the northern defences on 13 March, after which the defenders managed to halt further inroads. Kusmanek ordered a final desperate attempt to break through the Russian lines on 19 March, which came to nothing. Three days later, after an orgy of destruction, removing and burying the breech-blocks of the fortress guns, smashing all the small arms, blowing up ammunition dumps and setting fire to the last reserves of food and fodder for horses, the 117,000 survivors of the garrison surrendered.

They included nine generals and 2,600 other officers. Captain J.F. Neilson of 10th Royal Hussars, an officer on Knox's staff who supported his despatches with photographs and occasional watercolours, was present shortly afterwards and informed the War Office on 15 May:

> One cannot help feeling that there was much disgraceful in the surrender of this fortress … an impression heightened by the behaviour of the Austrian officers showing complete indifference, an utter lack of all natural pride or shame and complete callousness as regards their men. I have seen them here, sitting all day long in cafes, sleek, well-fed and complacent while their men (word illegible) along the street, half-starved and ragged, begging bread from passing Russians. (According to local people), the officers had lived in every luxury, including female society of the most aggressive sort.[14]

Among the Hungarian NCOs present at the surrender was Cpl Gyóni, who spent the next nine months as a POW being shunted further and further from home until reaching Krasnoyarsk, 2,000 miles east of Moscow. He was fortunate enough to be assigned as a batman to his younger brother Mihály, a career officer, and used the freedom and comfort this afforded to continue writing poems. One of them, entitled *Csak Egy Ejszakára* – meaning For Just One Night – was an invitation to all the war profiteers, and those who glorified war, to visit the front for one night, to see what the reality was like:

> Send them along for just one bloody night –
> your zealous heroes spoiling for a fight.
> Their former boasts within our memories ring
> as rending shells of shrapnel scream and sing,
> as mists of strangling poison slowly rise
> and leaden swallows swoop across the skies.[15]

Unfortunately his brother Mihály died in June 1917, leaving Géza Gyóni alone and sick in the limbo of the camp amid the endless wastes of Siberia. Two weeks later he too died, from causes unknown, on his thirty-third birthday. There are no records of how many thousands of POWs died in these camps.

NOTES

1. http://www.antikoerperchen.de/material/18/gedichtinterpretation-georg-trakl-grodek-expressionismus.html; also T. Cross, *The Lost Voices of World War 1* (London: Bloomsbury, 1998), pp. 112–23.
2. Knox, pp. 113, 115, 134, 137, 232 (edited, author's italics).
3. M. Occleshaw, *Dances in Deep Shadows* (London: Constable, 2006), p. 50.
4. Knox, pp. 181, 185, 190 (edited).
5. F. Farmborough, *Nurse at the Russian Front* (London: Futura, 1977), p. 92. Dates in the original are in the Julian calendar but have been adjusted to the Gregorian calendar.
6. Knox, pp. 216–19.
7. G. MacDonough, *The Last Kaiser* (London: Phoenix Press, 2001), p. 377.
8. Knox, pp. 139, 142–4, 147–9, 159 (edited).
9. Edited excerpts from letters on http:museum/omskelecom.ru/ogik/Izvestiya_8/Eperina.html.
10. Ibid.
11. Knox, p. 230.
12. Stone, p. 113, quoting *Kriegsarchiv B/50 Nachlass Pflanzer-Baltin Tagebuch 2 Februar 1915* (edited).
13. Knox, pp. 253, 255, 259.
14. WO 106/1122 and 1123 (edited).
15. Cross, p. 349 (trans. W. Kirkonnell) (abridged).

8

THE GREAT RETREAT

Not until April 1915 did OHL inform OAK in Vienna how it planned to use Mackensen's 11th Army, and only then because it required Conrad to transfer two corps of his 4th Army to Mackensen's command. Conrad again protested that the area of intended operations was on the front of which he was commander-in-chief, but had to accept this partial usurpation of his authority, since it seemed the only way to force Brusilov's retreat from the Carpathian passes, where he was little more than 100 miles from Budapest, twin capital of the dual monarchy.

On paper, the Central Powers now had a coordinated strategy from the Baltic coast right down to the Romanian frontier. In East Prussia, Hindenburg's forces consisted of the new 10th Army, 8th Army under von Below and 9th Army facing Warsaw. South of the salient, Austro-Hungarian forces were, from north to south, 2nd, 1st, 4th and 3rd armies. Russian forces holding the line were 10th Army in the north on the East Prussian border, 1st and 2nd armies defending Warsaw in the salient and the new 12th Army to the north-east of Warsaw. South of the salient, facing the Austro-Hungarians, were 5th, 4th, 9th, 3rd, 8th and 11th armies. However, in the terms of this history spanning the Russian fronts, a detailed account becomes confusing. Whose 10th Army? Which I Corps? And so on. So, some detail will be sacrificed to make a more readable account.[1]

On 2 May Mackensen's artillery loosed a devastating 4-hour barrage on a 35-mile stretch of the lines of Russian 3rd Army. He had tried to break through west of the River Narev in February and March, and was determined not to fail again. Mackensen had just over ten divisions in the line and another in reserve against the seven divisions of Russian 1st and 12th armies. He had 1,000 guns on this small front, with 400,000 rounds of shell, all coordinated by General Bruchmüller, the artillery expert, facing 377 guns with only forty rounds apiece. Immediately following the barrage, German infantry moved in, ready to tackle Russian survivors emerging from dugout shelters, but found instead almost all the men in the badly constructed front line, as well as the reserves, who had been held too far forward, lying dead because they had been cut to pieces in their trenches by shrapnel bursts and literally vaporised by high explosive (HE). It was about this time that the enormous numbers of casualties on the Russian fronts led to burials in 'brothers' graves', where dozens and sometimes hundreds of men were buried in the same mass grave without discrimination of nationality, race or religion.

For the reality of what lies behind the bland body counts we have an eye-witness account. For those not killed outright and lucky enough to be brought to a *letuchka*, or mobile surgical unit, everyday nursing was in the hands of the *krestovaye sestry* – Red Cross sisters. A few of these women who braved all the discomforts and dangers of working close to the front lines were English. Florence Farmborough was a 27-year-old governess employed by a surgeon in Moscow, who had volunteered and been given a few weeks' training in a hospital before spending a whole month in trains to reach the south-western front. Fortunately, she kept a diary, writing down events whenever she had time. With the general insufficiency of field hospitals, delay in treating even a small wound often meant death from infection. So the *letuchki* worked very close to the lines, moving frequently to keep up with advances and retreats. Florence's first base was in a well-built house with several pleasant, airy rooms, where the nurses' first task was to scrub every surface clean and paint or whitewash the walls. An operating theatre was set up and a pharmacy stocked with medicines and surgical material. They were told not to think they would be there long: the stay might be six months or six hours, depending on the movement of the front. Not knowing exactly what to expect, she took some solace in the scenery of the undulating Carpathian foothills.[2]

Mackensen pressed on with the German 11th Army in the centre, flanked by Austrian 3rd and 4th armies, demolishing any sustained Russian resistance with more massive artillery bombardments. Conventionally, Russian units north and south of the CP advance should have attacked the flanks, but Stavka was afraid of Brusilov's 8th Army being too exposed on the south-western front and ordered a general withdrawal to straighten the line, in the absence of sufficient heavy artillery – and especially sufficient stocks of shell – to even slow down the CP advance. Casualties rapidly mounted to the million mark, with reinforcements arriving and being thrown into battle after only two or three weeks' training.

Three days after Florence's arrival on this front, there was a sense of foreboding in her entry for 28 April, which recorded the arrival of a first batch of fifty wounded men, whose wounds had to be dressed before they were sent on to Yaslo. Against the booming of cannon fire, the soldiers voiced their dismay that German troops and heavy artillery had been sent to this section of the Front. 'We are not afraid of the Austrians,' they said, 'but the German soldiers are quite different.'[3]

Two days later, the new nurse of Letuchka No. 2 was shocked by a colossal influx of seriously wounded men after Russian 3rd Army was cut to pieces and 61st Division – to which the *letuchka* was attached – lost many thousands of men. The reality of a combat nurse's exhausting life had sunk in:

> We were called from our beds before dawn on Saturday 1 May. The Germans had launched their offensive. Explosion after explosion rent the air. Shells and shrapnel fell all around. Our house shook to its very foundations. Death was very busy, his hands full of victims. Then the victims started to arrive until we were overwhelmed by their numbers. They came in their hundreds from all directions, some able to walk, others dragging themselves along the ground. We worked day and night. The thunder of the guns never ceased. Soon shells were exploding all around our unit. The stream of wounded was endless. We dressed their severe wounds where they lay on the open ground, first alleviating their pain by injections. On Sunday the terrible word *retreat* was heard. In that one word lies all the agony of the last few days. The first-line troops came into sight: a long procession of dirt-bespattered, weary, desperate men. Orders: we were to start without delay, leaving behind all the wounded and the unit's equipment! '*Skoro, skoro!* Quickly! The Germans are outside the town!'[4]

Again and again, the surgeon, orderlies and nurses of Letuchka No. 2 fled eastwards out of towns and villages as the German spearheads entered them from the west. The arrival of a Cossack despatch-rider on his mud-flecked pony meant packing up the instruments and tents, always to head further east. Sleep-deprived, the nurses nodded off to get whatever rest they could in the jolting horse-drawn carts bumping over unmade roads. This was the Great Retreat of 1915.

In April 1915 Hindenburg also continued his push on the northern front into Russian-occupied Lithuania and Courland, relieving Königsberg and capturing the Russian naval base of Libau (modern Liepaja) on the Baltic coast in early May. On 2 May Mackensen's now very mixed armies opened an attack from the line of the Vistula River, all the way south to the Carpathian Mountains. Preceded by an enormous barrage, it was a huge success, with Russian 3rd Army suffering severe losses. The advance continued with the capture of the ruined fortress of Przemyśl – which could not be defended because of all the damage caused during the Russian siege and the demolitions carried out by the Austrian garrison before surrendering in March. Less than three weeks later, Lemberg was also recaptured. The joint German-Austrian attack continued its momentum, driving the Russians back to the River San just over a week after that. By the end of the month, the front had shifted 100 miles to the east.

By 15 June Letuchka No. 2 had moved so many times as the front collapsed that it was back inside Russia, but the retreat was not over yet. Asleep on their feet, the nursing sisters collected up all the equipment and re-packed again and again as the temporary haven of care for the suffering where they had worked the previous day fell into the hands of the enemy. Bumping along the bad roads in unsprung carts, two of the nurses were ill – partly, Florence thought, from the sustained anxiety. Trying at night to sleep on a carpet of pine needles in the forest, she heard the nurse lying beside her crying quietly. When dawn came, they merged again into the stream of humans and animals, all moving eastwards. Entire herds of cattle were being driven by their owners with droves of sheep and pigs. And always behind them black clouds of smoke rose into the sky as all the peasants' hayricks and barns full of straw were fired, to deny them to the enemy. She wrote:

> It was said that the Cossacks had received orders to force all the inhabitants to leave their homes so they could not act as spies. In order that the enemy should encounter widespread devastation, the homesteads were set on fire and crops destroyed. The peasants were heart-rending. They took what they could with them but before long the animals' strength gave out and we would see panting, dying creatures by the roadside, unable to go any farther. One woman, with a sleeping infant in her arms, was bowed almost double by a large wicker basket containing poultry, which was strapped to her back. Sometimes a cart had broken down and the family, bewildered and frightened, chose to remain with their precious possessions, until they too were driven onwards by the threatening *knout* of the Cossack or the more terrifying prospect of the proximity of the enemy.[5]

Near Lublin in the salient 5,000 Cossack cavalry and Russian artillery wiped out two crack Austrian cavalry regiments, mostly killed in medieval manner by sabre or lance. Knox described one Austrian officer taken prisoner after having the whole of his lower jaw carried away on the point of a lance. Joseph Bumby described his capture like this:

> I was left alone in front of the Russian trenches with six dead men on my left and the forest on my right. The Russians were 200 paces behind me when I was shot in the neck. In the evening when the firing died down, some Russian soldiers came close and called out to me. One escorted me to a house in the village of Něgartova where they gave me bread, tea and cigarettes, but they stole my gloves and some canned goods I had. Then they gave me some straw to sleep on.[6]

One always recalls the first night in captivity, after which it all becomes a blur.

After General Alexander von Linsingen recaptured Strij with the Galician oil-fields, which were 60 per cent British-owned, a cartel of businessmen in Berlin pre-echoed Hitler's plan to enslave the populations of Russia, Poland, Ukraine and the Baltic states. The southern end of the Russian lines was now floating unanchored and Mackensen continued pressing his advantage for four months with the tsarist forces retreating all along the Russian fronts – which ran from Latvia in the north, looped around Warsaw and, with most of Galicia back in Austrian hands, continued south to the Romanian border.

On 7 July Russian forces took thousands of POWs on the northern front and pressed on to take the key fortresses at Königsberg and Allenstein before being driven back. Florence Farmborough's mobile surgical unit was then attached to 5th Caucasian Infantry Corps. Her diary records that, of 25,000 men, only 2,000 were left.[7] But the major defeat of that terrible midsummer was due to a joint German and Austrian push towards Warsaw. Although Stavka managed to extricate three armies from encirclement, once the loss of the Polish salient became inevitable, an evacuation of all civilians was ordered, with the destruction of all homes, food and animals in the scorched-earth policy used against Napoleon. Knox recorded the start of the Third Battle for Warsaw on 13 July, of which the first warning came when human intelligence indicated that the frontier railway stations at Willenberg, Soldau and Neidenburg were being enlarged to handle more traffic. After a feint along the River Vistula, the Germans opened up a hurricane barrage on 12 July, which showed that they had no shortage of shells on this occasion. The weather had been dry and roads were at their best, so one corps of Russian 1st Army had to counter forty-two large-calibre enemy guns with only two of its own, with the result that an entire Siberian division was virtually wiped out amid widespread panic. The infantry attack came in on 13 July, when the Russian troops withdrew from the front line without pausing to defend a second defensive line that had been prepared on the line Przasnysz–Tsyekhanov–Plonsk–Chervinsk. The majority of Russian conscripts being of peasant origin, when a scorched-earth policy was ordered in retreats, they routinely drove off livestock and looted other possessions from civilians, which slowed down their movement, with the result during this retreat the enemy cavalry caught up and broke through in the centre of the line, attacking the slow-moving and vulnerable transport columns. The term 'scorched earth' requires clarification. It seems that poor peasants lost everything, as did the Jews. But noble estates belonging to rich Polish landowners who had connections with German, Austrian and Russian high commands, could 'arrange' for their lands and property to be left intact.[8]

On 16 July the fortified line Makov–Naselsk–Novo Georgievsk was reached, where Russian 4th Corps was sent immediately into combat as they stepped off the trains from Warsaw. Even this desperate measure was too little, too late. On the night of 18 July the retreat continued to the River Narev. After four German divisions forced a bridgehead on the right bank, it was decided to evacuate Warsaw. By this time, Russian 2nd Army had only a single corps remaining on the left

The great retreat of 1915.

bank, 4 miles outside the city. On the night of 4 August this too retreated to the right bank, after which the Vistula bridges were blown at 0300hrs on 5 August. The German scouts reached the left bank at 6 a.m.

By the time Warsaw fell to Mackensen that day, Russian losses in the war totalled 1.4 million casualties and nearly a million officers and men taken prisoner. The 'black summer' continued, but the German advance – in places up to 125 miles from the nearest railhead – was fraught with problems, corps commanders complaining that fodder for horses was impossible to obtain in sufficient quantity as they drove through primeval forest and hit the Pripyat marshes where, ironically, there was no drinking water for men or horses until it had been boiled.

On 8 August the largely obsolete Russian Baltic Fleet of five pre-dreadnoughts with four dreadnoughts, six ancient armoured cruisers, four light cruisers, destroyers, torpedo boats and a few small submarines – including three Royal Navy submersibles that had sneaked into the Baltic – found itself facing a strong German naval task force of eight dreadnoughts, three battle cruisers, some light cruisers and destroyers of the High Sea Fleet under the command of Vice Admiral Franz Ritter von Hipper. Hipper was attempting to break into the Gulf of Riga to destroy Russian naval forces based there and lay mines to interdict Russian use of the port of Riga – a strategically important communications hub. The Germans' first problem was negotiating the Russian minefields in the Irben Strait, which proved costly. After two minesweepers were sunk, the first attack was abandoned.

On 16 August a third minesweeper was lost but, more importantly, the ageing Russian battleship *Slava* was driven off by two German dreadnoughts while the main force stayed out in the Baltic. That night, two German destroyers broke through the Irben Strait, hunting the *Slava*. Battle was joined by Russian destroyers and one German destroyer was so damaged that it had to be scuttled. After daybreak, German dreadnoughts *Posen* and *Nassau* pursued *Slava* and scored three hits before it withdrew to the shelter of Moon Sound. After further mine-clearing, the first German warships were able to penetrate the Gulf of Riga and attack Russian shipping there. A blow for Britain was then struck when RN submersible E-1, captained by Lt Commander Laurence, scored a torpedo hit on the battle cruiser *Moltke*, damaging it in the bows.

On 14 August the British Admiralty had ordered Lt Commander Layton's E-13 and four other submersibles to sail from Harwich to reinforce the Baltic flotilla, but E-13 was not a 'lucky ship' and ran aground on the Danish island of Saltholm while negotiating the narrows of Øresund on the night of 18 August. In spite of Danish navy attempts to screen it, two German torpedo boats opened fire on the stranded vessel. Re-floated, E-13 was interned until the end of the war, when it was returned to Britain, its captain having meanwhile been allowed to escape and find his way home. Sister ships E-18 and E-19 arrived safely in the port of Riga the following month. The fate of the fourth British submarine is a mystery.[9]

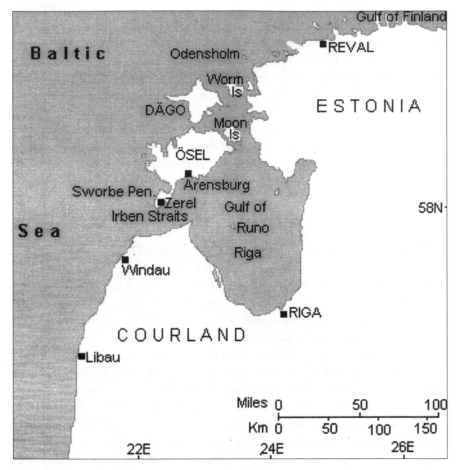

The Gulf of Riga (by courtesy of Gordon Smith and www.naval-history.net).

After the damage to *Moltke*, Hipper decided to break off contact in what was really a ground support operation, reasoning that the High Seas Fleet would have need of its capital ships for more important naval tasks ahead. On land, for most of the Russian troops food was poor or non-existent for days on end; there was no home leave; due to lack of medical facilities, a small wound often meant death from infection. But the main problem lay in the inability of the Russian munitions industry to supply guns and especially shells for the artillery. Because of the lack of rifles to issue to them, the proposed call-up of the 1916 class had to be postponed.[10] But there were signs of change. Some Japanese materiel was arriving from Vladivostok via the Trans-Siberian railway.

Lying on a mile-wide stretch of the estuary of the Northern Dvina, Archangel was not much of a harbour in European terms. This river was not a northern stretch of the Baltic Dvina, but a separate watercourse, the word *dvina* being apparently a pre-Russian word for river. Although devoid of wagon-ways along which ponies could haul freight, and lacking cranes, Archangel was an established town overlooking the water, over a mile wide at this point. The chaos here, caused by the impossibility of moving the stores away fast enough, made a negative impression on every visitor. The nearest railhead was across the river at Bakaritsa, to which freight had to be transported by barge or, in winter, hauled across the ice of the frozen river by pony-drawn sled for onward transportation along the ramshackle narrow-gauge railway leading to the south. In 1914 the railway had a capacity of twelve short trains a day; the requirement was for at least five times this level of traffic. An additional, seasonal problem was that the Bakaritsa terminal was flooded during the spring thaw, when freight transported across the estuary by barge was then hauled through mud and water 8 miles further south, to Isakagorka.

Given the vital necessity to import materiel for the Russian war effort, one would have thought that Nicholas II's government would have put in hand a priority programme of modernisation of the port, its freight handling facilities and the totally inadequate railway to the south. There was no such programme. Money was made available as and when: 1.5 million roubles to purchase two Canadian ice-breakers; 270,000 roubles to purchase metal barges to replace the rotten old wooden ones; another 20 million roubles for the widening of the rail-tracks – and so on. It was a Russian problem. No one was in overall charge, yet somehow by the spring of 1916 supplies were flowing in something like satisfactory manner.[11]

To get around the insoluble problem of Archangel being ice-bound for half the year, a contract was given to a British company for the construction of a railway reaching all the way from Petrograd to the ice-free fishing port of Aleksandrovsk (now Murmansk) on the Kola Peninsula. It lay 350 miles to the north-west of Archangel, but was ice-free all year, thanks to the mitigating effects of the Gulf Stream. This warm-water inlet was to become the home port for the Soviet Cold War nuclear submarine fleet. The British company backed out – either because of the nature of the near-impossible job or because of the difficulty of dealing with the Russian authorities. A larger than life character named Admiral Roshchakovsky[12] – big, bluff and with a chestful of medals – was given thousands of German and Austro-Hungarian POWs as forced labour to build a single-track railway from the fishing port of Aleksandrovsk to connect it with Petrograd and points south. As when Stalin ordered the construction of the White Sea Canal across the same region using Gulag labour in 1931–33 at the cost of 35,000 lives, so thousands of these POWs died during construction of the line.

There being no commercial docking facilities at Aleksandrovsk, Roshchakovsky's labour force built a port too – not that any westerner was other than depressed at the first sight of the unplanned sprawl of hastily built wooden shacks that was to be their home there. While the 600-mile railway was a-building, Roshchakovsky requisitioned thousands of Lapps and their reindeer to haul sledges laden with stores south towards the fronts. The Lapps had formally been exempted from this sort of exploitation and had to be threatened with the execution of their hereditary leaders before they gave in. It was at Aleksandrovsk that the Royal Navy based a flotilla of armed trawlers for minesweeping the shipping lanes around the northern tip of Norway. In 1916 a permanent town named Romanov na Murmane was founded, and later became modern Murmansk.

Aside from the appalling winter weather, there can be few more difficult terrains through which to drive a railway across the permafrost tundra, of which the top half-metre gradually thawed in summer to destabilise the rails and release swarms of vicious mosquitoes that tormented the labourers. In anticipation of its completion allowing freight to travel directly to Petrograd, the Royal Navy was sweeping German mines from the sea lanes to the north Russian ports – although, as Knox himself was to discover, not always successfully.

There was already trouble brewing in the subject nations on both sides. A Czech independence faction wanted to use the war to break away from Austrian domination. The Slovaks wanted independence from Hungary. If not the Tsar, at least the Russian government was aware that the Finns, Poles, Estonians, Latvians, Lithuanians, Ukrainians, as well as the Caucasian nations subdued in the nineteenth century, were all waiting for the right moment to escape from Russian hegemony. In a feeble attempt to purchase the loyalty of the vassal races, the tsarist government promised reforms – which stopped short of independence – to Poles and Finns, to the Slavs of Galicia and to the Jews, although Nicholas was a strident anti-Semite.

Morale in some Russian units was still good although losses already totalled 3.8 million killed, wounded and taken prisoner. Even these figures are to some extent conjectural. General Hindenburg wrote:

In the Great War ledger the page on which the Russian losses were written had been torn out. No one knows the figure. 5 millions or 8 millions? We too have no idea. All we know is that sometimes in our battles with the Russians we had to remove the mounds of enemy corpses in order to get a clear field of fire against fresh assaulting waves.[13]

On the day following the surrender of Warsaw, Colonel Knox lunched about 1,000yd from the firing line with the commander of the elite Preobrazhenskii Guards Regiment, founded by Peter the Great. They ate from a camp table covered with a clean white cloth and all the officers seemed in excellent spirits. When Knox asked about strategy, one of them joked: 'We will retire to the Urals. When we get there, the enemy's pursuing army have dwindled to a single German and a single Austrian. The Austrian will, according to custom, give himself up as a prisoner, and we will kill the German.' There was laughter all round.[14]

In another light-hearted moment Knox recorded two Jews discussing the progress of the war in a market. When one said, 'Our side will win,' and the other agreed, a Pole standing nearby asked which side was 'ours'. Both the Jews said: 'Why, the side that will win.'[15]

What was the truth of the Russian belief that Slavs in Austro-Hungarian uniform would willingly surrender at the first opportunity? Firstly, as Bolshevik commissars were to do with fellow Russians a few years later, the officers and senior NCOs of Conrad's predominantly Slavic units were ordered to shoot any men preparing to give up without a fight – as did also British and French NCOs and military police on the Western Front. Secondly, unless all the men in a particular group were agreed about surrender, there was always the possibility of an informer giving away the plan. Ferdinand Filacek was a Czech metal-worker from Litomysl who was called up, aged 18, in August 1914. Arriving at the front in mid-November, he was taken prisoner near Novy Sad on 5 December. It is true that he was temporarily out of danger, but the next year was spent in three different POW camps at Kainsk, Novo-Nikolajevsk and Semipalatinsk (modern Semeï in Kazakhstan) a sparsely inhabited area 2,000 miles east of Moscow, where the Soviet Union would explode hundreds of nuclear devices during the Cold War.[16]

At the second camp, he crossed paths with another Czech, Frantisek Tomek, who wrote in a letter home much later:

Dear friends, dear sisters and brothers!
It was 30 July 1914 when I left home, as they said, to fight for the emperor and my country. A soldier is not supposed to think, only to listen and obey, so I'm like thousands of others. I reported to my military unit, Č.K. Infantry Regiment No. 21 in Čáslav. Fortunately, I was posted to the Russian front and not Serbian, where I was originally supposed to go. I will not recount the hardships of war, for I have decided not to remember evil things. On 3 November I was happy to be taken prisoner. The first Circassian soldier I saw did indeed want to kill me, but the second was a friendly Cossack, who saved me and took me to the prisoner assembly point, where we were about a hundred in total. As he was leading us to the rear, a general kindly waved his hand and called 'Bohemia, Bohemia!' (This was a Czech independence slogan.) A band played Czech marches and we cheered him. For some days we were marched around Galicia before being transported to Kiev. On the twenty-first day of captivity we arrived in Novo-Nikolayevsk in Central Siberia, on the River Ob.

We left the transport and were conducted for the best part of an hour through the night out of the city and up a hill where there was *voyenny gorodok* – a military camp. The snow was already about one meter deep and still falling.

In our military greatcoats we were cold after being kept waiting half an hour, consoling ourselves with the thought that we should be staying in what we thought were empty barracks. No such luck! Marched out of the camp, through a gate into the forest, we found ourselves staring at dugouts with steps leading down into the earth and some smoke coming out of a hole – except it was not smoke, but steam from men's bodies.

'Everybody get down there!' said the old soldier who was guiding us.

Our quarters were in a dugout eight or nine metres across, with plank-lined walls and a roof which rose only half a meter above the ground, with small windows just below the eaves, all covered with snow. There was no flooring. Our feet sank into the mud floor and the foul air was almost unbreathable. At the entrance hung a small kerosene lamp, by the light of which I made out three-tier bunks occupied by POWs, which took up so much floor space that there was hardly room for men to squeeze past each other in the narrow corridor. As late-comers, we had to take the top bunks, climbing up makeshift ladders to get there. Up there the smell was worse and occasional drops of melting snow fell from the roof.

Thinking this place would be my grave, I lay down on a filthy bunk, using my cap as a pillow and wondering what to do. A batch of Czechs was already there and one of them told us that the dugout camp held 3,000 POWs – Czechs, Germans, Turks, Hungarians, Bosnians and Croats, all in dirty rags, sick and ill, but segregated by nationality.

To my question, whether it was possible to escape, he said: 'Running away would be possible, but that's even worse.' Escape, I thought, was the only salvation from death. I didn't even know where we were but, after a completely sleepless night, I ran away at five o'clock in the morning.[17]

In some of the POW camps, the death rate from malnutrition, exposure and disease – particularly typhoid fever – reportedly reached as high as 80 per cent until a tall, blonde, blue-eyed Swedish Red Cross worker named Elsa Brändström, who had been a volunteer nurse like Florence Farmborough, arrived with her friend Ethel von Heidenstam to organise medical supplies and food parcels. Nicknamed 'the angel of Siberia', she set up a Swedish Aid office in Petrograd, which the Bolsheviks shut down in 1917 – in the same way that they refused free food shipments for the starving peasants from the American Relief Administration. Undeterred, Brändström managed to return to Siberia in 1919 and 1920, when she was arrested in Omsk and finally expelled from Russia. Lecture tours in America and elsewhere on her experiences and the suffering of the POWs enabled her to raise funds to establish a home for 200 German and Austrian children whose fathers were dead or too traumatised by the war to provide for them.

Some of the Austro-Hungarian POWs were not even in camps, but lodged with Cossack families. Joseph Bumby described the extremely primitive conditions:

The house was a single room, half dug into the ground (for insulation in winter). The owners kept livestock in the house, so everyone was lousy. The only 'luxury' was the *krasny ugol* or 'beautiful corner', where the icon was kept. The bench and table were never washed, but scraped clean with a knife every Saturday. When the pig had to be killed, we POWs butchered it. Because our hosts did not eat offal, they let us make sausages out of the guts, which we ate with other POWs. One Cossack had taken a Kirghiz wife, which was a sort of custom, so one of our men 'bought a bride' for sixty roubles.

When a 21-year-old Cossack went off to the war, he was already married and had a child. Leaving home, he knelt down before his pony and kissed it, saying, 'To glory or death, comrade!' Then he rode off, probably never to return.[18]

NOTES

1. A detailed account in English of the Brusilov offensive can be found in T.C.Dowling, *The Brusilov Offensive* (Bloomington and Indianapolis: Indiana University Press, 2008).
2. Farmborough, pp. 32–3.
3. Ibid, p. 33 (abridged).
4. Ibid, p. 36 (edited).
5. Ibid, pp. 74–84 (edited).
6. Bumby account (abridged).
7. Farmborough, p. 88.
8. Stone, p. 184.
9. There is a blow-by-blow account on www.naval-history.net.
10. Knox, p. 294.
11. More about this from Stone, p. 157–8.
12. Some sources give his rank as captain.
13. B. Moynahan, *The Russian Century* (London: Random House, 1994), p. 65.
14. Knox, p. 308.
15. Ibid, p. 111.
16. Čestná vzpomínka 2005.
17. http:www.pamatnik.valka.cz (abridged).
18. Bumby account (abridged).

9

TREACHERY AND
A PLEA FOR HELP

Travelling about the fronts during the retreat, Knox was still conscientiously noting how the common soldiery was exhausted from retreating every night and digging trenches in the morning, only to be shelled in the afternoon by artillery to which the Russian guns could not reply. The Official Summary of Operations on 14 August reported an attack on 76th Division north of the Warsaw–Byalistok railway, where 'our artillery, owing to shortage of shell, is unable to develop a sufficiently intense fire in the sector of IV Corps to stop the enemy's continuous attacks'.

Like Florence Farmborough, he too noted the pathetic mass of fugitives heading east that blocked all the roads as the Russian troops withdrew, and was told that they were not ordered to leave their homes unless their villages were likely to be the scene of fighting. But with all cattle, horses, bacon, tea and sugar being requisitioned, it was impossible for the peasants to remain after being deprived of their means of livelihood. The sheer numbers involved made it difficult for the remaining civilian authorities to make provisions for what amounted to migration on a national scale. There were, of course, no trains running in this area. Even if there had been, they would have been of no use to the peasants, who transported as much of their property as they were able to load on long Polish wagons drawn by two horses. The father drove and the mother had to sit on top of the family's belongings with the younger children, while older sons and daughters drove flocks of geese or pigs along the roadside.

Somewhere near a village called Byelsk, Knox noted 20 unbroken miles of these wagons, nose to tail. Many families had been on the road for a month and had no idea where they were heading, except that it was away from the fighting. The Russian Red Cross staffed feeding-stations at intervals to serve the refugees tea and bread, free of charge, and most Russian soldiers treated them kindly enough.

Knox noted one peasant driving a cart on which lay the body of his wife, who had died of exposure, with her children lying on the bundles beside her. The father said he would keep going like this until reaching a Catholic cemetery, where he could bury the dead woman. Knox concluded this passage:

> It will never be known how many of these poor people died on their pilgrimage along roads studded every few hundred yards with rough crosses to mark the mass graves where cholera victims had been hastily buried.[1]

The refugees said with touching faith that their Russian brothers would at least not let them starve. This was far from sure. Already in the main cities the first tremors of revolution were being felt. If the war had ended earlier, it might even have counteracted the centrifugal social pressures, but the longer it went on, the more powerful these became. While most of the aristocracy at least talked loyalty to the Tsar, many middle-class members of the State Duma voiced their wishes to curb his powers radically. There was even a party calling itself the Constitutional Democrats, which was openly republican and wanted to reduce him to the role of a figurehead. Some major industrialists resented the government's haste in ordering from abroad materiel that they wanted to manufacture, but many whose factories were making munitions put prices up by 100 per cent and more; some even used the considerable advances paid on contracts for speculative investment instead of purchasing the raw materials and paying the workforce. There was a foretaste of the modern Moscow *v.* St Petersburg feuding when Moscow employers accused the government of unfairly favouring Petrograd factories. This was possibly a factor in the Duma's decision to take over the largest employer in Petrograd, the Putilov heavy engineering works, after which it was found that the bank accounts were empty and the two most important directors had flown the coop with a million roubles. With the currency plunging in value, inflation was biting hard, the prices of some foodstuffs increasing by 50 per cent, but wages had not been increased to keep pace and the influx of hundreds of thousands of refugees from the west was placing even more strain on the faltering economy.

Many historians have commented on the unsuitability of eighteenth- and nineteenth-century frontier fortresses for twentieth-century war, even on the static Western Front. On the Russian northern front, the fortress-city of Kovno (modern Kaunas in Lithuania) was relied upon by the government in Petrograd and by Stavka to be a significant obstacle for the German advance through the Baltic provinces. Its commander, 70-year-old General Vladimir Grigoriev, had 90,000 officers and men in a complex of walled citadel and outlying forts with interlocking fields of fire spread out at a radius of 8 miles from the city centre, somewhat on the model of Przemyśl. Although looking impressive, the defences were simply inadequate. Even more unfortunately, Grigoriev was a product of the appointment of Russian officers on grounds of birth and not military competence or even courage. On the morning of 15 August German forces carried the outworks south-west of the fortress. That night, they stormed the forts in this sector, but were driven back. Russian reinforcements began to arrive and were immediately sent into action but, once the outworks were abandoned, the concentrated fire of the enemy's artillery proved too much for the nerves of the half-trained and badly led defenders.

On 16 August the enemy captured Fort I in the south-western sector, and broke through between Forts II and III, attacking them from their unprotected rear. In the confusion, Russian forts fired on their neighbours which were still trying to defend themselves, thus aiding the attackers.[2] By that night all the forts in the first sector and most of those in the second sector had fallen. All was not yet

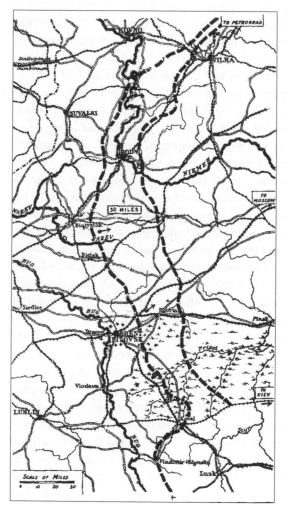

lost but the commander was a man sadly lacking in leadership qualities. At the very beginning of the German attack Grigoriev had created a panic by telling officers who had no intention of running away that the first man to bolt would be shot. The first man was he. On 17 August, accompanied only by a priest, he left by car for Vilna without telling his chief of staff, so no one knew for some time that he had gone. By 18 August it was all over, the last defenders literally running away, to save their lives. A survivor whom Colonel Knox met afterwards informed him that Kovno, although fortified at a cost of millions of dollars in today's money and having many guns and adequate shells, was

The great retreat after Kovno. Contemporary map with anglicised place names.

simply not constructed to resist modern artillery. The only concrete bunker was Grigoriev's personal quarters, and he never left it except at night.

In the headlong flight of the garrison, stores had not been destroyed, permitting the Germans to capture not only 1,300 guns, 53,000 rounds of large shells and 800,000 rounds of light shells, but also millions of cans of preserved meat, which provisioned their operations of the following month. Grigoriev was placed under arrest by Grand Duke Nikolai and court-martialled on two main charges: 1. That he failed to make proper artillery and engineering preparation for the defence of the fortress by massing his guns too closely and failing to clear the field of fire. 2. That he abandoned the fortress to report to the Army Command, instead of sending a staff officer, as he should have done, and that he failed to return to his post. A factor very much against him was that he had failed to blow up the railway tunnel east of Kovno, reputedly the only one between Ostend and Petrograd. It was said in evidence that the officer detailed to set the demolition charges had been told not to blow them until ordered. As he received no orders, he left the tunnel intact – a priceless gift to Ludendorff in his drive to capture the Baltic ports. Grigoriev was sentenced to eight years' imprisonment with hard labour.[3]

A few days later, on 23 August Tsar Nicholas sacked Grand Duke Nikolai and sent him off to command the Caucasus front, appointing himself commander-in-chief of all 16 million men in the Russian armies. It was a fatal error: his idea of raising morale was to visit troops, sometimes with the 11-year-old Tsarevich Alexei in tow – which was a nightmare for the aides-de-camp, since the boy suffered from haemophilia and could haemorrhage to death from the slightest blow. Instead of giving a rousing speech – one thing at which the Kaiser was good – Nicholas confined himself to frigidly holding aloft a holy icon, before which the soldiers knelt to receive his blessing.

The main problem was not the Grand Duke, but the inefficiency of the Russian munitions factories in supplying guns and especially shells for the artillery. It is true that the newspapers had been calling for Stavka to be held to account for the Great Retreat triggered by the fall of Kovno, but there were those who said that the Tsar had fired his uncle under pressure from the Tsarina, who resented the Grand Duke using his privileged family status to criticise the influence over her – and through her on the Tsar – of 'the mad monk' Grigori Rasputin with his constant urging to make peace with Germany. Of all Nicholas' poor decisions, this was arguably the worst since, from then on, he was perceived by the mass of his people as personally responsible for all the setbacks and all the losses of life.

With all their failings, the generals at Stavka were alarmed because Nicholas had neither experience nor interest in things military and was extremely indecisive by nature. After succeeding his assassinated father in 1894, he had actually said to one of his numerous cousins, 'I am not prepared to be Tsar. I never wanted this. Help me!' *Not prepared* was an understatement: his father had had so little faith in Nicholas that he had never been given any post that was remotely connected with the exercise of power. The advice from his cousin on that occasion was always to consult his uncles, the grand dukes, and accept their advice on the grounds that 'older heads' knew the ways of the world.

Russia's last Tsar was an inadequate person in every way, hesitant and insecure, therefore oscillating between inaction and inappropriately violent reaction. It is even conceivable that the wellspring of social tension in the corrupt and badly governed Russian Empire might have been converted into a positive social momentum under a modernising ruler with wisdom, vision and drive. Nicholas lacked any of these qualities – indeed any perceptible qualities except a disturbing humility at times, which was particularly inappropriate in an autocrat, let alone one who had just appointed himself supreme warlord of millions of men. As commander-in-chief, his 'management technique' consisted of sitting in on planning meetings at Stavka, but leaving without uttering a word for or against what was being discussed.

On 25 August the frontier fortress-city of Brest-Litovsk – destined to give its name to the treaty that ended war on the Russian fronts – also fell, while 150 miles to the south Russian forces were fighting through to Lemberg, where the Austro-Hungarians allegedly used Russian POWs as human shields. By the end of September 1915 Hindenburg's spearheads in the north, sped on their way by the premature fall of Kovno, had reached as far as the port of Riga in Latvia – a vital base for the Russian fleet's harassment of German ships in the Baltic when Petrograd was blocked by the winter ice – and also Vilna (modern Vilnius) on the Lithuanian-Russian border where, for the moment, they were held at a scant 300 miles from Petrograd.

The Kaiser, in his travels to show his keen interest in matters military, visited Brest-Litovsk at the beginning of November, and found the city a field of ruins, in which only a Greek Orthodox church had been spared in the Russian demolitions that preceded the retreat. Not until March 1916 would the Russian armies be anywhere near back up to strength after their terrible losses had been made good from the vast reservoir of men in Siberia and Central Asia. However, geography was now on their side: with no bulging Polish salient to defend, the front was significantly reduced in length and the opposing generals at both OHL and OAK were nervous of advancing too far on such a broad front as they now possessed, for fear of finding themselves in the position of Napoleon in 1812, when the Russian winter and overlong lines of communication had brought disaster to the Grande Armée – as they would again to Hitler's Operation Barbarossa in autumn 1942.

All the courage in the world could not make good the appalling lack of materiel in the Russian armies as 1915 came to its close. Colonel Knox calculated that, at the beginning of that winter, there had been along the 1,000-mile front from

Reval on the Baltic coast (modern Tallinn in Estonia) down to Czernovitz and the Romanian frontier, about 650,000 rifles, 2,590 machine guns and 4,000 3in field guns. This was manifestly inadequate, but replacement ordnance was not available to units in the line because the depots had been drained dry. As he said, even had more trained soldiers been available, there were no rifles with which to arm them.

Nor was this all. The number of officers of all ranks in a normal division of sixteen battalions and six batteries had fallen to an average of 110. Most infantry units had no more than 12 to 20 per cent of their original establishment of professional officers. The number of guns of 3in calibre or greater per army corps averaged at fourteen, three-quarters of which were light howitzers. Although Conrad was certainly wrong in thinking that morale outweighed all other considerations in war, Knox was worried that the multiple defeats at the hands of the Germans had instilled in many Russian officers a feeling that this enemy was invincible.

At the end of September, he spent a few days at Stavka, which was then in Pskov, and obtained from the Tsar a pass enabling him to travel to Petrograd in response to a summons from his ambassador requiring him to accompany a Russian delegation that was being sent to London and Paris requesting increased supplies of materiel, without which the offensives planned for the spring of 1916 could simply not take place.[4]

He arrived in Petrograd on 11 October and departed by train for Archangel six days later, in company with the delegation led by Admiral Aleksandr Russin, Chief of the General Staff of the Imperial Navy. Russin had a good command of English but was not, in Knox's opinion, forceful enough to deal with politicians like David Lloyd George, then serving as Minister of Munitions in the Asquith government, and his opposite number in Paris, Albert Thomas. The delegation arrived at Archangel after two days and nights on the train, the last 400-odd miles being on the narrow-gauge line from Vologda, which was scheduled to be converted to normal Russian gauge by the New Year. Ever a stickler for detail, Knox recorded that only 170 10-ton wagons then departed from Archangel daily for the south, although it was hoped, after the conversion to broad gauge, that the number could be doubled and 16-ton wagons used, to add another 50 per cent to every trainload.

Because of the delays due to the inadequate railway system, he noted an enormous backlog of materiel: copper, lead and aluminium, rubber and coal, and no fewer than 700 motor vehicles still in the wooden packing-cases, in which they had been shipped. Most of this stockpile was lying out in the open, but the delegation was assured that it would all be transported south during the winter months, when ships could not reach Archangel, due to the White Sea freezing up. It was to get around this that the line from the ice-free Kola Peninsula to Kandalaksha was being constructed.

The delegation spent two nights in the port of Archangel aboard HMS *Aegusa* – a vessel we have met before, when it was Sir Thomas Lipton's yacht *Erin*, transporting medical aid to Serbia. The captain of the ship was a former British admiral who had volunteered to serve again with far lower rank for the duration of hostilities. The atmosphere on board was congenial, rather like a gentlemen's club in London, except that there was one lady present – Mrs Blair, the wife of another of Knox's officers at the embassy in Petrograd.[5]

However, the Russian delegation, although accorded the best travel facilities available, was not to have 'a calm sea and prosperous voyage'. After trans-shipping to the converted passenger liner re-baptised HMS *Arlanza*, which Knox described as 'an enormous hulk', they enjoyed decent meals served at the captain's table in what had been the ladies' boudoir before the ship was requisitioned. The ship anchored each night, when minesweeping was not possible. Under way in daylight, *Arlanza*'s safety was theoretically assured by five British trawlers acting as minesweepers ahead and around the ship. Yet, on the very afternoon when the officer commanding the trawlers came aboard to inform them that the way ahead was clear of mines, there was an explosion at the bows which shook the whole structure of *Arlanza*. The weather being well below zero, the passengers ran to their cabins, to put on their fur coats before hurrying to the boat deck. There seemed to be no imminent danger of the ship sinking, so Knox and Mrs Blair climbed into one of the lifeboats, where he noted approvingly her calm manner in this emergency.

In the slight swell, their lifeboat crashed repeatedly against the side of *Arlanza* as they were lowered from what seemed an immense height, trusting to the skill of the crewmen manning the davits. They reached the water safely, to realise that there was no naval officer on board, so Lieutenant Lyubomirov, a junior member of the delegation, tried to direct the sailors in his incomprehensible English, but only added to the confusion. From the lifeboat, they could see German mines floating on the surface all round the ship, and waited until these had been dealt with by the trawler crews, after which they were hoisted back aboard *Arlanza*.[6]

After several other unsought adventures, Knox accompanied the Russians throughout the negotiations at the Inter-Allied Munitions Conference in London. Unfortunately, the dead weight of Russian bureaucracy obliged Admiral Russin to telegraph Petrograd for authorisations at every turn. Lloyd George promised the delegation 300 4.5in howitzers and 15 million rounds of Japanese small-arms ammunition by the following May, plus 25 million rounds in June and 45 million per month thereafter. On 8 December Knox and the delegation crossed to Paris, where the Russian officers were delighted to be smartly saluted by every serviceman they saw in the streets, in contrast with the near-total lack of this courtesy from British soldiers who had crossed their path in London.

The conference at the elegant Hotel Crillon included Lord Kitchener, Foreign Secretary Sir Edward Grey and other VIPs on the British side. Knox exceeded his function as an observer to ask Lord Kitchener to press the French for the 20 million rounds of Gras ammunition that the Russians needed in order to put their Gras rifles back into the firing line. When grilled as to when the Russians would take the offensive in 1916, Knox pointed out that it was impossible to expect them, outnumbered as they were by two to one, to take the offensive with any chance of success while the Allies in France, who themselves outnumbered the Germans by the same ratio, were unable to break the enemy front.

He was asked to return to the Hotel Crillon next morning, to be told that some of his despatches from the Russian fronts were too pessimistic – an accusation also levelled at His Majesty's Consul Robert Bruce Lockhart, and for the same reasons, namely that they confronted the wishful-thinkers in Paris and London with the hard realities of Russia's war! Defending himself, Knox tried to obtain an authoritative update of the situation on the Western Front – a subject about which he was constantly being asked in Russia. The delegation then departed for the French General Staff at Chantilly, where Admiral Russin reinterated the request to Marshal Joffre for more Gras ammunition and more heavy artillery, in what Knox felt was not a sufficiently forceful manner. From Chantilly they motored to the HQ of Marshal Foch, whom Knox knew from meetings at pre-war manoeuvres in Russia and France.

Invited back to dine with Foch after the Russians had left, Knox took the opportunity to emphasise their need for the Gras ammunition. Foch made a note and promised to speak to Joffre about it, telling Knox that he was convinced the Western Allies would soon break through, providing they were given sufficient reserves of guns and gas – a proviso that was all too familiar from the Russian fronts. A second proviso was that the next offensive in the West had to coincide with one on the Russian fronts, as agreed at the inter-Allied conference at Chantilly in November. The day of 12 December was spent visiting the sector of the front held by French 10th Army, lunching with General Neudon in command of the 70th Division and dining at St. Pol with General D'Urban, the army commander.

Returning to London, Knox accompanied the Russians to bid farewell to Lord Kitchener at the War Office, where Admiral Russin enquired about the 'monthly gift of 100 4.5in howitzers' that Lloyd George had promised to Russia. Kitchener was obviously unaware of this arrangement, and said bluntly, 'What howitzers?' When Knox explained, he took 'an angry note', to the dismay of the Russians present, who only cheered up on meeting the glibly persuasive Lloyd George at the House of Commons. The last visit was to Buckingham Palace, to be received by King George V, after which Knox wished his charges *Bon voyage!* for their return journey and departed himself to enjoy a spot of leave.[7]

As the year ended with a catastrophic shortage of ammunition of all calibres for the Russian armies, south-western front commander General Ivanov – a Santa Claus figure with a bushy white beard – was somehow managing to hold the CP forces on the western and south-western fronts from the Pripyat Marshes to the Romanian border. Russia had lost in this one year alone a total of 2 million men, but the Austro-Hungarians and Germans had manpower problems too. When Kaiser Wilhelm II ordered Hindenburg to drive on Dvinsk (modern Dauvagpils in Latvia), Hindenburg replied in his characteristic terse manner: 'Impossible without more men.' With the increasing demands on Austro-Hungarian man-power at the Italian front and the build-up of German forces in the west for what was intended to be the decisive Battle at Verdun, neither side had sufficient reserves of manpower.

NOTES

1. Knox, pp. 311–13, 317, 322, 323 (abridged).
2. Stone, p. 186.
3. Knox, p. 328.
4. Ibid, pp. 348–51.
5. Ibid, pp. 354–6 (abridged).
6. Ibid, pp. 357–8.
7. Ibid, pp. 361–3, 367 (abridged).

10

THE GREATEST CRIME
OF THE WAR

The risk run by those making strategic decisions is that the consequences of their errors are many times greater than those of wrong tactical decisions made by commanders in the field. After being appointed First Lord of the Admiralty in 1911, Winston Churchill set out energetically to modernise the Royal Navy, so that it would remain superior in numbers and performance to the growing Kaiserliche Marine. Measures he put in hand with First Sea Lord Admiral 'Jackie' Fisher included ensuring that new battleships would be oil-fired, rather than coal-fired, with investment in the Anglo-Persian Oil Company to ensure a 20-year supply. So far, so good. But Churchill was also a prime mover in the British government's decision to seize two battleships built in British yards for the Turkish navy, which decision is said by some historians to have been instrumental in the subsequent decision of the Ottoman Empire to declare for the Central Powers on 29 October 1914. Immediately, French Interior Minister Aristide Briant and Churchill decided to use that declaration as an excuse to storm the Dardanelles at the tip of European Turkey and force the Bosphorus, making a safe route by which supplies could be shipped from the Mediterranean to Russia's Black Sea ports.

Initially Churchill wanted to use obsolete Royal Navy battleships – which stood no chance against the dreadnoughts of the German High Seas Fleet – to bombard and destroy what he thought were lightly held Turkish defences at the Dardanelles – an idea that went into the waste-basket when several RN vessels were sunk by Turkish mines. Churchill's Plan B was the disastrous landing of British, British Empire and French ground forces at Gallipoli, which cost 130,000 lives and saw 261,000 men wounded in action before defeat was admitted and the Allied forces were evacuated at the end of 1915. Churchill was never forgiven by his political opponents for his responsibility in this disastrous adventure. Yet, there was another consequence of his decision to open a third front, many times more costly in human lives – and which has been called 'the greatest crime of the war'.

If there is one common factor in Russian strategic decisions during the First World War, it is the necessity, driven by shortage of materiel and the desperate need to make good those shortages with supplies from the Western Allies, for Stavka always to march in step with those allies. Timing offensives to suit them ran the risk of mis-timing them locally and making moves that were not in Russia's best interests. No one knew what a costly failure the Gallipoli intervention by naval and ground forces would turn out to be, but it fell to Stavka to create a diversion at the eastern extremity of Turkey that would draw Ottoman troops away from the Dardanelles, to give the Allied offensive at Gallipoli the maximum chance of success. For a few days after the Turkish declaration of war against Russia, Tsar Nicholas and his generals at Stavka hesitated, doubtless remembering the observation of the French King Henri IV about a projected campaign in the interior of Spain: 'Large armies starve there and small armies are defeated.'

The same applied to any invasion into the bleak and largely barren interior of eastern Turkey with its harsh climate and scant foraging. Russian border skirmishes against the Ottomans had been ongoing for centuries, but with his armies fully stretched on the Russian fronts, the Tsar did not declare war on the Ottoman Empire until 2 November 1914. At the time, a cartoon in *Illustrated London News*, which much later intrigued the author as a boy aged 4, browsing faded magazines in his grandmother's house, showed the Kaiser wearing a Pickelhauber helmet as he reclined on a dilapidated chaise longue of the type called an ottoman, exclaiming: 'I don't know how long this old Ottoman will support me.' Although some Turkish troops did serve with CP forces on other fronts, and caused heavy Allied casualties at Gallipoli, the main usefulness of Turkey for the Central Powers was to interdict Allied access to the Black Sea and prevent supplies reaching Russia that way.

Stavka had apparently no way of knowing that it would take until April of 1915 for France and Britain to muster and land an invasion force at the Dardanelles although it must have been obvious that such a force could not be assembled very much sooner. Russia's uneasy borders in the Caucasus were protected by an army with a peacetime strength of 100,000 men, but half of them had been sent north as replacements after the disastrous Battle of Tannenberg. Yet the logic of Russian-Turkish Realpolitik dictated an attack on Turkey before the Turks invaded Russian territory. Two weeks after Nicholas' declaration of war came the first Russian move on this front, when General Georgi Bergmann led 1st Caucasian Army Corps across the Georgian/Turkish border in a three-pronged attack with the main column driving towards the communications hub at Erzerum. The offensive came as no surprise to War Minister Enver Pasha in Constantinople, who had Turkish 3rd Army ready and waiting to repulse the incursion. Indecisive clashes continued until the end of the month, ending with heavy Russian casualties of around 40 per cent of the invading column.

With the aim of retaking territory lost during the recent Russo-Turkish wars, Enver planned to surround and destroy the Russian force at Sarikamiş, the western terminal of a Russian railway from Kars. In consultation with German liaison officers, whose interest was more oriented towards gaining access to the Russian port of Batum on the Black Sea coast, he planned an ambitious and over-complicated counter-attack that required synchronisation of three separate columns moving through the harsh, mountainous terrain. One column was held up at a mountain pass for twenty-four hours by a battalion of Armenian volunteers in Russian uniform. These men – and three other battalions of Armenian volunteers – had been recruited that summer on the initiative of Count Illarion Vorontsov-Dashkov, Viscount of the Caucasus Region. They were men who, although living in Russian-occupied territory, were not liable to conscription for various reasons, but volunteered to fight in Turkey in the hope of liberating their fellow Armenians, treated as second-class citizens or worse in the Ottoman territories, where they were known as *gavour*, or infidels. They and other Christians were discriminated against in law, routinely over-taxed, and forbidden to own weapons or ride horses, because that would make their heads higher than those of Muslims on foot. They could never consider themselves safe from robbery, rape or dispossession by their Turkish, Circassian and Kurdish neighbours.

With Enver's timetable out of joint due to those Armenian volunteers, the Battle of Sarikamiş began on 2 December 1914 and continued until 17 January 1915. The lack of metalled roads or Turkish railways in the region, on which Enver could move his troops and bring up supplies, the many deaths from exposure in the extreme winter weather at altitudes of 5,000 and 6,000ft above sea level and widespread sickness among his men all contributed to the Turkish counter-offensive grinding to a halt. They were also up against a newly appointed Russian commander, the 52-year-old Caucasian army chief of staff General Nikolai Yudenich. The scale of Turkish casualties is made plain by newsreel footage of thousands of Turkish dead abandoned in the frozen slush at the side of the road.[1] Since the footage was filmed mute, it is unclear whether they were killed in action, died of wounds later, or fell victim to the extreme cold. What statistics exist from this theatre are not reliable, partly because an outbreak of typhus killed thousands on both sides, but it is thought that Yudenich's losses were in the order of 16,000 battle casualties and 12,000 men lost through exposure and disease – as against Turkish losses more than twice as high.

Enver lost no time in claiming as his alibi for the defeat that it was due to the 20,000 Armenian irregulars, equipped with Russian weapons in the four volunteer battalions of which photographic evidence exists.[2] As a result, in February 1915 he ordered that all the young adult Armenians serving in Ottoman forces be disarmed as potential traitors and transferred to hard-regime labour battalions. Armenian males between 15 and 20 years of age and between 45 and 60 had traditionally been conscripted into labour battalions, but this new measure was the first step in a nationwide religious-ethnic cleansing programme being planned against the Christian Armenians living in Ottoman territory.

Neutral travellers and consular officials in eastern Turkey began to report that the Turks were using that alibi and the war with Russia as a cloak for genocide. These reports convinced, among others, US Ambassador Henry Morgenthau. It was finally estimated that somewhere between 1 and 1.5 million Armenian men, women and children were deliberately killed – along with several thousand other Christians in eastern Turkey. On one single day 716 leading Armenian intellectuals and political figures, rounded up in Constantinople (modern Istanbul) and elsewhere, were reportedly executed in order to 'cut the head off' the Armenian community in Turkey. Men arrested at this stage were formed into labour battalions under conditions that meant a slow death from exhaustion and starvation. Some were given the option of converting to Islam or being killed in various unpleasant ways while women were raped before death, some attractive young ones being spared as sex slaves. Uncounted thousands of mothers and children were afterwards marched several hundred miles with little or no food and inadequate water supplies through Anatolia into what is now Syria, Lebanon and northern Israel – until nearly all had died of exhaustion, exposure, illness and starvation.

As with the Final Solution during the Second World War, which consumed so much manpower, both among the victims and the perpetrators, one wonders why the Ottomans carried out this genocide at a time when the Russian Black Sea Fleet was forcing the Turks to transport men and materiel to eastern Turkey by bad roads over difficult country. The official rationale was that Christians of any ethnicity were potential traitors who had stored huge caches of arms and would rise up against their Ottoman overlords in sympathy with the Russian invaders, when given the chance. However, documented massacres of Armenians living in Turkey date back centuries and were particularly widespread during the reign of Sultan Hamid II, who created bands of Kurdish irregulars known as *hamidiye*, given carte blanche to 'solve the problem of the Armenian infidels'. From 1894 onwards, the *hamidiye* used armed violence against these non-Muslim citizens of the Ottoman Empire, who occasionally responded by procuring arms and fighting them off. Diplomatic pressure from the Great Powers was unable to curb the *hamidiye*, who continued what became known as the Hamidian massacres, in which neutral observers estimated that somewhere between 100,000 and 300,000 Armenian men, women and children were killed, mainly in eastern Turkey – or western Armenia, as the victims thought of it, for their ancestors had lived there many centuries before the Turks arrived, let alone when borders were drawn on a map. The Great Powers protested to the Sublime Porte in 1895, but without any real effect.

With the Young Turk Revolution in 1908, which deposed Sultan Hamid II, hopes rose among Armenians in Turkey that things were going to be different under a 'modern' government, more in keeping with Europe. Yet, the following year saw civil unrest that developed into a new pogrom in Adana province, where tens of thousands of Armenians died, their houses destroyed or burned down. The Balkan wars of 1912–13 saw an influx of Muslim immigrants driven home-less out of neighbouring states which fuelled even more ill-feeling against the long-established Armenian minority, the newcomers being particularly active in seizing property belonging to them. Although successive Turkish governments have denied that organised genocide or mass killings took place, according to Armenian sources the community numbered 3 million men, women and children in 1914, of whom more than half were killed. Understandably, Armenians regarded the Russian invasion in November 1914 as the coming of fellow-Christians to save them, especially after the Tsar made a point of meeting a group of Armenian notables on his visit to the Caucasus in December 1914 and played on the religious links between Orthodox Christians in Russia and the Christian Armenians in order to attract volunteers for the fight against Turkey, promising that they would not be sent north, but deployed on the Caucasian front.[3]

Yudenich's campaign was a relatively sophisticated combined operation, with a Russian battleship and destroyers of the Black Sea Fleet bombarding Turkish coastal positions along the way, from the border to Trebizond (modern Trabzon), all the while in radio-telegraphy contact with the northern wing of his land forces fighting its way along the littoral. Inland, the Russian ground forces thrashed the Turks at the heavily defended city of Erzerum, which finally sur-rendered on 16 February 1916 with the loss of over 300 artillery pieces and some 5,000 men taken prisoner in the city and surrounding forts. Nearby Muş also fell to Yudenich, whose Siberian fliers' aerial reconnaissance gave him the edge over his 'blind' enemy. By then, Turkish 3rd Army's strength had fallen from 118,000 to a low of between 25,000 and 42,000 men able to carry arms, as against Russian losses of 16,000 battle casualties and 12,000 men lost through sickness.

At nearby Bitlis, the Turks were in a stronger position, blocking a narrow valley in the belief that they could not be outflanked. So, on the night of 2–3 March, the Russian 8th Caucasian Rifles advanced silently under cover of a blizzard and, after several hours of bloody hand-to-hand fighting, took the town and 1,000 prisoners. Partly as a result of these Turkish reverses in the interior, Trebizond also fell to the Russians on 16 April. Russian intelligence officers in Bitlis found evidence of massacres by local Kurds and Turks, including the killing of 15,000 Armenians. A relief force under Mustafa Kemal, the victor of Gallipoli, who later became the president of Turkey under the name Ataturk, had been advancing to relieve Bitlis, but now had to turn back, although he did retake Muş and Bitlis that August.

Seeking to create a defensible salient, Yudenich now turned his attention to the major walled city of Van on the eastern shore of the inland sea called Van Gölü or Lake Van. On 19 April 1915 the local Turkish commander Jedvet Bey ordered the conscription of 4,000 men from the city. The Armenians in the city offered to supply 500 men and a large sum of money, to buy him off. The offer was refused by Jedvet. Knowing that arms had been accumulated and hidden in the Armenian quarter, he threatened to kill every Christian man, woman and child whose head was higher than his knee, if a single shot was fired from within the walls.

On the following day, two Armenian men were shot dead for attempting to protect one of their women being molested by Turkish soldiers. That was the spark that ignited the rebellion. Until then, the Armenian leaders had been divided between those saying they should 'wait and see', as in previous pogroms, and the younger element, who wanted to spill Turkish blood after years of humiliation.

Russian invasion of Turkey 1915 – 1918. Contemporary map with anglicised place names.

Within hours 300 rifles, hundreds of pistols and hunting shotguns were distributed to 1,500 men manning the walls of the Armenian quarter and barricades protecting a suburb outside the walls. Since, if taken prisoner, they would be killed, they were prepared to die at their posts, and held Jedvet Bey's soldiers at bay until Russian forces drove off the Turks the following month.

On 29 May the extremist Committee of Union and Progress (CUP) passed a 'temporary' law of deportation, under which anyone suspected of disloyalty to the Turkish government could be arrested and their property seized for distribution to Muslims. Later addenda to this law declared 'abandoned property' could be seized and sold by the state, especially the land, homes and livestock of arrested Armenians. One Muslim member of parliament had the courage to protest that arrested Armenians had not *abandoned* their property, and that its seizure in this way was contrary to Muslim ethics and Ottoman law. He was swimming against the tide. Evidence exists that Interior Minister Talaat Pasha authorised the setting up of twenty-five concentration and death camps for those arrested. It is only fair to add that, after the cessation of hostilities Sultan Mehmed VI did order the principal instigators of the genocide to be court-martialled in absentio.

Unfortunately for the people of Van, under pressure from Turkish 3rd Army the Russian force had to withdraw in August. Grand Duke Nikolai, arriving to take up his duties as viceroy of the Caucasus, left Yudenich free to pursue the campaign inside Turkey. As a result, not only was Van retaken in September, but Yudenich approved the establishment there of a puppet government for what was publicly renamed 'Western Armenia'. The eastern half of the once great Armenian Empire had become a province of the Russian Empire in 1829 but was since merged in the Caucasian *oblast* or administrative region. Unfortunately, the support of the Armenian population for this initiative was to lead to the entire city of Van being razed to the ground, in which condition it still is.[4]

The end of the 10-month struggle at Gallipoli came when British and ANZAC troops evacuated the landings which had cost a half-million Allied and Turkish lives, thus released thousands of Ottoman troops to confront the Russian invaders in a ding-dong campaign. They pushed the front back to the east, but on 17 July Russian troops routed a Turkish force at the key fortress of Erzincan, killing 17,000 men and taking as many prisoner. The Russian forces withdrew finally after the Treaty of Brest-Litovsk, leaving the Armenians in Turkey to their fate. It was former US President Theodore Roosevelt who categorised the genocide as 'the greatest crime of the war'.[5]

NOTES

1. Viewable on www.britishpathe.com.
2. It was later claimed at the Paris Peace Conference that 150,000 Armenians had served in the Russian armies.
3. M. Gilbert *The First World War* (London: Orion Phoenix 2008), p. 108.
4. The modern town is not built on the same site.
5. Letter to C.H. Dodge in *The Letters of Theodore Roosevelt*, ed. E. Morrison (Cambridge: Mass., Harvard UP, 1954), p. 6328.

PART 3

1916 – THE LAST CHANCE CAMPAIGN

1. Police arresting one of the conspirators, believed to be Gavrilo Princip, at Sarajevo 28 June 1914.

2. Ill-equipped Serbian troops in front line facing Austro-Hungarian artillery and aircraft.

3. Emperor Franz Joseph, 84-year-old ruler of the Austro-Hungarian Empire. He did not want war.

4. 'The loneliest man in Vienna', Prince Franz Ferdinand, shortly before the assassination.

5. There were atrocities on both sides in Serbia. Here Austro-Hungarian soldiers execute captured Serbs.

6. Invaded from west and east, thousands of Serbian soldiers and civilians fled their country in the terrible retreat of winter 1915.

7. Murdered by a Serbian conspiracy, their deaths triggered a world war: Prinz Franz Ferdinand and Countess Sophie shortly before the assassination.

8. The British cousin, King George V and his German wife, Queen Mary.

9. The Russian cousin, Tsar Nicholas II and his German wife Alexandra with the four princesses and Tsarevich Alexei – all to be murdered in Ekaterinburg.

10. The German cousin, William II, with his generals who gradually took away his power.

11. The first German chief of staff, Erich von Falkenhayn, who was ousted by generals Hindenburg (below left) and Ludendorff (below right).

12. Hindenburg and Ludendorff.

13. The reluctant Russian commander-in-chief. The Tsar's uncle Grand Duke Nikolai did not want the job.

14. After sacking the Grand Duke, the Tsar fatally took supreme command himself. Here, he pores over a map with Chief of Staff General Alekseyev.

15 & 16. The German and Austrian troops went to war by train. The Tsar's soldiers had to march hundreds of miles on poor rations to reach the front.

17, 18 & 19. The two Russian generals Pavel von Rennenkampf (top left) and Alexandr Samsonov (top right) refused to communicate with, or support, each other. As a result, Samsonov's army was destroyed at the Battle of Tannenberg, wasting the lives of many thousand Russian soldiers, buried anonymously in the forests of East Prussia (above).

20, 21 & 22. As a diversion to support the French at Verdun, the Tsar ordered his protégé General Aleksei Kuropatkin (top left) to attack a German army of 75,000 with a force of 350,000 men. General Aleksei Brusilov (top right) considered Kuropatkin unfit to command. He was proven right when the Germans broke through to Riga (above).

23 & 24. 'If the men will not fight, we women will!' With millions of Russian soldiers deserting after all the casualties, Maria Bochkaryova (left) formed the Women's Death Battalion (below). Mocked and harassed by male comrades, they were prepared to die for Russia.

25. As the appalling losses at the fronts continued, revolutionaries in cities like Petrograd armed themselves to arrest and assassinate Okhrana agents in the streets.

26. Lev Kamenev and other leading Bolsheviks arriving in Brest-Litovsk to negotiate the cease-fire with German and Austrian officers.

27. Berlin's money financed the Bolsheviks' rise to power. In return, Vladimir Ulyanov, aka Lenin, wanted peace at any price.

28. Israil Gelfand was a rich Russian-Jewish dissident who called himself Dr Helphand. He arranged the German subsidies for the Bolsheviks.

29. Like the picture of Lenin, this one of Leon Bronshtein, aka Trotsky, is a low-quality tsarist secret police mug-shot. After the cease-fire, he created the Red Army.

30. Left to right: an early picture of Stalin, Lenin and Kalinin. Under his real name Josef Djugashvili, Stalin may have been a police spy. There was alleged proof, but those who had it were murdered.

31. As Russia crumbled into anarchy, Admiral Aleksandr Kolchak's White Army seized the state treasury and much of the Russian Empire.

32. Official British observer Colonel Alfred Knox had little good to say about the Tsar's generals, except Brusilov, whom he respected.

33. Czech Legion soldiers hanging suspected Red sympathisers without trial in 1919.

34. Other Reds gloat over bodies of Czech legionnaires they have killed near Vladivostok.

35. Men of Denikin's White Army with a British Mark V tank in Don region, 1919.

36. Another Mark V tank preserved in Archangel as a reminder of the British intervention.

37. A Japanese propaganda poster shows local Russian civilians welcoming the first interventionist troops from Japan. It wasn't quite like that.

38. American 'doughboys' landed in Vladivostok, not to support the Allies, but to prevent the Japanese grabbing Russian territory.

11

THE VERY MODEL OF A
MODERN RUSSIAN GENERAL

During the uneasy inter-Allied conference at Chantilly in November 1915 the policy of coordinating Allied moves in the west and on the Russian fronts had been re-confirmed. Whatever Nicholas II's generals had thought initially about their role as decoys to relieve German pressure in Flanders and, to a lesser extent the Austro-Hungarian threat against Italy, their reliance on Western arms shipments again forced them to launch an offensive – this time to coincide with the planned Allied offensive on the Somme, which was intended to develop into the 'big push' that would end the war. With OHL giving priority to building up men and munitions for Falkenhayn's planned killing blow at the exposed fortress-city of Verdun in the spring – nobody then guessed that nearly a million men would die there, mostly blown to pieces by high-explosive shells – on the Russian fronts the winter 1915–16 passed in a series of small attacks of no great moment except to the thousands of men who were wounded, taken prisoner, died in combat or succumbed to exposure.

The Tsar paid a visit to several units on the south-western front, one of them 8th Army, commanded by General Brusilov, a slim and wiry cavalryman whose army career went back to the Russo-Turkish war of 1877. When the bodyguards' train arrived one hour before the royal train, the commander of the guard expressed concern that Austro-Hungarian aircraft might bomb the units to be inspected during the visit, putting the Tsar's life at risk. Brusilov pointed out that the low cloud would keep aircraft on the ground, so there was no danger of that happening. Accompanying the Tsar and crown prince, he noted how stiff and awkward they were when talking to the soldiers. A few overdue medals were presented and the royal train disappeared. Describing this in his memoirs,[1] Brusilov contrasts this pointless visit with the fact that the commander of the south-western front, General Ivanov, visited the front so rarely that he had no idea of the morale or capability of his troops. He not only failed to make any preparations for an offensive, but also openly voiced his opinion that his troops could not defend their own lines, if attacked. This was in distinct contrast with Brusilov, who was already mapping out plans for 8th Army to attack and drive Austrian 4th Army under Archduke Joseph Ferdinand back to the Styr and Stockhod rivers. His only reservation was that his right flank needed to be protected by 3rd Army, which was not part of Ivanov's command because it fell under the western front, commanded by General Aleksei Evert. Evert was an imposing man of fifty-nine whose chest was covered in medals and stars, but who was equally as lacking in fighting spirit as Ivanov. As time would tell tragically, Brusilov was right to suspect Evert of failing to support an attack by a neighbouring unit or army, even when ordered to do so.

As a sop to Brusilov, front commander Ivanov allotted *sotni* of Cossack cavalry to patrol on 8th Army's right flank. As Brusilov pointed out, they were intended for fast-moving manoeuvres in open country and could not be of much use in the Pripyat marshes there. Instead, these bands of horsemen mainly roamed about behind the Russian lines, raping and looting the property of the remaining inhabitants. Their only successful operation against the enemy that winter was a raid by three dismounted *sotni*, who used local guides to follow secret paths through the marshes and raid the HQ of a German infantry division, capturing several officers including the commanding general. Generally, officer POWs were well treated when captured by regular troops but these prisoners must have been ill treated by the Cossacks because the general committed suicide, cutting his throat with a razor after receiving permission to shave himself. At the end of the winter, these irregulars were disbanded, with some men sentenced to death by court martial or exiled to hard labour for robbery and rape. As Brusilov commented in his memoirs without actually mentioning Ivanov, it is amazing how many otherwise intelligent people have stupid ideas![2]

He, as commander of 8th Army, spent the winter overseeing the construction of better shelters, both for the men's comfort and health, and to protect them from artillery fire when winter gave way to spring and the front heated up again. However, when he later saw the reinforced concrete shelters constructed by the Austrians, he admitted that they were a great deal more impressive – especially the plentiful bathhouses which enabled the enemy troops to keep cleaner and less lice-infested than Russian infantrymen. It is true that there was less disease in the tsarist armies than in previous wars, yet outbreaks of typhus, cholera and smallpox recurred, as Florence Farmborough was to find. Nevertheless, Brusilov considered that morale was good, while regretting the lack of sufficient heavy artillery and aircraft for reconnaissance and artillery observation on south-western front and a total lack of armoured motor vehicles. These last had been promised from France, but did not arrive during the time he was commanding 8th Army.[3]

When Falkenhayn at OHL began his Verdun offensive on 21 February 1916, Tsar Nicholas informed his generals that, in keeping with the 'request' of General Joffre at Chantilly, a new offensive must be launched on the Russian fronts to immobilise German forces that could otherwise be transferred to Verdun. The most promising sector for such an attack was on the northern front in the area of Lake Narotch (modern Narach in Belarus), where elements of two Russian armies totalling 350,000 men faced a German line held by General Hermann von Eichhorn's 75,000-strong 10th German Army. The northern front was commanded since von Plehve's health had given way by General Aleksei Kuropatkin, a man so disgraced during the defeat by the Japanese a decade earlier that he should not have been given any command, in Brusilov's opinion. Grand Duke Nikolai had rightly refused to appoint Kuropatkin, but had been over-ruled by the Tsar when he took over as supreme commander.

On 17 March at the lake – now a peaceful and verdant tourist area – Russian 2nd Army opened the offensive. With conditions seemingly favourable for a rapid victory to raise Russian morale and please the French, a two-day preparatory bombardment that used up much Russian ammunition was so badly directed that it caused scant damage to the German artillery. The price for this was paid when the infantry went in, in tightly grouped squads. Not only did they suffer as obvious targets for the German artillery, but the failure to spread out and use what cover was available caused a terrible slaughter from well-sited German machine gun positions with interlocking fields of fire. The few local gains made were all subsequently lost in German counter-attacks. Early in April, this sector of the front went quiet, having cost another 100,000 Russian casualties, including around 10,000 men who died of exposure in the harsh weather conditions. For this further blot on his record, Kuropatkin was later relieved of his command and sent to distant Turkestan as its Governor-General.

On the day before the Lake Narotch offensive opened, Brusilov received an encoded telegram from Stavka, in which Chief of Staff General Mikhail Alekseyev informed him confidentially that he was being appointed commander of the whole south-western front, replacing Ivanov, who had had a nervous breakdown – as a result of which he was being transferred to a sinecure post in the Tsar's household. Ten days later, 120 miles behind the lines at Berdychev, Brusilov arrived at Ivanov's HQ to take formal command of the whole front. He found Ivanov living in a railway carriage, ready to depart, weeping and asking repeatedly why he had been sacked. This embarrassing behaviour continued at dinner in front of his staff. As Brusilov dryly commented, he could give no reply to Ivanov, not being privy to the precise reasons for Alekseyev's decision.

The Tsar had not been keen on Brusilov's appointment, but refrained from blocking it. He arrived on another tour of the south-western front and insisted on inspecting 11th Army, speaking to the troops paraded for the occasion without a glimmer of charisma. As Brusilov commented, the speech was not such as to lift the spirits of the men. During the visit, enemy aircraft appeared but were driven off by Russian artillery. To his credit – or perhaps his lack of imagination – the Tsar remained with 11th Army for two days and nights. Kaiser Wilhelm was also visiting German troops on the other side of the lines, where his gruff man-to-man manner had always gone down well with the rank-and-file, although on this visit he noticed for the first time an unpleasant surliness in his troops due to the high casualties, the harsh weather on the Russian fronts and news from home of social unrest and the imprisonment of revolutionary socialists like Karl Liebknecht and Rosa Luxemburg.

Brusilov's next meeting with Tsar Nicholas was on 14 April, when attending his first meeting of Stavka as commander of the south-western front. This took place in Mogilyov (modern Magilyou in Belarus), described as a depressing town, chosen because it had some large buildings to accommodate the various staffs, and was presided over in his usual indecisive manner by Nicholas. Among the officers present was General Evert, commanding the Russian western front, who supported Kuropatkin's claim that the failure at Lake Narotch had been due to inadequate reserves of artillery shells. They both agreed that this made further offensives pointless. As chief of staff, Alekseyev nevertheless ordered a summer offensive on the northern front by 2nd and 10th armies when new conscripts had replaced casualties and missing in action, to bring strength up to between 700,000 and 800,000 men. The right flank of this offensive would drive on Vilna while the rest of this force, outnumbering the Germans by a ratio of 5:1 or better, was tasked with playing a waiting game to interdict movement of enemy forma-tions against the right flank. But there was a trade-off. There always was with Alekseyev, an unpretentious man of humble origin who tried to avoid contact with his own staff and felt embarrassed if he did not pay his own mess bill, unlike many of the noble officers he commanded, who took it as of right that the army should feed them. In his favour, it has to be said that he had effected an excel-lent clear-out of the aristocratic cavalrymen who had scavenged at the table of his predecessor, yet was unable to impose his will at times like this. He agreed to a two-month delay and accepted the need for 1,000 more heavy guns for the preparatory bombardment.

At this conference, Brusilov surprised the other front commanders by volunteer-ing to direct a simultaneous offensive on his front to prevent the enemy moving reinforcements on the railway network in Austrian Galicia to reinforce their posi-tions on the northern front. After he refused to be deterred by Alekseyev's warning that he could expect no priority in reinforcements or materiel, Kuropatkin and Evert rubbished the idea of Brusilov's offer. At dinner that evening one of the senior generals – in his memoirs, Brusilov does not name him, for whatever reason – gave some advice: 'You've just been appointed front commander. Your reputation stands very high, why take a risk like that which could tarnish it and cancel out all your achievements so far?' Brusilov replied that he saw it as his duty to attempt to win the war, whatever the problems of manpower and materiel.[4]

He reasoned that the crippling shortage of artillery, rifles and ammunition that had beset the Russian armies earlier in the war was being steadily overcome, and that the situation would continue to improve because the retreat of 1915 had shortened the front, making re-supply more rapid, and Russia's indigenous armament industry was at last producing 1.5 billion cartridges and 1.3 million rifles per annum, with a further 2 million in process of importation from abroad.[5] The standard of recruit training was also much improved and a policy of initially drafting 'new meat' to quiet sectors of the front meant that raw recruits no longer de-trained to find themselves thrown into combat the next morning. Ivanov, still not recovered from his breakdown, was in habitual negative mood and asked the Tsar to veto Brusilov's proposal. As usual, Nicholas refused to throw his weight on either side, so Brusilov left Stavka to present his plan to his own staff.

Alexei Brusilov was unlike most of his fellow generals in the Russian forces in not being an alumnus of the General Staff Academy. He also did not share their conviction that endless bayonet charges would win the war by killing more of 'them' than 'us'. To his way of thinking, new materiel like tanks and aircraft offered more efficient possibilities. To some extent, this was because he was familiar with Western European military thinking, having visited the German, French and Austro-Hungarian cavalry schools before the war and had made his own independent analysis of the Japanese defeat of Kuropatkin and his army commanders Rennenkampf and Samsonov in the war of 1904–5. Britain's senior soldier of the Second World War, Field Marshal Bernard Montgomery considered that Brusilov was one of the seven outstanding commanders of the First World War. It is certainly arguable that the eventual result of the war in the east might have been very different, had Brusilov been given overall control at the outset and authority to override the blinkered nineteenth-century thinking of the generals senior to him, particularly at Stavka.

The third generation of his family to serve in the tsarist army – his grandfather had fought against Napoleon in 1812 – Alexei was born in 1853 in Tiflis of a Russian father and Polish mother. Orphaned young, he was raised by relatives in Georgia until the age of 14, when he was sent to continue his education with the prestigious Corps of Pages in Saint Petersburg – a promising first step to a military career. There, a tutor's report on him contained the comment: 'Of high potential, but inclined to be lazy.' The slur hardly fits with the man he showed himself to be in 1916. His rejection by the Tsar's prestigious guards regiments had more to do with lack of family money to subsidise life as a guards officer than any character defect. Instead, he was posted with the rank of ensign to a lowly dragoon regiment back home in Georgia.

There, keenness and efficiency saw him rapidly promoted to regimental adjutant with the rank of lieutenant. In the Russo-Turkish War of 1877–78 he was awarded several medals and ended the war as a captain. He must have caught the eye of some senior officers, for this was followed by a posting to the prestigious cavalry officer school in St Petersburg, leading to an appointment on the staff of the college, where he spent the next thirteen years. By 1902 he was a lieutenant general commanding the school. It was at this time he was able to travel to France, Austria-Hungary and Germany, ostensibly to study horse breeding and other harmless matters, but also to observe first-hand, in Germany and Austro-Hungary, the manoeuvres of the very armies he would almost certainly be confronting one day, and thus gaining an appreciation of their commanders' thinking.

Although not as shattering to Russian society as the 1917 revolution, the revolution of 1905, triggered by Russia's defeat and appalling death toll in the Russo-Japanese war, caused much disruption of life in St Petersburg, as it then was. Coming after the death of his first wife, this caused Brusilov to seek a posting away from the capital. He was rewarded in 1912 with appointment as deputy commander-in-chief of all Russian forces in the strategically important Warsaw Military District. It was, however, not a happy time because his superior, Governor-General Georgi Skalon, was an autocrat whose brutal repression of civil unrest there at the time of the 1905 Russian revolution had led to an attempt on his life by Polish nationalists. Brusilov simply did not fit in the rigid pomp-and-circumstance hierarchy of Skalon's command and had himself transferred to Kiev in the Ukraine.

On mobilisation in July 1914, he was promoted to command Russian 8th Army on the south-west front in Galicia, which smashed its way through the opposing Austro-Hungarian forces, rapidly advancing nearly 100 miles, but had to retreat in the general withdrawal after Tannenberg. Early 1915 saw the same script replayed, with Brusilov's spearheads advancing through the Carpathian passes to threaten Budapest until forced back in the general retreat. Never the sort of commander to stay back at HQ all the time, he had thoroughly reorganised 8th Army before handing over command to his successor and made a complete tour of inspection of the whole south-western front after his promotion to front commander. He felt confident that, although his two previous successes had been forfeited by the shortcomings on his flanks and shortages of materiel, this time Evert would have to attack simultaneously, so that he could again push the opposing German and Austro-Hungarian forces back to the Carpathians and this time hold them there.

Brusilov disagreed with the customary Russian practice of concentrating an offensive on a small sector of the front for the good reason that this left the advancing troops vulnerable to counter-attack on the flanks. What he was planning, was an attack that would hit the enemy in many places over the whole

280-mile length of the south-western front, reasoning that this would prevent the enemy moving forces to strengthen weak positions, one of which would give way and lead to a collapse. His artillery was also to be deployed differently, not to make saturation barrages but to target strategic points such as road junctions and command posts of the German units they were facing. Brusilov even accepted the transfer of some divisions to Evert's front on the assumption they would be attacking at the same time as he did and securing his right flank.

On 17 April at front HQ in Berdychev he therefore informed his four army commanders that the offensive would be launched simultaneously in a number of places from the southern limit of the Pripyat marshes down to the Romanian border, with 8th Army targeting particularly the railway junctions at Lutsk and Kovel – an axis that had the potential to split the opposing CP forces in two. The army commanders' reaction mirrored that of the generals at Stavka. In fairness to them, the enormous scale of previous losses in this theatre and the fact that every advance made had, sooner or later, been repulsed by the enemy, had eroded whatever aggressive spirit they once had. Traditional military thinking was that an attacking force should be roughly three times as strong as the defenders. With a manpower ratio of roughly 1:1 – each side had about 135,000 men in the line on this front – General Aleksei Kaledin, commanding 8th Army because of family connections with the Tsar, who had blocked Brusilov's choice of appointee for that post, said openly that the offensive could not succeed. He was pulled up sharply by Brusilov, who reminded him that he had just handed 8th Army over to him and was personally aware that it was well prepared to attack – and also that he was familiar with every mile of 8th Army's front. The commander of 7th Army, General Dmitri Shcherbachev was the only one initially favourable to Brusilov's plans, and even he allowed himself to be talked round until Brusilov found all four of his army commanders speaking out openly *against* them. He then informed them all that he was not asking for their advice, but ordering them to prepare the offensive.

His four armies gave him forty infantry divisions and fifteen cavalry divisions. The four opposing armies they would be taking on consisted of thirty-eight infantry divisions and eleven of cavalry. In artillery, Brusilov's 168 heavy guns and 1,770 light guns roughly matched the Austro-Hungarians' 545 medium and heavy guns and 1,301 light guns on that front.[6]

Time spent in preparation is seldom wasted. The old maxim from Caesar's day, or earlier, was Brusilov's credo. He commenced by ordering reserves brought forward all along the line, so that enemy aerial reconnaissance could not determine at what point the offensive was likely to come. Once 'up', these troops were set to excavating sheltered *places d'armes* or assembly areas for thousands of men, with the displaced soil piled up into berms running parallel to the front line, both to impede observation from the ground and to afford some

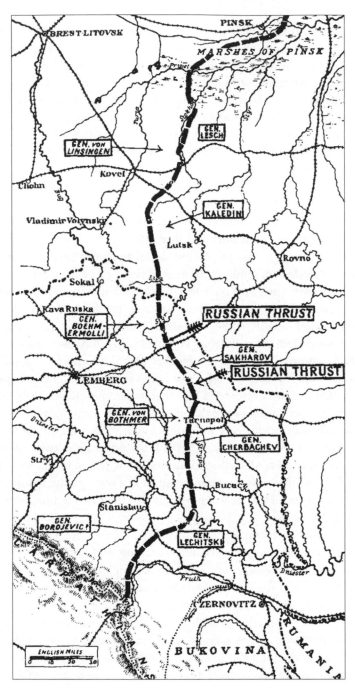

South–western front when Brusilov took command. Contemporary map with anglicised place names (e.g. Pripyat marshes are labelled 'Marshes of Pinsk').

protection against incoming artillery fire. From these areas, communication trenches were dug to the front lines. Not content with that, Brusilov ordered saps, or tunnels, to be dug out into no man's land. The purpose of these was to bring the jumping-off points for his infantry within 50–100yd of the enemy lines and thus radically reduce the time they were exposed to machine gun fire during the assault.

Always keen to exploit new technology, Brusilov ordered aerial reconnaissance not only of the enemy front lines, but also in depth to the rear, so that he could see where the opposing commanders were concentrating reserves, where they planned to retreat or make a stand and, especially, chart their artillery dispositions. The result was a series of accurately plotted maps of the enemy positions, enhanced by interrogation of deserters and prisoners. This done, he shared the maps with his four army commanders and delegated to them the choice of axes for their attacks, each hitting between 8 to 25 selected miles of front. This enabled General Shcherbachev, for example, to designate a small salient in the south of his line where the opposing troops were of Slav origin – and therefore believed likely to surrender rather than fight – and where the topography favoured the Russian attackers, giving good cover for their troop movements while affording a clear field of fire for their artillery.[7]

With his passion for detail, Brusilov ordered full-size mock-ups of the enemy positions to be constructed behind the lines, so that the assault troops could make repeated mock attacks until they knew their way around in them as well as in their own lines. It was impressed on them that they should press on to the second line of defence with minimum delay, and not linger in the front lines – which, once taken, were vulnerable to counter-attack and pre-set artillery barrage. In his words: 'We have to consider that our opponent normally places his strongest defence in the second line, so that assault troops halting in the front line only serve to concentrate the enemy's fire.'[8]

It would have been futile to try and conceal all these preparations from enemy reconnaissance over-flights, so Brusilov confused the photographs thus taken by what would later be called a deception operation. He had dummy batteries constructed to deceive enemy observers and concealed the real batteries until the day of the attack. Misleading radio traffic was also generated specifically for Austrian interception. False 'deserters' crossed the lines with misleading disinformation. Movement of reinforcements was similarly passed off as one body of men apparently relieving another, so that the enemy command had no suspicion of the massive troop movements which had previously given away preparations for a massed Russian attack.

A picture of what conditions were like on the south-western front at the time comes from a soldier's graphic letter dated 30 March 1916[9] that was read out in Russian by military historian Professor Narskii at a 2004 symposium in Berlin:

This is a landscape of trenches, dugouts, artillery of all calibres, mortars, flame-throwers, yet by daylight you might think you had landed on an uninhabited island. Everything has gone underground, masked from predatory binoculars, observers in aeroplanes and balloons tethered above the treetops. A man on foot could pass near the battery and see nothing; the horse lines are hidden in thickets; soldiers wait in their deep, narrow trenches. But at night, out of nowhere come infantry columns marching along the roads, food convoys, canteens, machine guns, carts, artillery batteries on the move. Soldiers in a great grey mass, even their faces all alike. Then come the first rays of dawn and the landscape, as if transformed by a magic wand, becomes again a desert island.[10]

NOTES

1. Brusilov *Vospominaniya* (Original Russian text downloadable from http://militera.lib.ru/memo/russian/brusilov/index.html. No page numbers. Dates are given according to the Julian calendar, but have been adjusted here by thirteen days to synchronise with the Gregorian calendar, adopted in Russia in 1917.
2. Ibid.
3. Ibid.
4. Ibid.
5. N. Stone, *The Eastern Front 1914–1917* (New York: Charles Scribner's Sons, 1975), p. 212.
6. Various sources give conflicting numbers.
7. Dowling, pp. 43–5.
8. Ibid, p. 45.
9. It is actually dated 17 March according to the Julian calendar.
10. Narskii.

12

BRUSILOV'S PLAN

The gunners on Brusilov's south-western front also used the mock-up enemy positions to familiarise individual battery commanders with the weak points of their allotted targets because the traditional massive barrage on the enemy wire had been discarded by Brusilov as inefficient – which, as at Lake Narotch, it all too often was, with tragic results for the attacking infantry. Each battery was therefore allotted specific targets and was instructed by experienced gunners brought in for the purpose, including some Japanese veterans of the 1904 war. Light batteries were placed under the command of the local infantry commander and were tasked with creating gaps in the wire in specified places, rather than wasting shells on a general barrage. After this, they were to deal with the enemy machine gun posts, which posed a major threat for the infantry. Meanwhile the heavy guns were to destroy the well-mapped communications trenches to interdict movement of reinforcements and create chaos behind the enemy lines, only then hitting the front line just before the infantry went in and laying down a creeping barrage just ahead of them – a tactic that Brusilov copied from the German defence at Lake Narotch. Although a cavalry man himself, Brusilov put a lot of thought into the role of artillery. He ordered the heavy batteries to be no more than 3 miles behind the lines so that they could afford some protection to the attacking infantry by targeting the Austro-Hungarian field guns on its flanks.[1] At this point the lighter guns in forward positions were to silence the enemy's heavy batteries.

Whether because the plan required tight coordination of all arms, or due to their ingrained defeatism, Brusilov's army commanders were still not impressed, except for 11th Army's General Nikolai Sakharov. The dissenters' arguments varied: the enemy had more artillery; his defences were too well constructed; there was an inadequate supply of shells; and so on. Brusilov dealt with them all, at one point threatening Kaledin with dismissal, never mind that he was the Tsar's appointee. However, once the confrontation was over, he did everything possible to bolster Kaledin's flagging spirits and made more trips to 8th Army's front than to the other armies, all of which he regularly visited.

Each attack was to be made in four or more waves. The first was by 'bombers' – shock infantry whose task was to clear the first trenches with plentiful use of hand grenades and to deal with those forward artillery positions that had escaped the Russian counter-battery fire. The second wave followed 200 paces behind and moved through the first to attack the second line of trenches. A breach achieved, the third and fourth waves widened it and brought forward machine guns to protect the cavalry, whose function was to funnel through the breach and fan out to take the enemy in the rear.

Meanwhile, what preparations to resist a Russian spring offensive had been made on the other side of the lines? The answer is, so little that Conrad von Hötzendorf could have been collaborating with Brusilov. After the Italian declaration of war, he had become obsessed with the Isonzo front, where the fifth major battle was about to begin early in March 1916. Since Falkenhayn had no men or resources to spare for that front – and technically Italy was not at war with Germany, but only with Austria-Hungary – Conrad posted his XIV Corps and two infantry divisions from the Russian front to the Isonzo in October 1915, replacing them on paper with Hungarian Reserve or Honved Infantry Divisions (HID) who had never been in combat. To compensate for this, some experienced battalions were embedded in the reserve divisions, but at the cost of weakening their parent formations. As historian Timothy C. Dowling comments:

> Not only did this weaken the units from which battle-hardened officers were drawn, it also failed to provide career officers in sufficient numbers for the new units to operate with confidence. When the Austrian 4th Army amalgamated the 70th HID, it assigned three staff officers from each of three units … to the new troops. This left each regiment with an average of one-quarter of an officer per company in the best case. In 7th Infantry Division most regiments counted one career officer for every two companies. By the winter of 1915–16 the vast majority of officers in the Austro-Hungarian 8th Cavalry Division were young and untrained.[2]

The resultant lack of contact between officers and men and the insufficient attention given to training the reservists led to a considerable diminution of fighting spirit throughout the ranks.

By January 1916 Conrad had withdrawn three more divisions and eventually fifteen heavy artillery batteries from the Russian front to strengthen his Italian front. The rugged mountains of the Austro-Hungarian positions on the Isonzo front made this a cruel posting for the gunners. Contemporary photographs show up to 2,000 men harnessed by long cables to one heavy gun in the attempt to drag it up steep, snow-covered slopes.

Falkenhayn was equally obsessed with his planned 'killing blow' at Verdun, for which he had withdrawn eight German divisions from the northern sector of the Russian front. So when Conrad asked at a planning meeting in February 1916 for German reinforcements and artillery to strengthen the south-western front that he had enfeebled, Falkenhayn told him that, should conditions on the northern front demand it, he would *withdraw* German forces from the south-western front – a total of 13,000 men. The two CP supreme commanders parted frostily after Falkenhayn suggested that Conrad had his priorities all wrong and should simply hold the Italians on the Isonzo front while concentrating his strength on the main enemy: Russia.

Conrad ignored this advice completely, withdrawing four more divisions from the Russian front in March 1916 in preparation for the massive attack against the Italians which he planned for May. Recalling the Christmas/New Year attack by General Platon Lechitsky's 9th Army, when Russian infantry marched practically in parade-ground order over a mile in open country, exposed to Austro-Hungarian artillery and were then mown down by Austrian Schwarzlose water-cooled machine guns before reaching the first trenches, he was confident that Russian losses of 70,000 men in two days during that offensive had taught his enemies that they would require at least thirty additional divisions in order to launch a significant attack. Without them, he considered in March that, given the comparative strengths on the south-western front, 'a Russian offensive (of the available strength) would have to be considered pointless'.[3]

To compensate for moving the heavy guns to the Italian front, he increased Austrian 4th Army's remaining artillery by nearly 50 per cent, many of them being light guns of improved new types. Ammunition supplies were also increased. As to manpower, new levies produced three-quarters of a million 'other ranks' and 15,000 fresh, but untried, officers. The first months of 1916 also saw German forces on the south-western front increased by 38,000 men and 400 officers. Although nominally *Korsettenstangen*, these were not in fact first-class troops, who were prioritised for Verdun.

In addition, most of the new troops, both German and Austro-Hungarian, were set to practise drill and digging in, with snow-shovelling as light relief – hardly the best preparation for the offensive bound to come when weather conditions improved with the coming of spring. The new 'other ranks' grew tired and bored; the new officers appear to have concentrated on making their own quarters comfortable and homely, with good cuisine and ample cellarage. What is interesting to the historian is the lack of whistle-blowers. It is as though there was an unspoken conspiracy, with reports of inspecting officers glossing over the near-total lack of combat training and all ranks placing their faith in the supposed impregnability of the new fortifications, as though this obviated the need for combat-readiness.[4]

The senior German commander on the south-western front was General von Linsingen, whose *Heeresgruppe* (Army Group) held the left flank of the CP forces, facing Russian 3rd Army. On his right or southern flank was Archduke Joseph Ferdinand, commanding Austrian 1st and 4th armies – the latter including as corset stays the German troops of Group Marwitz – facing Kaledin's 8th Army. Refusing to accept a German officer as senior commander of the south-western front, Conrad promoted Joseph Ferdinand, in defiance of his poor record in the war, to the new rank of colonel general, so that he could outrank Linsingen. OHL's riposte was to promote Linsingen to the same rank and back-date the promotion, making him theoretically senior to the archduke! Tension between commanders had been a significant factor in the Russian defeat at Tannenberg, and the tension between Linsingen and Joseph Ferdinand was on a par with that, the two men refusing to communicate except by telegraph.[5] South of there was Eduard Freiherr von Böhm-Ermolli, commanding Austrian 2nd Army opposite Russian 11th Army and the German Südarmee facing Sakharov's 11th Army. The very south of the front, in the Bukovina-Carpathian sector, was held by Austrian 7th Army, commanded by General Karl Freiherr von Pflanzer-Baltin, opposing Russian 9th Army, commanded by General Lechitsky, a veteran of the Boxer Rebellion in China and the Russo-Japanese war.

Brusilov kept a careful watch on the German and Austrian winter–spring construction programme of defensive works in three strips, each of three lines deep with a gap of between 50 and 100m between the lines to serve as a killing ground for the field artillery in the event of any Russian breakthrough. In front of the forward trenches was Brer Fox's briar patch: three extensive separated strips of wire, 10m deep. The forward machine gun positions and observation posts overlooking this were not made of logs with an earth covering, as on the Russian side, but were reinforced concrete bunkers, camouflaged with a covering of earth and vegetation. The new idea of foxholes, some as deep as 4m, intended to protect forward infantry from the effects of new artillery firing more powerful shells, was expected to provide better shelter than conventional trenches and dugouts. In order to try and compensate for the loss of the heavy guns sent to the Italian front, artillery dispositions were reorganised and it was also planned to 'seed' first-line infantry units with *Infanteriegeschütz Abteilungen* (literally, infantry-artillery units). These were field artillery batteries of ten 37mm guns each, integrated with infantry units. Fortunately for Brusilov's plans, the introduction of these was incomplete when his offensive began, Army Group Böhm-Ermolli having only five among its eight infantry divisions.[6]

Of necessity, military history deals mainly with the big issues. But even at this time of comparative quiet on the eastern front men were dying, many of them simply vaporised by the enemy artillery. On 31 April an otherwise unremembered infantryman somewhere on that long front wrote home:

18 April, I write to you.[7] Hallo, my dear godfather Ivan Kuzmich and dear godmother Agrafena Ivanovna. Greetings also to … wishing everyone the best of good health. We marched for ten days with Vasily Pustovoit but now I do not know where he is. And now we are in position in a forest, the thunder of the guns going on day and night. Artillery, there is nothing else. My field post office address is … Please write to me, Vasily Lodshina.[8]

Surprisingly, at this time of preparation for the great offensive of 1916 – and even more surprisingly in view of the millions of casualties already suffered and men taken prisoner – Russia was sending troops abroad. When Vasily Lodshina was being deafened by the guns in the forest, 1st Special Brigade of the Russian Expeditionary Force landed at Marseille to fight on the Western Front. Visiting Russia in December 1915 future French president Paul Doumer had asked for 300,000 men, which ridiculously high figure was based on the assumption that Russia had unlimited reserves of trained manpower. At Stavka, General Alekseyev was understandably against sending any men to France, in addition to those already destined for the Salonika front. The Tsar, however, overrode his objections in return for Doumer's promise of armaments and eventually compromised on sending a brigade, providing it was to serve under Russian officers, be equipped by the French, and be transported by the French navy.

Comprising one regiment from each of Moscow and Samara, the brigade numbered 8,942 men, with factory workers predominating in 1st Regiment and peasants in 2nd Regiment. Contemporary photographs show French officers on the quayside at Marseille in April 1916, saluting the new arrivals after their ten-week journey from Moscow, via the Trans-Siberian railway and by sea from Dal'ny around China, across the Indian Ocean, through the Red Sea and Suez Canal. On board one of the four French ships, some Russian officers return the salutes, while most of their men see Europe for the first time with no apparent emotion. They parade through the Old Town in front of curious, but not very large, crowds before being transported by rail to Mailly le-Camp in Champagne, preparative to being sent into the line. Killing time for a few days there, they eat, smoke and watch two burly NCOs doing energetic Cossack knees-bend dancing to music played on an accordion. In a safe trench on the French–held sector of the Champagne sector of the line, their commander, General Nikolai Lokhvitsky, poses for a photographer. For him and the other officers, with fluent French as their second language, liaison was not a problem. For their conscripts in the brigade, it was a different story. At that point, the photographic record ends, but the documentary record continues, to end in tragedy.

A few days after setting foot on French soil, 1st Special Brigade was transported to Châlons-sur-Marne and attached to General Henri Gouraud's 4th Army, 'going up' to the line around Auberive at the end of June. Like their brothers-in-arms on the Russian fronts, the men of 1st Special Brigade fought and suffered in the trenches, being joined later by 3rd Special Brigade, shipped from Archangel to Brest in September, while 2nd and 4th Russian Special Brigades were in Macedonia, fighting the Bulgarians. In all, some 45,000 officers and men were sent to fight in France. There is a military cemetery at Mourmelon-le-Grand containing the graves of 1,000 Russian officers and men. Somewhat belatedly, the French nation erected a memorial equestrian statue on the bank of the Seine in Paris in 2011.

News of the Tsar's abdication in March 1917 and of the mutinies on the Russian fronts divided the men's loyalties, with many of the more politically active townsmen in 1st Brigade refusing to fight and demanding to be repatriated while the peasants of 3rd Brigade remained under the discipline of their officers, prepared to continue the war. The generals might have been able to fool themselves that the loss of millions of lives was justified in some unprovable way, but the men in the front lines had long ceased believing in anything, except the likelihood that they would soon be corpses. Because the French army was suffering mutinies with many men being summarily shot in front of their comrades *pour encourager les autres*, the mutinous Russians were moved to where they were less likely to spread dissent at the front. At the huge military camp of La Courtine in Central France, attempts were made by Russian and French officers to restore order in 1st Brigade. After 3rd Brigade was ordered to surround the mutineers' camp, there ensued five days of scuffles and argument before a Russian-manned battery of French field guns shelled the mutineers, causing fifty casualties.

The surviving mutineers were despatched to concentration camps, some as far away as the Sahara desert, then policed by the French Foreign Legion, where conditions were horrific. Most officers and some men, however, volunteered to form the Légion Russe, which continued the fight until the Armistice in November 1918. By then, few of these legionnaires thought it was safe to return to Russia under the Bolsheviks. Since France had been a *pays d'accueil* for refugees from European monarchies ever since the Revolution, they opted to stay there on demobilisation. This produced the strange phenomenon between the wars, when it seemed that the majority of taxi-drivers in Paris were former Russian officers, as were many of the commissionaires outside posh hotels.

At the end of April 1916 came a distraction that Brusilov would rather have done without. Notified by Stavka that the Tsar and Tsarina, accompanied by two of the princesses, were going to inspect the Serbian Division at Bender near Odessa, he had to make a round trip of some 600 miles to welcome them, the hinterland of fourteen provinces coming under his authority as commander of south-western front. To Brusilov's military mind, it was incredible that the supreme commander of the Russian armies should travel as far as the Crimea just to alleviate the boredom of his wife and daughters, who had spent the winter at Tsarskoye Selo (modern Pushkin). This was an eighteenth-century fantasy village used as a country residence of the tsars outside Petrograd. The visit was as boring as one may imagine, except that Brusilov was interested to review this division composed of some 10,000 Serbian volunteers.

Briefed twice a day on developments at the fronts, the Tsar seemed otherwise unconcerned with the progress of the war. Sharing two meals a day with him and the princesses, Brusilov had little contact with the Tsarina – *nemka*, or 'the German woman', as she was known in Petrograd – until she summoned him to her carriage on the royal train and asked frigidly whether his offensive was going to be ready on time. He prevaricated, saying that it depended on many factors, but in any case would hardly have divulged this Top Secret information to her. That was, as he said in his memoirs, the last time he saw Nicholas' consort.[9] When she asked whether the royal train with its ample stores of provisions and bath-coach could be of use at the front, he replied that it would certainly enable some wounded men to be better cared for. There were already several hospital trains near the front paid for by her and a number of other noble ladies, who had taken this upon themselves in the belief that the war would be short. Since some of their grown daughters served as nurses on these trains, looking after men wounded 'above the belt', the situation presented a rare opportunity for a worker or peasant to actually meet a grand duchess.

As winter turned to spring the Central Powers' commanders on the south-western front seemed to wake from a long hibernation. Forward observers of army group Böhm-Ermolli noted Russian 8th Army saps in no man's land. Aerial reconnaissance by Austrian 4th Army noted the construction of Brusilov's *places d'armes* and many saps being dug towards its front lines. Attempts to hamper Russian preparations at this late date came up against OAK bureaucracy. When Linsingen requested more shells for the purpose, he received the reply that use of munitions for aimless firing and registration firing had been restricted. One can imagine his fury at having to rely on Austrian logistics. It can have been of little comfort that Archduke Joseph Ferdinand and Böhm-Ermolli also received the same response from OAK when requesting supplies of howitzer shells – for no good reason at all, since there were at that time adequate reserves. Bureaucracy and complacency in the invulnerability of the defence fortifications pervaded the meeting between Falkenhayn and Conrad on 23 May, at which they both considered that all was well on the Russian south-western front.

NOTES

1. Dowling, pp. 44–5.
2. Ibid, p. 55 (edited).
3. Ibid, p. 50.
4. For greater detail, see Dowling, pp. 55–6.
5. Ibid, p. 57.
6. Some sources say ten infantry divisions.
7. Letter dated according to Julian calendar.
8. http:museum/omskelecom.ru/ogik/Izvestiya_8/Eperina.html.
9. Brusilov *Vospominaniya*.

13

BRUSILOV GOES IT ALONE

On 24 May Stavka received cables from the Italian high command requesting a diversionary attack to relieve pressure on the Isonzo front. The same day, Alekseyev informed Brusilov that the other front commanders would not be ready to coincide their offensives with his target date of 1 June. Alekseyev suggested that the offensives be staggered, Brusilov to delay three days and Evert on the western front to follow ten days later, on 14 June.[1] Brusilov, now beset by both his superior and his subordinates, none of whom wanted the attack to go in when he judged was the best time for it, agreed to postpone the offensive for the three additional days on condition that neither Evert nor anyone else sought further postponement. Yet Alekseyev telephoned Brusilov just hours before the postponed H-Hour to say that he should change his plan and attack in the conventional way, concentrating all his forces on one axis for each army. Brusilov refused on the grounds that any further delay would irreparably damage his men's morale. When Alekseyev played the Tsar card, saying that Nicholas II was behind the complete change of plan and foot-dragging, Brusilov offered his resignation. Alekseyev backed down, saying: 'Then God be with you. I shall inform the Tsar of our conversation in the morning.'[2]

Böhm-Ermolli's front-line observers belatedly realised that Russian 8th Army troops were cutting passages through their own wire. It is true that occasional patrol activity brought in genuine Russian prisoners – often at considerable cost in Austrian lives – whose interrogation made it plain that Russian units in many places were preparing an important offensive, but the intelligence officers compiling and forwarding these reports were wasting their time because Conrad and Hindenburg both considered that Brusilov was only preparing a reconnaissance in force.[3] Bolstered by this, the CP army commanders on the south-western front regarded the situation complacently, secure in the illusion that their reinforced defences were impregnable anyway.

As D-Day approached, Brusilov felt reasonably confident that his deception strategy had prevented the enemy from deducing exactly where the attacks would go in. Overall, he believed that, with adequate support by Evert's 3rd Army on the right flank of 8th Army and Sakharov's 11th Army advancing on its left flank, his forces could reach the Carpathian passes again and this time press right through onto the Hungarian plain, threatening Budapest and even Vienna, which could lead to the collapse of the Hapsburg dynasty and the surrender of the Austro-Hungarian armies, after which Germany would be obliged to sue for an armistice. That was a gamble well worth taking.

From south to north, 9th, 7th and 11th Russian armies were to immobilise the forces opposing then and prevent reinforcements being sent northwards to where Kaledin's 8th Army – supported by more than half of all the artillery on south-western front, totalling about 1,000 pieces – was to attack Böhm-Ermolli's Austro-Hungarian 2nd and 1st armies, with particular emphasis on the axis Tarnopol – Kovel. Kovel was not only an important rail junction, but also Linsingen's HQ. Since this advance would be close to the demarcation line between the Austrian troops and neighbouring German units, Brusilov strengthened Kaledin's right flank with two extra cavalry divisions.

Back in Russia, Alfred Knox – now promoted to major general – noted the opening salvoes at many points along the front at 0400hrs, after which the enemy artillery bombarded the Russian observation posts and forward batteries. Russian firing of HE, shrapnel and gas shells continued until 0700hrs, pounding the specific targets allotted to each battery. When it ceased, Austro-Hungarian troops hurried into their first line of trenches in expectation of an immediate infantry attack, but this did not come, except for a number of probing patrols. After the Russian artillery observers had evaluated the damage, the barrage opened up again in the same targeted way – most unlike the previous blanket barrages of the western front.

Return fire did not last long. As was afterwards learned, this was because all the enemy telephone cables to the batteries had been cut by the bombardment, thanks to accurate mapping. The carefully corrected Russian artillery continued all day. After dark, the targets were mainly the gaps cut through the enemy's wire during the day, to prevent their repair by working parties.[4]

Suffering the brunt of the Russian shelling on the first day of the offensive, Hungarian troops of General Baron Sándor Szurmay's army corps were cut to shreds in their trenches. About 1800hrs Brusilov's interest in new weapons took tangible shape in the form of a column of thirteen lumbering armoured vehicles advancing on the enemy lines. That does not sound impressive today, but the arrival of this column on Sakharov's centre, driving from Tarnopol towards Lemberg, had a big psychological effect, panicking the defenders and opening up a gap between Böhm-Ermolli's forces and Felix von Bothmer's Südarmee just as Austrian 1st Army's exposed bridgehead on the eastern, or Russian, bank of the River Ikvanie was nipped off. It was possibly after this engagement that an undated and unsigned letter home described life as one ordinary Siberian infantryman from faraway Omsk saw it:

Dear Shura,

In my previous letters I asked you to send tobacco and cigarette papers. Of course, it would be nice if you enclosed some Siberian canned goods also. Maybe I am not going to come back alive, but all is in the hands of God. I am living in a tent in the forest, with combat all around against both Austrians and Germans too. Many prisoners. There are no civilians here because the Austrians took them all as forced labour. We had an air raid the other day – thirty-two aircraft. What's the news in Siberia and what are people thinking in Omsk? I am happy that you are starting your studies. Work hard at them, my brother! At the time of writing I am sitting in the trees and above our heads is an aerial battle. Our planes are being attacked by five Austrian bandits. The other day one of their planes killed several of our horses and one man. On the ground the Austrians run away, but we pursue them. So far I am healthy.[5]

At OHL and OAK the reports of this activity were still not considered to be preparation for an imminent offensive, but possibly a rehearsal for a later attack when Stavka was required to take the pressure off the panicking Italians on the Isonzo front or off the Western Allies in Flanders. Yet someone at OAK must have had a suspicion that more was afoot, because supplementary stocks of shells were released for the Austrian units most concerned – with the contradictory habitual caution from OAK that local artillery commanders should use only the minimum of shells. When Archduke Joseph Ferdinand's staff finally deduced from the artillery concentration hitting their positions that the axis of attack must be towards Kovel, a prepared plan was put into action to impede this. At his HQ there Linsingen read the reports coming in without alarm. Although aware that the Russian forces opposite them outnumbered their own men, both he and Archduke Joseph Ferdinand were still confident that the defences prepared during the winter months would eventually slow down and then halt any advance by Kaledin.

When the Russian artillery again ceased firing after midday, Austro-Hungarian troops were once more ordered into the front-line trenches, while their artillery pounded no man's land in expectation of the customary infantry attack. Nothing happened along Kaledin's front of nearly 80 miles, apart from a few more probing attacks. Then pre-aligned Russian mortar fire began taking a further toll on the Hungarian troops of Corps Szurmay, causing those not killed or wounded to scuttle back to their dugouts, unable to retreat as what was described as 'a curtain of fire' cut them off from the rear. In the centre of 8th Army's front, shelling continued for the rest of the day and night.

Further south, Lechitsky's 9th Army and the opposing Austrian 7th Army were so equally matched – ten or eleven infantry and four cavalry divisions on each side – that army commander Pflanzer-Baltin had taken the risk of posting 79th Hungarian reserve infantry brigade to the front line in place of combat-toughened formations siphoned off to the Isonzo front by Conrad. These Hungarian rookies had spent most of the winter digging in and shovelling snow, which had not prepared them to resist Lechitsky's 3rd Transamur infantry division they were facing in the line. In addition, the reservists were twice as numerous as the troops who had dug the defensive positions into which they had moved. Crowded into the far-too-small dugouts, they emerged with relief when the first barrage lifted, to be caught unawares and shredded by the second barrage that followed fifteen minutes later from nineteen heavy guns firing HE concentrated on a sector less than 3 miles wide. When the Russian infantry advanced across the short expanse of no man's land between their jumping-off saps and the Austro-Hungarian front line, the broken ground afforded them protection from the enemy artillery, so that losses were slight.

The shock of the attack by the Russian and Transamur troops shattered all resistance by the defenders. The Transamur infantry were Asiatic troops from the Amur region of the Russian Far East and had a reputation for savagery unusual in modern European warfare, terrifying the enemy by taking no prisoners, even after surrender. Pflanzer-Baltin lost 90 per cent of the Hungarian reserve brigade, killed or taken prisoner and Russian troops also overran four of his artillery batteries. The Austrian reserves sent forward to plug the gaps were just untried troops who could do little to stem the tide when Lechitsky broadened the front to support the initial advance. By mid-afternoon his troops had taken 4,000 prisoners, advancing 4 miles in places.

Back on 8th Army's front, Knox noted on the night of 4–5 June that fire was lifted to enable scouts to examine results between 0030hrs and 0230hrs. After dawn on the second day of the offensive, the enemy's front lines were again bombarded, with the first line of trenches entirely destroyed and the second and third lines obliterated, except for some of the dugouts.[6]

At 0830hrs the barrage increased until by 0900hrs it was, in the words of General Kralowitz, chief of staff of Austrian 4th Army, 'a firestorm of unprecedented intensity (which) crackled along all lines of the position, stirring up thick yellow sand and dust clouds that then hung over the field'.[7]

At Olyka, the Russian saps reached within fifty paces of the Austrian front line. Men leaped out of them and ran through the smoke, dust and debris to surprise the defenders before they could emerge from their shelters. More than half the men of 70th HID were taken prisoner while still cowering in their foxholes. Austrian

2nd Infantry Division was also pushed back with little effort. It was reported by prisoners taken by Russian troops that their officers had disappeared to the rear with most of the artillery, leaving their men with no chain of command and abandoning the remaining field guns to the Russians. A local counter-attack, hampered by communications to the rear being cut in the barrage, as reported by Knox, saw part of the front line retaken until a second Russian push cleared it again.

When Linsingen sent reserve units forward blind at 1330hrs on 5 June, Kaledin's troops in the centre had already penetrated 2 miles into the enemy positions, meeting little resistance from the shattered remnants of Corps Szurmay. The arrival of the eagerly awaited reserves achieved so little that local commanders decided to retreat during a rainstorm at 2230hrs in considerable chaos. Fortunately for them, Kaledin did not pursue immediately. The centre of Austrian 4th Army eventually stabilised at its prepared third band of fortifications on the eastern bank of the Styr River, 25 miles southwest of their position that morning. There, at daybreak, they found themselves under fire from Russian artillery that was now installed on high ground to the south. Some units retreated even further. That morning, Conrad asked OHL for German reinforcements, which Falkenhayn refused on the grounds that OAK would do better to order back to the east its own experienced troops posted to the Italian front. No reinforcements were to be expected from Linsingen, he said, unless Russian forces they faced in the line opposite them were suddenly posted south. However, as a stop-gap measure, OHL ordered Bothmer to release some units from Südarmee to strengthen Austrian 4th Army.

In slight contradiction to this, Linsingen's appreciation of the risk to his right flank after the collapse of the Austrians caused him to move five infantry divisions from his apparently unthreatened left flank to make a counter-offensive on 4th Army's centre, together with German units under the archduke's command. It was too late: the Austrians were already retreating across the Styr on pontoon bridges, fleeing from the two infantry divisions of Russian 22nd Corps. It seemed for a while that their advance was a mistake as it placed them within range of Austrian artillery on the western bank of the river – until the bombardment stopped abruptly because the available stock of shells had been exhausted. When the defending troops realised this, many abandoned their positions in their haste to get away and others simply surrendered en masse. By 0900hrs Kaledin's troops had opened a breach that left the road wide open to Lutsk, with its thirteenth-century castle and cathedral, and also captured thirty-eight artillery pieces.

The archduke ordered his last reserves to plug the breach and informed Linsingen that he *might* have to pull back even further. If the following few hours are difficult to unravel in print, that is nothing like the demoralising confusion on the battlefield. In vain, Linsingen tried to impose some control over the disorganised units of the archduke's army to his south. At 1000hrs 70th HID was again on the retreat, obliging the survivors of Corps Szurmay also to withdraw in order to avoid exposing its flank, but opening a breach 4 miles wide between it and X Corps. The belief that Russian forces were already forcing a passage through the gap convinced General Martigny to pull back X Corps at 1115hrs. Half an hour later, he was ordered to stand fast in the position X Corps had already abandoned!

With Szurmay and X Corps in full retreat, the gap to the north widened, with units that had not even been attacked falling back in order not to be outflanked. At 1500hrs the completely disorganised rump of a few hundred men – all that remained of 70th HID – broke and ran. Like water down a plug-hole, neighbouring units were drawn into the rout, in turn pulling their neighbours into a swirling vortex of uncontrolled and uncontrollable men, horses, wagons and guns.

Linsingen's professional opinion was that the archduke and General Martigny of X Corps deserved to be court-martialled. The true problem, however, was much more serious. Despite having started the whole war, Franz Joseph's government had counted on a swift victory and made no provisions for prolonged hostilities. As a result, by spring 1915, there was already a severe manpower crisis and growing shortage of materiel, especially shells for the artillery, complicated by the dual monarchy's artillery using guns of forty-five different models, many of them obsolete. Vienna expected Berlin to make good shortages of materiel, but Germany needed every shell and bullet for its own forces, so OHL was not sympathetic to its ally's blackmail on the line of *Help us, or we fold*. Exaggerating the problem, Austrian arms manufacturers actually cut back production under cartel agreements with German firms in order to force prices up, with the Austrians sharing in the profits of their German partners.[8] Austrian shell output never exceeded 1 million rounds per month, even in 1916 when German production was 7 million and even Russia managed 4 million rounds of shells.

The background to the situation in which Linsingen now found himself dated back to when Italy had finally been bribed by the Western Allies into declaring against the Central Powers in May 1915. Then, OAK was obliged to balance the possible loss of Adriatic territory to Rome against weakening its southern flank in Galicia. In this dilemma, the other half of the dual monarchy was worse than useless, the government in Budapest refusing to loan rolling stock to speed up movement of men and supplies because it feared a Romanian attack on Hungary.

Demanding that both the archduke and General Martigny be immediately relieved of command, Linsingen attempted desperately to repair the damage by using as reinforcements one infantry division from Böhm-Ermolli's 2nd Austrian Army and two from General Paul Puhallo's Austrian 1st Army. Having completely lost control of his army commanders and the situation, Conrad had to agree to this but Linsingen's intervention came too late to save the day. The only stroke of luck for the CP forces on that awful day of shattered formations and headlong retreats was that Kaledin wished to consolidate his forces' new positions, to avoid his advance forces possibly being cut off and so did not order his cavalry to pursue the fleeing enemy until dawn of the following day. Mentioning Russian cavalry leads to a factor that played in favour of the CP commanders: the need to feed 1 million horses with thousands of tons of fodder was occupying half of all Russian rolling stock and at times bringing to a standstill the railway system, whereas the German forces opposing them had a more efficient rail network and used less than a fifth of their rolling stock for animal feed. The German railway troops were also more effective than their opposite numbers. Norman Stone cites more efficient German usage of Russian rail tracks in conquered territory than had been managed by the Russians themselves – and this despite the different gauge.[9]

Further south on 9th Army's front, Lechitsky seems to have reverted to traditional tactics on 5 June: badly targeted artillery barrages and 'human wave' infantry tactics. Positions changed hands three and four times during the day, with mounting casualties on both sides. Pflanzer-Baltin reacted to this in the conventional way by shortening his line, pulling back to new positions across the Dnyestr River, but was hit at 0400hrs next day by Shcherbachev's assault on the Austrian left flank where the line was held by 80 per cent Slav units. Hungarian 15th Infantry Division was driven back 1½ miles on a 4-mile front until accurate counter-battery fire halted the Russian advance. *Only* 12,000 men were reported as killed that day on both sides along this sector of the front, but the Hungarian infantry was so disorganised by dusk that its commander informed Pflanzer-Baltin that he could not hold and was told, in turn, that no reinforcements were available, as they had already been despatched to other threatened parts of the line.

Both Hindenburg and Falkenhayn had a low opinion of their allies' troops and commanders, but needed to keep Austro-Hungary in the war or see Germany stand alone like a stag brought to bay with a whole pack of hounds tearing it to bits. On 7 June Falkenhayn therefore telegraphed Conrad that he was sending 100 trains of reinforcements from the western front, due to arrive on 14 June, to block this possibility. Conrad detested being summoned to Berlin like a naughty schoolboy sent for by the headmaster. He had already ordered back from the Isonzo two infantry divisions, as required by Falkenhayn, but now had to put in an appearance at OHL in the humiliating position of a supreme commander who no longer held the supreme command, and listen to Falkenhayn's lecture on how to redress the appalling defeats of the Austro-Hungarian forces. Falkenhayn also required Linsingen to be given direct command of all the Austrian troops of 1st and 4th armies, with General Mackensen given overall control over the 200-mile front between the Pripyat River in the north and the Dnyestr in the south. As to the southernmost sector, he wanted Pflanzer-Baltin sacked and replaced by a German general.

Confirming Falkenhayn's fears, by noon on 7 June 15th HID was wiped off the map by Shcherbachev's 2nd cavalry corps, 7,000 men surrendering and the rest fleeing to put the River Strypa, a left-bank tributary of the Dnyestr, between themselves and their pursuers. The panic spread further. Brusilov confines himself in his memoirs to summing up the progress thus:

> By noon on 7 June we had taken 900 officers and 40,000 other ranks, seventy-seven artillery pieces, 134 machine guns and forty-nine mortars. Three days later, this had increased to 1,240 officers and 71,000 other ranks and another seventeen guns and forty-five machine guns, plus a lot of other booty. At this stage I was called to the telephone for a somewhat unpleasant conversation with Alekseyev, to the effect that Evert would not attack on 14 June because of bad weather (which had made the ground too soft), but would postpone his advance until 18 June. He called again to say that Evert's intelligence officers reported a huge build-up of enemy forces and artillery at the point of his planned offensive towards Baranovichy. If ordered to attack, he would do so, but without any chance of success. He had requested the Tsar's permission to change the focus of his attack, and the Tsar had given his consent.
>
> I (told Alekseyev) that this was exactly what I had feared. Even an unsuccessful attack on the other fronts would immobilise enemy forces that could be moved against me, whereas the failure of Evert and Kuropatkin to attack at all left the enemy free to move forces from their sectors and concentrate them against me. For Evert to decide on a new point at which to attack and re-position his forces would mean a delay of six weeks, during which time I should suffer heavy losses.
>
> I therefore requested that the Tsar review his decision. Alekseyev replied that it was not possible to question a decision of the Tsar, but Stavka would send me two additional army corps as compensation. I said that moving two corps with all their logistics and support on our inadequate railways would give the enemy, on his far more efficient rail system, time to move not two, but ten, corps against me. I knew very well that the Tsar was neither here nor there in this matter, since he understood little of military affairs, but rather that Alekseyev, who had been subordinate to Kuropatkin and Evert in the Russo-Japanese war, knew exactly what was going on, and was covering up for them.
>
> General Aleksandr Ragoza, who had been my subordinate in both peacetime and war, told me afterwards that he had personally gone to Evert at this time to inform him that his attack at Molodechno (modern Maladyechna in Belarus) was well prepared, had sufficient resources to succeed, and that delay would affect his men's morale adversely. He requested permission to make a report to this effect for forwarding to the Tsar. Evert at first agreed, then refused to forward the report. Ragoza believed that Evert's motive for repeatedly postponing his attack was jealousy of the success of my offensive and fear of being shown up by me. Be that as it may, when Alekseyev eventually prevailed on Evert to make the long-delayed attack on Baranovichy, it failed with enormous losses.[10]

Contact having been lost the previous evening, soon after first light five Russian corps advanced cautiously in the direction of Lutsk and Kolki until coming under accurate fire from Linsingen's artillery on the right flank. On the left flank, General Puhallo's Austrian 1st Army held firm. In the centre, however, Austrian 13th Infantry Division was defending the Central Powers' bridgehead on the eastern bank of the Styr, having just moved into position after losing contact with its supporting artillery. Unfortunately it was still taking orders from Archduke Joseph Ferdinand's HQ at Lutsk because Emperor Franz Joseph in Vienna had not yet approved his dismissal. The archduke decided to demonstrate firmness by ordering the bridgehead to be held at all costs by General Martigny's exhausted and demoralised troops, whose artillery had already crossed the Styr and thus had no communication with the units remaining in the bridgehead. About midday, he then moved his HQ away to safety after giving one more fatal order that caused another breach in the line.

The Germans often referred to their Austro-Hungarian allies as a comic opera army. If it had not been tragic for the thousands of men caught up in the farce being played out between Martigny's corps HQ, the archduke's army HQ and Conrad at OAK, the next few hours would deserve to be a Marx Brothers film. Having withdrawn himself and his staff to comparative safety, the archduke was apparently completely out of touch with conditions at the front and refused to accept Martigny's plea that the shattered X Corps be allowed to retreat across the Styr. Instead, he relieved Martigny of command. Martigny had, however, already ordered the demolition of the bridges across the river at 1440hrs. Shortly afterwards, the archduke learned that Emperor Franz Joseph had approved his own removal from command, causing him to depart from army HQ in high dudgeon.

As effective CP commander of the entire front, Linsingen did his best to salvage the situation, appointing Junior Field Marshal Sellner to take command of X Corps. Sellner, already on the sick list, ordered that the bridgehead be held under increasing pressure from Kaledin's infantry and field artillery, but by 1900hrs demolition on both sides of the river included the rail tracks to Kovel. Still, after what had happened to the archduke and General Martigny, no local commander dared to abandon the bridgehead on the east bank until, at just before 2000hrs Sellner bit the bullet and ordered a complete evacuation. Once again, an order arrived too late. By the time it had reached the ragged remnants of Austrian 4th Army on the eastern bank, Russian artillery had destroyed two bridges and Austrian engineers had demolished most of the other crossings now desperately needed by the men stranded in the shattered remains of the bridgehead. How many thousand men threw away their weapons and heavy kit before jumping into the deep and swollen river under fire from Russian infantry and field artillery is unknown, but the majority never made it across. It was calculated that as many as 11,000 Austrian troops drowned, were killed or taken prisoner on that day.

With the archduke gone, Austrian officers went round the town of Lutsk, ordering the destruction of entire warehouses of food and ammunition, which might have made a difference to the men in the front line, if it had not been kept uselessly back in base. One eyewitness described the scene thus:

> Towering columns of smoke shot up to the sky. Pressure waves raised the roofs of houses when the magazines exploded. Flames shot up from the row of munitions dumps. All of the wonderful white flour, the hay and straw for fodder, the bread, the meat and whatever else lay in these rooms, more than enough to feed thousands and to let thousands forget their wants. All of the fruits of uncounted days of labour by innumerable hands, assembled with care and effort, were destroyed.[11]

With the abandoned stores being consumed by flames, local commanders requested Linsingen's permission to withdraw to prepared positions further west. At 2200hrs this was authorised. Kaledin's forces were already crossing the Styr, untroubled by any defence because Austrian X Corps continued running away in defiance of an order to stand and fight. In the afternoon of 8 June, the retreating Austrian and German units were pushed back a further 3 or 4 miles.

NOTES

1. Some secondary accounts differ as to dates. In this account the dates are taken from Brusilov's own memoirs, adjusted to the Gregorian calendar.
2. Brusilov *Vospominaniya*.
3. P. von Hindenburg, *The Great War* (London: Greenhill, 2006), tr. F.A. Holt, ed. C. Messenger, pp. 93–4.
4. Knox, *With the Russian Army 1914–1917* (New York: Arno Press, 1971), p. 441 (abridged).
5. http:museum/omskelecom.ru/ogik/Izvestiya_8/Eperina.html.
6. Ibid.
7. Dowling, p. 78.
8. Stone, p. 123.
9. Ibid, p. 134.
10. Brusilov *Vospominaniya* (abridged).
11. Dowling, p. 84 (abridged).

14

BREAKTHROUGH

On 8 June, after being notified that one of his corps commanders north of the breakthrough was making a tactical retreat to protect his right flank, Pflanzer-Baltin decided that the time had come to make a strategic retreat of more than 30 miles, permitting his shattered forces to regroup behind the lines of the Dnyestr and Prut rivers and then be in position to attack the left flank of the Russian advance, which he believed was aimed at Lemberg. Since this was opening up a 70-mile breach between his forces and Bothmer's Südarmee to the north, Bothmer was furious and demanded to be given command over the disorganised Austrian forces in retreat, to close the breach and save the situation. For the usual reasons of national pride, Conrad refused to authorise this and tried to make amends by ordering Pflanzer-Baltin not to lose contact with Südarmee – which was pretty meaningless in the circumstances.

In the chaos of the Austrian retreat, strategic or otherwise, Lechitsky's cavalry and infantry was pushing steadily westwards on a front of 20 miles or more, taking prisoner tens of thousands of 'other ranks' and several thousand officers. Momentarily, Pflanzer-Baltin's left, or northern, flank stabilised, holding a new line with just enough men to stay in contact with Südarmee. Each time this happened, Lechitsky piled on the pressure against the other flank until the Austrian right flank collapsed. After a bombardment that began at dawn on 9 June and lasted three hours, three Russian infantry divisions attacked at 1000hrs and were briefly held by the largely demoralised defenders, reinforced at the last minute by the last five battalions of reserves in the sector. A lieutenant trapped in the midst of this chaos afterwards wrote, '(Our) units in the trenches had no ammunition; the reserves lay fully exposed; the regimental command had allowed a squadron to be posted to another sector in return for another, at the time unserviceable, unit.'[1]

The struggle had now become extremely unequal, with 122 Russian battalions against only fifty-four battalions of defenders. When the centre cracked at around 1030hrs on 10 June, the same lieutenant was unable to control his men, who streamed away from the trenches, and Florence Farmborough wrote:

> Alexander Alexandrovich, one of our transport heads, offered to drive us to see the deserted Austrian dugouts. One excelled all others in luxury and cosiness. We decided it must have belonged to an artillery officer. It contained tables, chairs, pictures on the armoured walls and books; there was even an English grammar. We toured some of the smaller trenches; these too were amazingly well constructed. I thought of the shallow ditches with which our soldiers had to be content; even their most comfortable dugouts were but hovels compared with these.[2]

By noon the Russian breakthrough was so evident that Pflanzer–Baltin realised he had only two options: to retreat in as orderly fashion as possible and protect the Carpathian passes to his rear or see his troops annihilated where they stood. Conrad would not hear of it. Countermanding the decision to retreat south-west towards the passes, he ordered Pflanzer–Baltin to retreat in a north-westerly direction in order to maintain contact with Südarmee and prevent the Russians capturing the rail junction at Stanislau (modern Ivano-Frankivsk in Ukraine). It was too late. By now Austrian 7th Army was chronically reduced in numbers and the remaining forces had already begun moving southwest. The order to change direction completed the demoralisation of the rank-and-file by revealing to them that their commanders were now clutching at straws. One Hungarian division lost half its strength in twenty-four hours.

Also on 9 June Böhm-Ermolli sought permission to reinforce the rump of Corps Szurmay. Before permission was granted by Linsingen's HQ, it was too late because the corps had been cut off from Austrian 2nd Army. Early on 10 June a sustained attack by Kaledin's infantry forced a breach between the lines of Austrian 1st and 4th armies. By late afternoon, the gap was 35 miles wide, but the sheer speed of the Russian advance had outpaced the horse- and ox-drawn supply trains, so that it was necessary that evening to pause and consolidate the enormous salient almost 35 miles deep and 50 miles wide, in which 44,000 POWs had been taken – at a cost of 35,000 Russian casualties. Kaledin was also faced with a difficult choice: his mounted scouts reported the roads open north-west to Kovel and south-east to Lemberg. Which way to turn?

This pause allowed some respite to the retreating Austrians of X Corps, reduced to some 3,000 men. On its flank, II Corps was even more depleted in manpower. Some units were so shattered and separated from their official position in the line that they had to be absorbed into fresh formations and lost any independent identity. Russian 8th Army's chief of staff was General Vladislav Klembovskii, who had been Brusilov's personal choice to succeed him as army commander. He urged Kaledin to press on. Brusilov agreed with him that doing so at that moment might have brought the Hapsburg dynasty to its knees. On the other side of the lines, Böhm-Ermolli also shared this opinion, due not only to casualties and men lost as prisoners but also the effect on morale of all Austro-Hungarian units from the repeated retreats.

However, Brusilov decided that prudence was the better part of valour, and held back, unwilling to deepen the salient and make it more vulnerable to counter-attack on its exposed northern flank. A factor in his thinking was Kuropatkin's failure to attack on the northern front and Evert's continued delays in launching his offensive, which would have obliged Linsingen to keep north of the Pripyat River some formations that now threatened the new salient from the north. At Stavka, Alekseyev was unable to force Evert and Kuropatkin to move, but did scrounge a mixed bag of troops from their fronts as reinforcements for Brusilov. He used them to strengthen the northern flank of the salient, meanwhile regrouping for an attack towards Kovel.

The next moves depended on whether the Russians or CP forces were able to consolidate and regroup first.[3] Throughout 11 June, gaps opened up in the new Austrian line. Pflanzer-Baltin did his best to plug them with fast-moving cavalry until the cavalry also had to retreat or be cut off. One soldier afterwards described the confusion of the retreat: '[There were] endless columns of wagons … with artillery placed among them. The troops came from all sides, tired and harassed.'[4] And behind them, driving them on, were Lechitsky's Cossacks riding down the fleeing infantry with sabres slashing in downward blows that could decapitate a man or lop off his arm and lances impaling bodies, then flicking them off before 'pig-sticking' a new, living human target. Tens of thousands of luckier 'other ranks' and thousands of officers went 'into the Russian bag', life as a POW being preferable to a painful death on the battlefield.

Four divisions of German reinforcements arrived at the Galician front under Linsingen's command on 12 June. By then, one gap in the Austrian line was already 20 miles wide. By dawn on 14 June Lechitsky and Shcherbachev had to split their forces as the front widened even more. Even the unbroken enemy line was thinly held, Pflanzer-Baltin relying on the natural barriers of the Prut and Dnyestr – and on the sheer exhaustion and heavy losses of the Russian troops. By 14 June both sides had fought themselves to a standstill, but on the following day a random charge by a Cossack *sotnya* of probably less than 100 riders triggered another panic retreat, which was only stemmed by a timely reinforcement of the southern flank of Südarmee. By this time all units of Austrian 7th Army were severely under strength, so that, although the front seemed to have stabilised for the moment, the situation was summed up in negative terms by the new chief of staff imposed on Planzer-Baltin. Monocled Major General Hans von Seeckt was of strict Junker military stock and described by those who knew him at this time as having 'an icy stare'. Certainly, he saw little to please him at Austrian 7th Army HQ, where his new commander labelled him 'no friend of Austria'. Seeckt's new colleagues at 7th Army found their German chief of staff abrasive and downright rude because he made no effort to conceal his contempt for their inefficiency. On 16 June, he wrote:

> Whether (7th Army) still has the internal disposition to hold against a strong, well-prepared overall attack is doubtful. I fear that in the task of covering the area between the Prut and Dnyestr with its main force and securing the Bukovina region the army will be split in the middle.[5]

The chain of command on the Russian side was hardly less acrimonious, in this case because the delayed offensives by Evert and Kuropatkin still did not take place despite Brusilov's protests to Alekseyev. On 14 June, when Evert's delayed attack was supposed to go in, he had had the nerve to telephone Stavka and beg for another delay of four days on the grounds that the marshes around Pinsk, across which he was supposed to advance on an axis threatening Brest-Litovsk and Warsaw, were too wet! With very little sleep, master-minding his own offensive, Brusilov was understandably furious, and called Alekseyev, demanding that Stavka formally order Evert to attack without further delay. Alekseyev prevaricated. Brusilov did the unthinkable in writing directly to the Tsar for help, but Nicholas, as usual, refused to make any decision. As a sop to Brusilov, he was sent some more reinforcements and firmly told that Evert would attack the next day.

On 18 June, Evert had another excuse for not moving: the Germans forces in the line where he had intended to attack, had been reinforced; he wanted time to redirect his attack to a weaker point. Given permission by Stavka, Evert promised the attack would go in at latest by 3 July. Coming from the man who had repeatedly let him down, Brusilov placed little faith in that. He was right. As he recalled these events in his memoirs:

> I did not consider that the Tsar was guilty, he being a mere amateur in military matters, but Alekseyev understood very well what was going on and how criminal the behaviour of Evert and Kuropatkin was. If we had had a different supreme commander, Evert would have been dismissed immediately for his indecisiveness and Kuropatkin should never have had a place in the active army (after his failures in the Russo-Japanese war).[6]

By the afternoon of the following day, Russian troops were across the Prut in three places and continued pushing Austrian 7th Army's lines south and west for the next week. However, the three days required for regrouping constituted a near-fatal delay for Kaledin's 8th Army facing Austrian 4th and 1st armies now commanded by General Karl von Tersztyansky, a Magyar nobleman whose extremely short temper had caused him problems in the past and was to cause him more in the future.

As further sop from Alekseyev, to compensate for Evert's delays, Brusilov had been given temporary control of Russian 3rd Army, until then under Evert's orders as part of western front. Its new commander was General Leonid Lesh, who was now ordered to make a diversionary attack near Pinsk – perhaps the ground had suddenly dried up? – while Kaledin's 8th Army with some reinforcements advanced toward the rail junction at Kovel. South of there, Sakharov's 11th Army attacked the Austrian 1st Army and Shcherbachev and Lechitsky kept up the pressure on the Central Powers line in the south of the front, to prevent troops being moved from there northwards. Unfortunately, Lesh had not been brainwashed by Brusilov in the preparatory stage and therefore attacked in traditional Russian fashion with human waves after a badly focused barrage, losing 7,000 casualties without making any real advance. To the south of that fiasco, 11th Army broke through on an axis aimed due west at Volodimyr-Volynsky, rather than either Kovel or Lemberg, but Tersztyansky blocked this move with adroit deployment of his mixed formations of German and Austrian troops.

Next morning, Sakharov threw elements of 11th Army against Austrian 1st Army, but not until late on the afternoon of 15 June, and after taking heavy casualties, did he achieve a breakthrough exactly where it could do most harm – on the demarcation line between the enemy's 1st and 4th armies. This compelled General Puhallo to make a tactical withdrawal. That, in turn, forced Linsingen to plug the gap between the two armies, more than 8 miles across, at the cost of weakening the centre of his line. This would have been exactly the moment for Kaledin to pile on the pressure while the forces facing him were either disorganised or re-positioning themselves. Brusilov later wrote that the problem with Kaledin was that he was indecisive and always complaining, which had a negative effect on the troops under his command. Kaledin's alibi was that by this stage he lacked the manpower to press on.

Desultory attacks continued throughout the day, but failed to prevent the Austrian 4th and 1st armies stabilising in new positions. In two weeks of heavy casualties on both sides, the only real change to the line was that Kaledin had gained the large salient that extended 20 miles west of Lutsk and Shcherbachev had gained a much smaller salient south of Tarnopol.

What does not show up on a map is how thin the CP lines were in places, nor how depleted were some of Kaledin's units. By now, Brusilov's forces had captured 4,013 officers and 200,000 men, together with booty of 219 cannons, 644 machine guns. 196 mortars, 150,000 rifles and other materiel. 'Heroic' is not a word often used in the context of this kind of slogging match, yet one has to admire the way exhausted men of both sides stumbled forward and were pushed back in places on 16 June. Then, something shameful happened overnight. Many officers in the Austrian forces reported sick and abandoned their men, who surrendered. This allowed Kaledin to expand the Lutsk salient to the north and to the south, where it reached almost to the town of Redkov (modern Ridkiv in Ukraine).

Linsingen begged desperately for more German reinforcements, but was told none were available. Attempting to snatch victory from the jaws of defeat, he used whatever forces he could re-position to keep up the pressure on the Russian advance, again at a heavy cost in casualties. This continued for another four or five days, with a small advance being pushed back again and again in a strong-arm contest where neither contestant had enough strength remaining to push his opponent's arm down to the table. Despite all the thousands of casualties and having taken those 200,000-plus prisoners, the majority of Brusilov's forces were now ordered to dig in and prepare for a new offensive after reinforcement – whenever that might be.

On 24 June Russian 7th and 9th armies were ordered to advance while 11th Army held its position. Russian 8th Army was beating back repeated powerful counter-attacks intended to drive it back to Lutsk. Hindenburg sent two divisions of German reinforcements south in an endeavour to nip off the salient. Incredibly, a pompous officer in Austrian 4th Army, newly arrived in theatre, commented that the exhausted men shambling forward towards the line 'did not march like Imperial troops, but like a flock of sheep. Stretched out all across the street, followed by countless stragglers, these columns offer a model of how not to march.'[7] Two days later, Tersztyansky answered Linsingen's order to attack with a report that he had neither sufficient ammunition for his artillery nor the men to execute it.

By 29 June, Lechitsky had overrun nearly all the Bukovina with Austrian losses of 40,000 taken prisoner and more than 120,000 dead. But the cost in Russian lives had also been enormous and Lechitsky no longer had the manpower to press on through the well-defended Carpathian passes or to drive into the widening gap between the two rivers as the Austrians retreated. Determined to throw Russian 8th Army back over the Styr at Lutsk, on that day Linsingen attempted to use a German battle group, relatively fresh to the front, to stiffen a new assault on the Russian line, only to find that Brusilov had scrounged fresh troops on his side also. A barrage by heavy guns preceded the attack, but little ground had been gained before the Russians drove back the Austrian troops who had briefly won a short length of their front line. Under withering fire from well-sited Russian artillery, one Hungarian reserve division refused to advance; the rest of Tersztyansky's forces moved forward, however reluctantly, when ordered. But, as the afternoon wore on, Linsingen's hope of retaking Lutsk became more and more impossible, the Austrian local commanders openly declaring their exhausted men incapable of further combat.

Not only the men in the line were exhausted. So also were the nurses of Letuchka No. 2. On 17 June, Nurse Farmborough fell asleep from exhaustion in the operating room and slept for hours. At 0600hrs more wounded arrived, one with an entry wound at the shoulder blade, with the bullet going down his right side to lodge in his thigh, causing much trauma on the way. Disregarding the groans and cries from her patients of, 'Sestritsa, bolit!' – little sister, it hurts! – she was washing the face of another soldier, covered with dust, grime and dried blood, when he said: 'Leave it. I shall not go visiting (girls) any more.' Seeing the ugly gash on his head that had been concealed by all the filth, she understood what he meant. A young officer was brought in, severely wounded in both legs, with fragments of rusty metal protruding from the swollen, discoloured flesh. The surgeon amputated one leg above the knee but, out of the patient's hearing, the medical staff made no secret that he was going to die of gangrene anyway, having been left for twenty-four hours with open wounds in mud and filth near the wire.

At this point, an ominous note creeps into the diary for the first time. To comfort the wounded Austrian prisoners, Florence talked to them in German, but was warned by the chief dispenser that talking with prisoners in their own language might make her suspect. When she protested that, if they were English or French, she would speak to them also in those languages, he added: 'A word to the wise.'[8] Russians had always been xenophobic, but this was the beginning of the paranoia that would characterise Russia after the Revolution.

By July 1916, Brusilov's offensive seemed to be well on the way to total success. Kaledin's 8th Army was in position to drive right towards Kovel or left towards Lemberg. Choosing the easier option towards Kovel, it seemed possible to split the Central Powers' front in two. In the south of the front, Russian 7th and 9th armies, suitably reinforced, looked able to reach the Carpathian passes. On the central and northern fronts, Evert and Kuropatkin had the resources easily to apply sufficient pressure to prevent German reinforcements being shipped south.

By 3 July Linsingen had to face the facts and commanded both his German and Austrian forces to dig in and await reinforcements before making any further moves. By 14 July elements of Russian 3rd and 8th armies had reached the left bank of the Stokhod River. During this time, Sakharov's 11th Army made three brief attacks, advancing the line, taking 34,000 German and Austrian prisoners and capturing forty-five cannons and seventy-one machine guns. Russian 7th and 9th armies also regrouped to launch a new offensive along the line of the Dnyestr River, but Lechitsky was delayed by heavy rains until 28th July, which lost the element of surprise and gave the enemy time to move reinforcements to the threatened sector. On 28 July Russian 3rd Army and the Guards Army drove towards Kovel, meeting stiff resistance from the reinforced enemy positions and heavy artillery fire. Although Kaledin's 8th Army had some success and the left flank of 9th Army did advance in a southwesterly direction, no progress was made towards Vladimir-Volynskii.

Altogether, from 4 June to mid-August Brusilov calculated that his armies had taken prisoner 8,255 officers and 370,153 other ranks – and captured some 500 cannons, 144 machine guns, vast quantities of rifles and ammunition and much other materiel. He was aware that the enemy was receiving reinforcements from other sectors of the front and some from France, but Stavka knew that the Western Allies planned a massive offensive along the Somme in July, which should prevent OHL moving any more German reinforcements to the east. Brusilov was not worried about Austro-Hungarian reinforcements. Although he now had 3rd Army added to his front as well as the freshly reconstituted Guards Army, whose various regiments looked marvellous on a parade ground, with every man tall and well-fed compared with the peasant conscripts of most other regiments, what worried him was the quality of their commanders. He wrote in his memoirs:

> The commander of the Guards Army, General Bezobrazov had been sacked on several occasions for incompetence, but was an honourable man, though rather stupid and unbelievably stubborn. Count Ignatiev, his chief of staff, had never served on a staff and thus had no idea of the work despite having gradu-ated from the General Staff Academy 'with honours'. The commander of the Guards' artillery was the Duke of Mecklenburg-Schwerin – a stout fellow, but who had only the faintest idea of the modern uses of artillery. Commander of 1st Guards Corps was Grand Duke Prince Pavel Aleksandrovich. Although a sensible and personally courageous man, he understood nothing of military life. Commander of 2nd Guards Corps was Rauch, a clever, educated man who had a fatal flaw: he lost his nerve as soon as he heard the first shot and completely went to pieces once personally in danger, after which it was impossible for him to exercise command.[9]

With reinforcements like that, Brusilov hardly needed an enemy. He protested to Alekseyev that, to make the Guards Army of any real use, he needed to replace its commanders. They, however, were appointed by the Tsar personally, so only the Tsar could authorise that – and Alekseyev lacked the courage to ask him.

In one respect the Russian armies were better off than at any time since August 1914. That was in the supply of shells. In-country arsenals were now manufactur-ing them at the rate of 2.9 million in September 1916 alone. By the end of the year there was a reserve at the fronts of 3,000 shells per gun. Everything else needed for the war effort, from barbed wire to bandages, seemed to be available at last – although not always where it was most needed.[10] Notwithstanding all the problems of command, Brusilov's offensive was the great Russian success of 1916, causing transfer of an estimated 30 CP divisions from the Western Front by the end of August and compelling OAK to cancel a planned offensive on the Isonzo front because sufficient forces could not be sent there. The battle lines had been moved an average of 20 miles and in places as much as 100 miles to the west with Central Powers' losses of 200,000 casualties and 400,000 taken prisoner. Yet, the price for the success of the south-western front was high: in addition to 600,000 battle casualties, widespread desertion, punishable by firing squad if caught, had cost Brusilov a further 60,000 men. It is generally accepted that total Russian losses – dead, wounded and taken prisoner – were somewhere between 7.5 million and 11 million men, with 3 million of these happening in 1916. Nobody, apparently, had any thought at the time that this was the tip of an iceberg that was going to sink the Russian ship of state.

NOTES

1. Lieutenant Alphons Bernhard, quoted in Dowling, p. 74.
2. Farmborough, p. 193.
3. Dowling, p. 87.
4. Anonymous soldier, quoted in Dowling, p. 77.
5. Dowling, p. 77 (abridged).
6. Brusilov *Vospominaniya* (abridged).
7. Dowling, p. 97 (abridged).
8. Farmborough, pp. 204–5, 211–12 (edited).
9. Brusilov *Vospominaniya*.
10. Stone, pp. 211–12.

15

LAST TRAIN TO BUDAPEST

The British military attaché in Bucharest, Lt Colonel Christopher Thompson, had been sent in 1915 from London to manoeuvre the Romanian government into making a pro-Allied commitment, both to secure its army of 650,000 men and to prevent the Central Powers getting their hands on the partly US-owned Romanian oilfields at Ploești – which would be bitterly fought over again in the Second World War. Once in post, he quickly realised that bringing the country over to the Entente had more disadvantages than advantages. Firstly, to mobilise the armed forces for combat would require deliveries of around 300 tons of materiel *per day* from the Western Allies – an impossibility, since Romania was geographically isolated from the Entente, with the exception of Russia, which was its traditional enemy. Secondly, the Romanian army was riddled with corruption. Thirdly, it was appallingly badly trained for modern war. Thompson's realistic reports to this effect were simply disregarded by his masters in London who had sent him to Bucharest.

The Romanian army was largely equipped with German and Austrian weaponry, and the country had a treaty of alliance with the dual monarchy that obliged it to go to war if Austria or Hungary was attacked. Since they had not been attacked, but had initiated the war, King Carol I played a waiting game at the outbreak of hostilities – for reasons similar to those of Italy. It was in Romania's interest to see which side would offer the better chance of reuniting within his country's borders the Romanian-speakers who made up the majority of the population in the Hungarian province of Transylvania to the north and the many thousands of Romanian-speakers living in Russian-occupied Bessarabia to the east of Romania. Carol thought the best chance for his country was to side with the Central Powers, but his politicians preferred to take their chances with the Western Allies. When Carol died on 10 October 1914, the throne passed to his nephew, Ferdinand of Hohenzollern-Sigmaringen, who also sat on the fence, all too aware that a premature declaration for the Triple Entente could see his country invaded from the south by Bulgarian and Turkish forces and from the north-west by Austria-Hungary, whereas a declaration for the Central Powers could see Russian forces pouring over the border from the north-east and east. It was a typically Balkan dilemma.

The resounding success of the 1916 Brusilov offensive finally tipped the balance in Bucharest in favour of declaring for the Entente. On 13 August 1916,[1] as ordered by London, Thompson signed a treaty of alliance, none of whose terms were ever implemented by the Allies. At Stavka, the news was received with horror: Russia had lost a neutral buffer at the southern end of its long front lines and gained a highly unreliable ally.

Preceding by a few hours King Ferdinand's formal declaration of war on 28 August, three Romanian armies – which looked far better on a parade ground than in the field – attacked positions of the Austro-Hungarian 1st Army on the Carpathian front, where the Romanian-speaking inhabitants acclaimed their 'liberators'. Initially London and Paris considered this favourably, on the assumption that Austria-Hungary was overstretched already on the Galician and Italian fronts and Germany fully committed on the Western Front and the several Russian fronts. Despite Knox's despatches, considered 'too pessimistic' by his masters in London, the general ignorance about conditions on the Russian fronts was such that no one seemed aware that the only reinforcements immediately available to support the Romanians in Transylvania were three ill-equipped divisions made available by Stavka.

These moves coincided with the sacking of Falkenhayn as Germany's chief of staff in punishment for the costly failure of his attack on Verdun. On his replacement at OHL by Hindenburg. Falkenhayn was relegated to the command of the CP forces on the Romanian front, Hindenburg's position as Oberbefehlshaber Ost – commander-in-chief of what the Germans called 'the eastern front' – being taken by Prince Leopold of Bavaria. Somehow, he managed to scrape together eight German divisions. Augmented by four Austro-Hungarian divisions, this force halted the Romanian advances in Transylvania by mid-September. Meanwhile Mackensen, promoted to the rank of field marshal, moved into Romania from the south on 1 September with a German brigade, Bulgarian 3rd Army, some Austro-Hungarian units and two divisions of Ottoman troops.

Within a month this disparate force had reduced the Romanian fortress of Turtuciaia (modern Tuturka in Bulgaria) largely by use of the 10cm M1917 gun, which was designed for counter-battery fire. The fortress was a complex of fifteen forts built by Belgian engineers overlooking a narrow stretch of the Danube, which was Romania's southern border, but on the Bulgarian side of the river, having been seized by Romanian force of arms at the end of the second Balkan

Romania in 1916.

war in 1913. To reduce the fortress took a 5-day siege that cost 1,764 Bulgarian soldiers' lives, as testified by the impressive and impeccably maintained memorial on the site.

Crossing the Danube, Mackensen next used reconnaissance aircraft to map every move of the enemy as he bore in on the Romanian defensive line along the strategically important railway line from the Black Sea port of Constanza to Bucharest. He also had a small air force of four Zeppelins and twenty-four bombers, which were handicapped by bad weather, although on 9 October 1916, the latter dropped four tons of bombs on a rail junction north-west of Bucharest. Other targets were the important rail and road junction at Cernavoda and the crucial port of Constanza. Strangely for a country still primitive compared with Western Europe, Romania did have an air force of sorts, having commissioned ten aircraft from an in-country inventor named Vlaicu. It also allegedly procured the improbably large number of 322 aircraft during the war from France and Britain, including Nieuport fighters and Breguet-Michelin heavy bombers.[2] If this was correct, it is extremely surprising that the Romanian pilots did not greatly trouble Mackensen's reconnaissance and bombing missions, only one German pilot being shot down during the whole campaign.

Romanian 3rd Army made several stands, giving way each time to Mackensen's forces. In fairness to them, it has to be recognised that the combined Romanian frontiers included 1,000 miles of enemy borders, across which German, Austro-Hungarian, Bulgarian and Turkish forces could invade, so the available manpower was thinly spread. A week after the surrender of Turtuciaia the Romanian high command halted the Transylvanian advance in order to regroup against Mackensen and deploy a mixed Romanian/Russian force to prevent him cutting the railway from Bucharest to Constanza while setting up a seeming master-stroke to take the invaders in the rear. At first, all went well, with Bulgarian 3rd Army halted at Cobadin after a 2-day battle and forced onto the defensive for more than three weeks. On 1 October two Romanian divisions crossed the Danube at Flămânda, making a bridgehead in Bulgarian territory 10 miles wide and 2 miles deep, but a storm that same night smashed the flimsy pontoon bridge they had used, and prevented the arrival of reinforcements. Heavy fighting for the next two days, and the news that the Romanian/Russian offensive north of the river had stalled, caused the Flămânda manoeuvre to be abandoned. In the Second Battle of Cobadin 19–25 October the Bulgarians took the vital port of Constanza and cut the railway line to the capital. By then nearly all Romanian forces, effectively cut off from the outside world, had been driven back inside their own borders and the re-supply position was hopeless. Contemporary photographs show long lines of Romanian dead along the sides of the unpaved roads where they had succumbed to poison gas, artillery and strafing from the air.[3]

On 23 November Mackensen crossed the Danube near Svishtov and advanced rapidly in the direction of Bucharest, threatening to split the Romanian armies in two. A last desperate effort was made by the Romanian high command at the beginning of December, throwing all its reserves into the battle, but this failed when Stavka withdrew its support. Seeing no possibility of holding both Mackensen's and Falkenhayn's forces, Alekseyev thought it preferable to strengthen the Russian lines in Moldavia against an eventual incursion from Romania, should the CP forces there be victorious. Making a scorched-earth fighting retreat, King Ferdinand and the government with their remaining armies fled to Iaşi on the Russian border shortly before Bucharest fell on 6 December. The oil wells and refineries at Ploeşti that had largely caused this national tragedy were sabotaged during the retreat with the help of British officers. Amazingly, the Romanians continued fighting throughout December and January as French and British support began arriving in the shape of materiel including 150,000 rifles and 2,000 machine guns. A French military mission under General Henri Berthelot also arrived and set about retraining the demoralised Romanian troops.

The onset of winter slowed down most military operations in the mountains, where not all Romanian-speaking soldiers were fighting for their country. As in Poland and elsewhere, for whom one fought and maybe died depended on the sheer chance of being conscripted by one side or the other. Extracts from the diary of an unnamed Austrian 2nd Lieutenant posted to the Carpathians tell of the conditions under which his Romanian troops were fighting:

November 17th
Sergeant Corusa reported some thirty Russians in front of our line, who called out, in German and Hungarian, 'Cease fire!' At this double command, fifty of our men left their shelter behind the trees. The Russians opened rapid fire on our poor simpletons and then bolted. Hardly fifteen men came back untouched. Poor Michaelis, the bookseller, hit in the left shoulder by a bullet which came out the other side, was killed and buried there. A Romanian stretcher-bearer laid him on straw at the bottom of a trench and recited a paternoster over him. Two of the other officers had been seriously wounded, so I was the only one left, out of all those who had left Fagaras (modern Făgăraş in Romania) with the battalion.

In the afternoon I took fifty men to hold a slope covered with juniper trees. The men hastily dug trenches, and I made a shelter of boughs. There was no question of lighting fires, so when it snowed once more, everything was wrapped in a mantle of snow. In the evening, when I went to inspect the men lying in their coffin-shaped scrapes covered with juniper branches, they looked to me as if they had been buried alive. Those poor Romanians![4]

The diary entry for 20 November describes the area of operations in the thickly wooded hills between the road to Radoszyce (now in Poland) and one which leads to Dolzyca on the frontier. Visibility was so reduced by the juniper bushes growing thickly everywhere that the Austrian force had to fire blind through the undergrowth whenever they heard what appeared to be enemy movement. When the lieutenant went with a major to reconnoitre a suspected enemy position, they narrowly missed being shot by a 300-strong battalion of their own infantry. Although the enemy was only thirty paces distant, the undergrowth was so thick that nothing could be seen of them.

Back in their own trenches, the two officers were aware that there were gaps in their line, but could do nothing about it, so many men had been lost. Relieved next morning by another company, the exhausted survivors rested in reserve, filling their empty bellies with bread and canned goods. Issued also with winter underclothes:

defying the cold, the men lost no time in undressing to change their linen. I saw human bodies which were nothing but one great sore from the neck to the waist. They were absolutely eaten up with lice. For the first time I really understood the popular curse, 'May the lice eat you!'

One of the men, when he pulled off his shirt, tore away crusts of dried blood, and the vermin were swarming in filthy layers in the garment. The poor peasant had grown thin on this, with projecting jaw and sunken eyes:

Even we officers were infested. Lt Fothi counted fifty on him yesterday, pulling them one by one from the folds of his shirt collar and throwing them onto the fire. About midday I decided to change also. I began by washing, for I was filthy. From the time of our arrival at Laszki-Murowane, six weeks earlier, I had not been able to wash out my mouth. The field postal service having brought me from Hungary a toothbrush and some paste, it was a joy once again to have white teeth and a clean mouth! At home one cannot imagine that such pleasures exist.

I had just put on my shirts again – I always wear two or three at a time – when Private Torna came to our shelter to announce, 'Sir, the Russians are breaking through our line on the top of the hill!'

I asked my friend Lt Fothi to take command in the trenches, pulled on my boots, took my rifle, and ran to the edge of the woods. I could hardly believe my eyes. Along the whole company front, men in Russian uniform and some of our men were threatening each other with fixed bayonets and, in places, firing at each other. In one place, some Russians [sic] and some of our men were wrestling on the ground to get at a supply of bread intended for 12th Company. This struggle of starving animals for food only lasted a few seconds until they stood up, each man having at least a fragment of bread, which he devoured voraciously. This is how bread reconciles men, not only in the form of Communion before the holy altar, but even on the field of battle, when they make peace to get a scrap of bread.

Some of the Russians now tried to surround us. One young conscript came quite close and raised his rifle at me. I levelled my rifle at him in response. Something in my look stopped him firing, and I too refrained until he ran away. But the shock of that sudden confrontation had been too much for me. Like a savage, I yelled, 'Disarm them!' Fothi and I wrenched the rifles out of the hands of two Russian soldiers, after which they all surrendered like lambs. We took sixty of them. All our men wished to escort the prisoners to the rear. I selected three as guards, the third to walk behind and carry the Russians' rifles. I then marched them off in file to the Commander-in-Chief.[5]

This sector then fell quiet as the men who had been able grab a whole loaf shared it with the prisoners, who offered them tobacco in exchange. They said that their unit was about 400 strong, so the lieutenant requested reinforcements. An hour later, a group of men in Russian uniform appeared 200 paces away on the edge of the woods with rifles shouldered, beckoning his men to approach. A party of twenty men under a sergeant major was ordered to surround the Russians with fixed bayonets and bring them in. The diary continues:

> I clambered over the body of a man whose brains were sticking out of his head, and signed to them to surrender, but they still called to us without attempting to move. I thereupon gave the order, 'Fire!' and held my own rifle at the ready. At this point my Romanians refused to fire, and, what was more, prevented me from firing also. One of them put his hand on my rifle and said, 'Don't fire, sir. If we fire, they will fire too. And why should Romanians kill Romanians?' He meant that those men were from Bessarabia (and spoke a dialect of Romanian).
>
> I tried to make my way towards them but two of my men barred my way, exclaiming, 'Don't go and get yourself shot!' It was incredible. Our men were advancing towards the enemy with their arms shouldered, and were shaking their hands. It was a touching sight. I saw one of my Romanians kiss a man in Russian uniform and lead him back to our lines. Their arms were round each other's necks, like brothers. It turned out they had been shepherd boys together in Bessarabia. We took ninety Russians [sic] as prisoners in this way; whilst they took thirty of our men off with them.
>
> After I again requested reinforcements, a machine gun and a 125-man company of the 96th Infantry Regiment arrived almost immediately under Lieutenant Petras. They reinforced our right wing and the Major sent me to the left, to command two machine guns, with which to cut off the retreat of those Russians who had remained in the wood. Instead, it was a Russian machine gun that welcomed us as soon as we reached the trenches. The bullets whizzed by, thick and fast. One grazed my leg, another came within a hand's-breadth of my head.
>
> The Russian snipers creep into advanced positions and pick off officers only. Major Paternos had the fingers of his left hand shot off in his observation post. They are wonderful shots, and I showed my respect for them by not leaving the trench until nightfall, when I returned to my sector. Lt Petras had meanwhile attacked the Russians, losing all but twenty-five of his men. Those who entered the forest, never came out.[6]

That inconclusive day was considered a victory because the company had prevented the Russian troops from out-flanking their positions. So the commanding major ordered a list to be drawn up of men who had distinguished themselves, all receiving the second-class medal for valour. Three officers, including the writer of the diary were also awarded the Signum Laudis bar. After that, they marched through thick forest to divisional HQ at Hocra. That sounds easy enough, but the winter conditions in the forest made it a different hell. By the time they arrived late at night, company strength had dwindled to a quarter of what it had been at the start of the march. Not only city men from Budapest but also some of the veterans dropped out weeping from exhaustion and were abandoned en route. It was, as the lieutenant said, by the mercy of God if they survived the freezing night and the wolves in the forest.

On 25 November the company was dissolved, being reduced to the strength of a platoon, and the survivors were absorbed into two new companies attached to the 1st Honved Regiment. On 27 November they left Havaj early for Stropka-Polena in a thick mist, cold and penetrating. Marching was difficult, for the men were worn out and the lieutenant admitted to being 'nothing but a shadow'. During a halt at Polena, Austrian bureaucracy caught up with these exhausted men, who were required to make a full return of all missing kit. This was a nonsense for men whose uniforms were in rags, and filthy, with lice swarming all over them. Most of them were fighting in the snow-covered forest without boots, and had wrapped rags around their tattered socks to avoid losing their feet to frostbite.

At midday the lieutenant and his men set off again up a forested hill badly cratered by Russian artillery, with shells of all calibres falling thick and fast and machine gun bullets penetrating the undergrowth from hidden positions. At the top of the hill, the unit came under the orders of a colonel, who ordered several men to take a house about 1,000m behind the Russian front line, saying that they would be shot if they returned, having failed in the mission. They realised that he had gone mad, but the men obeyed and few returned.

The diary described the terrors of night fighting in forests so thick that one could not see far even in daylight, and only muzzle-flashes betrayed the enemy's whereabouts after dark. To add to the horror, it was rumoured that the Russians were using dum-dum bullets. That night, a squad was ordered to fix bayonets and drive the Russians from a neighbouring trench. Just before they attacked, the scouts called out that the trench was occupied by 24th Honved Infantry, who had been firing at Russian troops in the same trench.

Withdrawing to Havaj, thought to be safe until they were shelled by Russian artillery in the next village, men on sentry duty had to be relieved every two hours on account of the bitter cold. By this time – it was the end of November – of all the officers in the battalion only the sub lieutenant and the surgeon were left; of the 3,500 men on the original roll call a mere 170 remained. Of the sub lieutenant's company, which had been 267 strong, only six now survived, including himself. A bag of bones shaking with fever, he was given permission for convalescent leave, said farewell to his last few men and had to walk for two whole days to reach the town of Bukocz. From there, he was driven to the railhead at Eperjes, where he caught the last train to Budapest. He ends his diary: 'God had willed that I should return alive.'[7]

By late spring of 1917, freshly equipped and retrained by the French mission, the strength of the two Romanian armies in the east of the country had grown improbably to nearly a half-million men and the air force had also been reorganised. With the support of a million Russian troops from Moldavia, they were to attack the CP occupation troops in the summer of 1917. Unfortunately, Russian soldiers were not always welcomed with open arms by their Romanian allies. Florence Farmborough's *letuchka* was with the Russian 8th Army in north-eastern Romania, where the nurses found the villagers – all of whom kept chickens – refusing to sell them eggs. When they complained of this to a French-speaking Romanian officer, he told them politely enough that his own people had not enough food for themselves. So, the nurses were reduced to living on *kukuruza* – a gruel made from maize. Although Jews would usually rent them accommodation, the peasants refused to, on the grounds that Russian soldiers regularly looted private property at gunpoint and had broken into official food stores.

Managing to set up a dressing-station nevertheless, the nurses found two Russian female soldiers among their first batch of wounded. They belonged to the Women's Death Battalion, formed and commanded by an amazing woman called Maria Bochkaryova. After leaving two wife-beating husbands, she had been given the Tsar's personal permission to enlist in 25th Tomsk Reserve Battalion, where she defied abuse and harassment by her fellow soldiers, fighting alongside her third husband until he was killed in Galicia. Appalled by the number of soldiers deserting on all the fronts, she had returned to Moscow with her slogan 'If the men will not fight for Russia, we women will'. Her original 2,000 volunteers were whittled down by harassment from their male comrades and also by the ferocious discipline Bochkaryova imposed. Finally, their numbers dwindled to a hard core of less than 300 fighting on the Galician and Romanian fronts. Both the women soldiers being treated for wounds by Letuchka No. 2 were, Florence noted, too shocked to say very much about their experiences in combat, but the driver of their ambulance cart said that the Women's Death Battalion had been 'very cut up' by the enemy. Nor were they the only women in combat in Romania, where some local women were fighting alongside their menfolk in the region of Ilişişti. Their wounded were also treated by the *letuchka* nurses.[8]

The poverty of the Romanian peasants was epitomised when Florence, a keen photographer in her spare time, wanted to take the picture of a woman in traditional dress, who agreed to pose for her providing the family's most precious possessions – her husband's boots – could be prominent in the shot. The nurses' patients were not only adults of both sexes, but also young children, usually the victims of shrapnel bursts. Increasing numbers of unkempt and filthy Turkish prisoners were also brought in and cleaned up. Their wounds were dressed and they were given clean shirts and trousers. Even when the wounded being treated at the *letuchka* were deserters with obviously self-inflicted wounds, the nurses increasingly came in for verbal abuse from mutinous Russian soldiers, who were stirring up trouble among the Romanian soldiers. What she described as 'strange-looking men', some in uniform and some in civilian clothes, harangued large numbers of angry soldiers at unofficial meetings, making revolutionary speeches and urging them to desert in order to save their own lives.

Despite all the casualties at the front and the wrecking of Romania's primitive infrastructure, one way or another a million CP forces had been tied down in this unknown theatre of the war, which greatly helped the Western Powers in France and Italy. But as tens of thousands of Russian soldiers downed arms and walked away from their positions, the Romanian government had to negotiate an armistice, signed on 9 December 1917 – but not by King Ferdinand, who refused to append his signature. German technicians then repaired the installations at Ploeşti, which supplied more than 1 million tonnes of oil for the CP war effort. In addition, 2 million tonnes of grain were requisitioned, as were 300,000 animals for slaughter, leaving the country in a state of famine.

Nothing about Romania's actions in the First World War was predictable. In May 1918 the Central Powers imposed the Treaty of Bucharest, under which ironically a part of Romania's motive for going to war was gifted – on paper – when Russian-occupied Bessarabia was declared Romanian territory. King Ferdinand's country re-entered the war one day before the General Armistice went into effect on 11 November 1918, in order to claim at the negotiating tables its reward as a victorious belligerent. Romanian-speakers in the Bukovina voted for political union with the mother country, as did those in Transylvania in December. These moves were approved by the Treaty of Versailles in keeping with US President Wilson's 'Fourteen Points'. The Transylvanian region was, however, one-third populated by Hungarian-speakers, which triggered fresh hostilities between Romania and the Hungarian Soviet Republic, already at odds with Czechoslovakia and the Kingdom of Serbs, Croats and Slovenes over territorial disputes. This new war dragged on through 1919.

Yet, despite the Romanian government and high command doing nearly everything wrong and despite the appallingly high casualties suffered by its armies – estimated at 220,000 deaths, or roughly 6 per cent of all Entente military losses – and the hundreds of thousands of deaths among the civilian population, the nation ended this chapter in its turbulent history in far better shape than it had been in 1914, both geographically and politically.

NOTES

1. Some sources say 17 August.
2. The author does not give great credence to this information.
3. Neiberg and Jordan, pp. 110–11.
4. Extract from the diary available on http:www.firstworldwar.com/diaries/carpathianmemoir.htm.
5. Ibid.
6. Ibid.
7. Ibid.
8. Farmborough, pp. 302–7.

PART 4

REVOLUTION

16

ISKRA – THE SPARK

As to the lives of the predominantly peasant population of eastern Poland and the Bukovina, fought over for the second or third time in this war with all the men of military age conscripted by one side or the other, the suffering of the women, children and the elderly defies description and even imagination. Successful Brusilov's offensive undoubtedly was in military terms, but with Russian losses in the war so far amounting to something like 5.2 million dead, wounded and captured, even the long-suffering subjects of Tsar Nicholas II were aghast at the scale of fatalities. Bereaved families from the Baltic Sea to the Pacific Ocean and from the White Sea to the Caucasus mourned the loss of fathers, sons, brothers, uncles and cousins. Throughout the empire, just about every commodity was in short supply or impossible to obtain; even basic food had to be queued for; hundreds of thousands of refugees from the German-occupied provinces added to the strain on the system; inflation mounted; wages did not. Dissatisfaction with the empire's leaders from the Tsar downward, and with the many obviously incompetent generals, had led to massive desertion and open mutinies at the front and strikes at home. Particularly in the war industries, these became increasingly disruptive. Rebellion on a national scale had not actually broken out, but its seeds were there and germinating as the New Year of 1917 dawned.

The Duma warned Nicholas II that society was collapsing and advised him to form a constitutional government, as was done after the 1905 Revolution, but Nicholas had recently discovered dominoes and was currently devoting more time to mastering the intricacies of the various games than to the war or affairs of state. Denial or dimwittednesss? It is impossible to say. The Tsarina Alexandra was in deep mourning for Rasputin, who had been assassinated rather messily in December by a cabal of nobles, determined to rid the court of his defeatist influence.[1] In between visits to his tomb, she blamed the social unrest on the rabble in the Duma and advised her husband by letter that the workers would go quietly back to work, if he threatened to send every striker to the front. With desertion running at the rate of 30,000-plus every month, or a third of a million men in one year, that was hardly useful advice.

On 4 March 1917 workers at the Putilov heavy engineering works – Petrograd's largest factory – demanded a 50 per cent rise, to catch up with inflation. This being refused, 30,000 went on strike on 7 March[2] and were locked out the following day, which provoked disturbances at other factories. On 9 March women textile workers demanding bread for their hungry children turned International Women's Day into a huge demonstration of more than 50,000 people chanting revolutionary slogans. The Duma pleaded with Nicholas to release emergency stockpiles of food, which he refused to do, ordering the strikers back to work. A reassuring telephone call from the Tsarina informed him that there was nothing to worry about. When the workers refused, troops were ordered to fire on the demonstrators, but instead went over to their side, triggering the February Revolution, March not having yet begun under the old Russian calendar. Informed of this, Nicholas dissolved the Duma, thus severing the only link with any legitimate form of government. Every factory in Petrograd was closed, as were most shops and offices. Banners in the streets demanded food for the soldiers' children and payment of the long arrears in their pay. After widespread looting of bakeries and other food shops and nearly empty grain stores – the 1916 harvest had been good, but the chaos on the railways had prevented food reaching the towns – clashes broke out between police and loyal forces on the one side and armed students from the technical institute with mutinous soldiers on the other, who rounded up at gunpoint in the streets the formerly all-powerful Okhrana agents sent to spy on them.

On 11 March 1917 the Duma refused to obey the Tsar's decree of dissolution – which some historians consider the first overt political act of the February Revolution – and instead voted to form a provisional government replacing the Tsar's authority. On 12 March men of the elite Preobrazhenskii Guards Regiment, together with the Volinsky, Semenovsky and Ismailovsky regiments all mutinied and switched sides to support the workers. With a little prompting from, among others, General Alekseyev, Russia's last Tsar formally renounced his throne and titles on 15 March. On leaving Stavka just after midnight, he noted in his diary, 'All around me is treachery, deceit and cowardice'.[3] Succession should have passed to the *tsarevich*, for whom, on account of his invalidity, Nicholas renounced the right to succeed – which was probably unconstitutional, not that anybody worried at the time. Instead, the act commanded Nicholas' brother, Grand Duke Mikhail, to succeed him but, since Nicholas had already abdicated and was no longer Tsar, that was probably also illegal. The Grand Duke was charged with 'conducting the affairs of state in complete and inviolable union with the representatives of the nation in the legislative institutions'.[4] If only Nicholas himself had followed such a policy, all might have been different. Appropriately, the act of abdication ended, 'May God help Russia!'

After Grand Duke Mikhail sensibly refused the honour the following day, three centuries of Romanov rule came to a sordid end with the royal family under house arrest, ostensibly for its own protection, at Tsarskoye Selo. On hearing of the abdication, Britain's King George V sent a telegram to Nicholas, extending to his cousin an offer of asylum in Britain. Arrangements were made by the neutral Swedish government for a Royal Navy cruiser transporting the former Russian royal family not to be attacked by the Kaiserliche Marine during the voyage to Britain.

By discreet manoeuvring, on 16 March members of the Duma managed to put together a provisional government chaired by liberal aristocrat Prince Georgi Lvov, who belonged to no political party or group. He then prevaricated until the British offer was withdrawn. It was rumoured that George V regretted his humanitarian impulse to save his cousin's family, in case he was tarred with the same brush as the autocratic Romanovs. Whatever the reason, the British Embassy in Petrograd cancelled the invitation on 13 April and Nicholas, Alexandra and their children were transported by train nearly 1,300 miles eastward to Tobolsk in Western Siberia, where they were placed under house arrest in the governor's mansion to await their unhappy fate.

Embroiled in the chaos that March were numerous British civilians and more than a few British servicemen. Several officers were staying at the Astoria Hotel in Petrograd, where foreign observers and Russian officers and their wives had been quartered during the war. They included Commander Francis Cromie, commanding the Royal Navy submarine flotilla at Reval, and Commander Oliver Locker Lampson, who commanded the Armoured Car Division of the Royal Naval Air Service. The ever-active General Knox came and went. Outside this temporary haven, conditions in the streets were unpredictable, with bursts of machine gun fire and snipers shooting from rooftops. On one occasion a mob including many mutinying sailors from the Kronstadt naval base broke into the Astoria, shot a woman in the neck and killed a Russian general before seizing all the tsarist officers' swords and side-arms. After this disgrace, some of the officers killed themselves. The mutineers then placed armed guards on every floor, preventing entry by anyone who did not have the right room key.[5]

A young Able Seaman (AB), who had landed at Murmansk, since Archangel was iced-in at this time of year, travelled by rail to the capital and was on his way to join the British submarine flotilla at Reval. He recorded his impressions on arrival at Petrograd:

It was snowing fairly heavily. We made some tea while waiting for our baggage, and had to go underneath [sic] the station to get the water. What a sight! Everything was smashed up, evidently there had been a large food store there. All the shops were closed, except the bakers, outside of which people were formed in long queues. Occasional shots were still being fired. (At the Baltic station) just before our train left (for Reval), some excitement was caused by several machine guns opening fire outside the station. It appears a police spy was seen on the roof of a house and they meant to make sure of him. The belt of one of the machine guns jammed and there was not one soldier there who knew what was the matter. One of our Petty Officers set it going again.[6]

The party of British naval personnel including the anonymous AB joined their subs safely, after which Commander Cromie thought it prudent to remove his flotilla and its Russian depot ship to Helsingfors (modern Helsinki) to avoid problems with mutinous Russian sailors roaming the port of Reval. However, this hardly made a difference since the ratings of the Russian fleet in Helsingfors were also in full mutiny.

In shattering the infrastructure of the tsarist regime, including its secret police, the March Revolution produced a brief interlude of personal freedom, in which eventually 3 million inhabitants of the former tsarist empire took the chance to flee abroad, leaving their homes, property and businesses. They were right to leave, for many who did not were arrested as 'counter-revolutionaries', and imprisoned for years or executed.

The Romanov dynasty had ruled with a medieval sense of what was formerly called 'the divine right of kings'. For the Tsar and his family to become overnight homeless refugees left the devout but illiterate peasants who made up the majority of the Russian people confused and all the more easily influenced by the educated revolutionaries from the cities who talked so convincingly of a New Age dawning, where everyone would be equal. The revolt that began in Petrograd and Moscow spread rapidly to every city in European Russia and beyond the Urals. The moderate liberals and socialists in the Duma were trying to make the best of a bad job but the infrastructure of Russian society was in shreds, with the *soviety* of workers and soldiers defying any sign of legitimate authority. The Russian word *soviet*, plural *soviety*, means literally 'council', but perhaps 'self-elected committee' would be a more helpful translation. Order No. 1 of the Petrograd *soviet*, dated 1 March, stated explicitly that the Duma's authority was subordinate to 'the orders and resolutions of the Soviet of Workers' and Soldiers' Deputies'.[7]

The anarchy this caused was witnessed by another young Englishwoman serving as a volunteer nurse at a hospital for wounded soldiers in Petrograd. Meriel Buchanan was the daughter of the British ambassador and thus reasonably safe herself, but she described how 'ruffians with unshaven faces took control of the streets, blocked by overturned cars and trams'. When the wounded men for whom she was caring caught the revolutionary fever, they became so insubordinate and threatening to the doctors and nurses that the hospital had to be closed, leaving them without any medical care.[8]

Not having been elected by vote, the provisional government lacked the authority to challenge the power of the Petrograd *soviet*. That it maintained the semblance of a provisional government was because the *soviet* consisted of 2,500 members too busy with their internecine jostling for power to show much interest in the administration of the empire for some time to come.

An accomplished 35-year-old socialist lawyer-politician called Aleksandr Kerensky, judged by Knox to be the best of the leading politicians – and also, coincidentally the only clean-shaven one among a forest of moustaches and beards, worn to demonstrate mature masculine power – managed to have himself elected Minister of Justice in the provisional government and also vice chairman of the *soviet*. After it passed a resolution banning committee members from serving in the provisional government, Kerensky made a brilliant speech that won him the right to be the sole exception to that rule. It seemed briefly that Russia had found a leader acceptable to both liberal socialists and revolutionaries, although Lenin was subtly undermining all other claimants to power with his *Ten Theses* published in April, confusing many with his talk of 'the traitors to Socialism', 'the deception of the masses by the bourgoisie' and 'placing power in the hands of the proletariat and the poorest strata of the peasantry'.[9]

On 7 May a dictatorship of the *soviety* was declared in Petrograd at the same time as a crisis inside the provisional government over whether or not the war should be continued led to Kerensky becoming Minister for War and setting out a few days later to tour the fronts, exhorting mass meetings of other ranks to 'do their duty', no matter what was happening on the home front. It was, to say the least, a mixed message because Kerensky, who had served a term in prison as a revolutionary himself, abolished the death sentence for military offences and undermined the authority of officers by replacing them with *soviety soldatov* – soldiers' committees. Nevertheless, General Brusilov did manage to assemble thirty-one divisions on the front opposite the Austro-Hungarian 2nd and 3rd armies, which he regarded as the sector most likely to crack and open the way to Lemberg and the Drohobych oil fields, the capture of which would possibly have strengthened the provisional government's fragile power base.

The result, which is referred to as the Kerensky offensive, was an insufficiently strong attack launched by Russian 7th, 8th and 11th armies against Bothmer's Südarmee and Austro-Hungarian 3rd Army under Böhm-Ermolli to the south of Tarnopol on 1 July. Brusilov was using the same logic that had won such success the previous year: attacks and diversions to wrong-foot the enemy along a 100-mile front, of which the main axis was on a front of 30 miles, heavily supported by artillery. Perhaps unwisely seeking to share the glory of a victory he wrongly anticipated, Kerensky toured the first-line units in military uniform, haranguing them to fight for Mother Russia and their own freedom – with no mention of the Tsar. It was widely believed that he leaped onto the parapet in full view of the enemy when one regiment refused to emerge from the probably illusory security of their trenches and there implored them to follow his example. Truth or spin? It is hard to say.

The indisputable truth is that the offensive was crippled by increasing desertion and open mutinies in many of the Russian units involved and refusal to obey orders among Ukrainian soldiery, attempting to force the provisional government to cede autonomy to their country. But mutiny also affected the other side. For two long years, because he feared nationalist feelings among the minorities of his own empire, the Tsar had refused pleas from Czech and Slovak POWs to be allowed to fight against their common overlords in the dual monarchy, but now they were armed and allowed to play their part in brigades formed from POWs who preferred to take their chance on the field of battle, rather than waste away in Siberian camps for the rest of the war. Brusilov had placed the Czech Legion in the line opposite two Czech regiments in Austro-Hungarian uniform. After they refused to fire on their own countrymen in Russian uniform, 3,000 of these men walked across no man's land to surrender, some changing uniform there and then to turn their weapons on yesterday's comrades in the opposing trenches.

In the first week of July, it did seem that Brusilov's luck of the previous year was holding: a 20-mile-wide breach was forced in the enemy front, splitting Böhm-Ermolli's troops from Südarmee. The most significant advance was achieved on the left, or southern, flank of the offensive by Cossack General Lavr Kornilov, whose 8th Army pushed back the enemy 20 miles. OHL rushed German reinforcements from the Western Front and on 19 July Südarmee counter-attacked with two German and nine Austro-Hungarian divisions. With their supply lines over-extended, the right flank of Brusilov's advance crumpled. With tens of thousands of soldiers deserting, this retreat turned into a rout characterised by sabotage of military equipment and mutinies which made it plain that, although some units would still defend their lines if attacked, hardly any were prepared to accept again the far higher casualties inevitable in an offensive. Sick and exhausted, Brusilov attempted to control this uncontrollable situation, while Kornilov argued that attack was all that mattered. Kerensky sacked Brusilov and attempted to restore discipline by reintroducing the death penalty, which Kornilov imposed rigorously for mutiny or desertion, causing an even further drop in morale. Back in Petrograd, already on 2 July 1917 the first provisional government met its inevitable end amid the widespread disorder of what were called 'the July Days'. Prince Lvov resigned and was superseded as prime minister by Kerensky on 22 July. Astute politician though he was, things in Russia had gone too far from autocracy to stop at any form of democracy.

On 2 May 1959 the author was being interrogated in the Stasi prison on Lindenstrasse in Potsdam. He mentioned to the interrogating officer that he had heard, in his cell, the sound of many bands playing in the May Day parades of the town – and was reprimanded: 'Mr Boyd, parades are militaristic. We do not have parades in the peace-loving German Democratic Republic. What you heard were spontaneous demonstrations by the workers.'[10] Photographic evidence later seen showed stoney-faced party functionaries marching along the streets of Potsdam bearing 3-metre-high portraits of the leadership – an impressive accomplishment for a spontaneous demonstration. Similarly, according to the revisionist history imposed by the post-Revolutionary regime in Russia, the October Revolution was a spontaneous process – aka the force of history, more or less as prophesied by Karl Marx. However, a major factor in the October Revolution, which took place in November under the Gregorian calendar, was what is now called a 'deniable dirty trick'.

At the beginning of August 1914, among the dissidents who fled Russia to escape the Okhrana secret police was the 47-year-old brother of Aleksandr Ulyanov. He had been one of five terrorists belonging to the Narodnaya Volya – or People's Will movement – who were hanged in 1887 for plotting the assassination of Nicholas II's father. Aleksandr's younger brother Vladimir, who used the revolutionary name Lenin, was arrested in Kraków by the Austro-Hungarian authorities as a suspected spy, but released two weeks later when they realised that, if his anti-tsarist political activities could be harnessed to destroy the Russian armies' will to fight, it might be possible to force their surrender. This, in turn, would allow the Central Powers to transfer most of their forces on the Russian fronts to the Western Front and Italy, thereby winning the war.

Lenin had enjoyed a privileged upbringing, including secondary education in Switzerland. He was a disputatious man, who refused to listen to anyone else's ideas and was perpetually quarrelling with all his fellow-revolutionaries. For this reason, after he settled in neutral Switzerland, he was subsidised by Okhrana agents as a way of sowing dissension among the other revolutionary schisms who had sought sanctuary there. No one is sure who originated the incontrovertible slogan 'A bayonet is a weapon with a worker at both ends' yet, despite having agreed at pre-war international meetings that they would exploit the opportunity of an imperialist war to overthrow the governments involved, as the battle lines were drawn in August 1914 socialist parties on both sides chose to support their national war efforts. From the safety of his Swiss retreat, Lenin called in vain for them to transform the imperialist war just beginning into civil wars in their countries, arguing that the true enemy of the worker was not the worker in the opposite trench but the capitalist at home. He argued that rank-and-file soldiers should turn their weapons on the vulnerable members of the bourgeoisie and aristocracy wearing officers' uniforms who exercised the power of life and death over them and, by killing them all, seize this chance of destroying the capitalist system that was plunging the world into the greatest carnage ever known.

A number of ultra-rich German businessmen like millionaire industrialist Hugo Stinnes and banker Max Warburg were prepared to use their own wealth to turn the Russian dissidents into a fifth column – although that expression had not then been invented – to stab the Russian armies in the back. On 30 September 1915 an Estonian independence activist called Kesküla, aka A. Stein, informed the German Foreign Ministry that Lenin was prepared to sign a peace treaty with the Central Powers if a revolution in Russia brought his Bolshevik Party to power. He relayed to Berlin Lenin's programme, which included:

Point 4: Full autonomy for all nationalities of the Russian Empire;
Point 7: Russian troops to move into India[11] in a move to force Britain to withdraw troops from the Western Front for the defence of the Raj.

Whether the latter was sincere, or included in the programme as bait to loosen the German purse-strings, is unclear.

The Russian word *bol'shinstvo* means 'majority' but, as applied to the party, did not refer to any majority following among the population, or even among Russian revolutionaries. It referred instead to a vote won by Lenin's group over the editorial policy of a revolutionary publication called *Iskra* – meaning the spark that would ignite revolution. The losers in the vote were called Mensheviks – from *men'chinstvo*, or minority – and kept their distance from the Bolsheviks. With a shrewd feeling for public relations, the latter clung to their fortuitous title, which suggested widespread support although at the first meeting of the Petrograd Soviet in the State Duma building a large banner was displayed reading *Doloi Lenina* – Down with Lenin![12]

To convert their minuscule membership into a forceful power base, was going to cost a lot of money for what would today be called a massive public relations campaign. In January 1915 Germany's Under-Secretary for Foreign Affairs Arthur Zimmermann was already exploring the possibility of getting a German passport for a Russian-Jewish revolutionary named Israil Gelfand, who called himself Dr Helphand and had made a name for himself as a left-wing writer in Germany under the pen-name of Parvus, meaning 'poor man'. Persona non grata in both Russia and Germany, he wrote a memorandum dated 9 March 1915 setting out at considerable length the possibilities and methods of using the expatriate dissidents to organise social and political unrest inside the Russian Empire that could lead to an early withdrawal from the war.[13] Such was the importance attached to this approach, and its urgency, that on 26 March arrangements were being made to pay over 2 million marks to subsidise the Bolsheviks and Mensheviks inside Russia.[14] In May Helphand met Lenin to compare notes. As was his habit,

Lenin rejected anyone else's ideas. Yet Helphand pressed on with his design. As a result, by 9 July the Kaiser's Foreign Secretary, the normally diffident Gottlieb von Jagow, upped this budget to 5 million marks from secret funds designated 'Article VI, Section II of the extraordinary budget'.[15] This money began to be channelled into Russia through various deniable middlemen.[16]

Stinnes actually 'lent' 2 million roubles out of his own funds to the Foreign Ministry for setting up in Russia a publishing house that would print and distribute anti-war propaganda. Warburg also allocated substantial funds for 'publishing activities' there.[17] From the various German sources, Lenin's associates in Russia were amply provided through the discreet chain of bankers moving funds covertly through cut-outs and front companies so that the money could not be traced back to the German government. In all, these laundered 60 million gold marks for the Bolsheviks – equivalent to about $1,000 million today. Much passed through Swedish Nya Banken – whose director Olof Aschberg admitted to being the Bolsheviks' banker[18]– and ended in Russia in the accounts of various sympathisers, who passed it on to the Bolsheviks. One bagman alone, N.M. Weinberg, who was Petrograd agent for Berlin bankers Mendelssohn & Co, paid out 12 million roubles to 'Lennin, Trotski and Derjinski' [*sic*].[19] After the Revolution he was tortured by the sadistic Felix Dzherzhinsky, a minor Polish nobleman who was head of the Cheka secret police, in an endeavour to force him to hand over the signed receipts. Because the embarrassing paperwork had already been sent back to the accounts department in Berlin, Weinberg could not comply and was murdered by Dzherzhinsky on Lenin's orders to eliminate a potentially embarrassing witness to the real funding of the Bolsheviks.[20]

That was still in the future, with Lenin in Switzerland and Trotsky in Canada when the spring of 1917 became the moment for the expatriate revolutionaries to risk all or lose everything. Lenin and the other Russian expatriate revolutionaries in Switzerland had been negotiating with German Foreign Office officials for safe transport back to Russia – safe in the sense that they could not be arrested en route by Allied authorities. With both OHL and the German Foreign Office in agreement that the reappearance in Russia of these professional agitators was certain to increase the industrial unrest there, foment mutinies in the Russian armed forces and possibly force the provisional government to sue for peace, on 25 March 1917 it was agreed that a 'sealed train' would be made available to take Lenin and his party from Switzerland through Germany to the Baltic coast and then via neutral Sweden and Finland to Russia.[21] The only risk was that British officials in neutral Finland might be able to prevent transit of the last stage. Plan B was for the whole party to be smuggled through the German and Russian front lines, if necessary. Proving that there is nothing new about deniable clandestine operations, the mission had been approved by German Chancellor Theobald von Bethmann-Hollweg, but the Kaiser was not initially informed of this ungentlemanly ploy,[22] which was later repeated with other groups from Switzerland and Belgium – the only criterion imposed by the German authorities being an anti-war stance on the part of the returning dissidents.[23]

With all arrangements made, the German Foreign Ministry now found its plan jeopardised by the paranoia that is characteristic of revolutionaries. Lenin's group feared that their return to Russia at German expense would be exploited by their revolutionary rivals there as proof that they were agents of German capitalism. Yet, he, Zinoviev and others considered that staying longer in Switzerland would risk them being sidelined by rivals inside Russia who were as avid for power as they were. On 4 April they therefore insisted on paying their own third-class fares for the trip![24] On 16 April 1917, Lenin and some thirty other revolutionaries departed from the Swiss capital Berne to travel across Germany in complete secrecy in what became known as 'the sealed train'.

Complete secrecy? That's another myth. An expatriate community is a gossip factory and conspirators and their enemies gossip more than most. In addition, Swiss counter-intelligence had naturally been closely watching all the Russian conspirators. Here is the official police report of their departure:

> Today, I learned of the departure of a number of persons and at 3.20 p.m. proceeded to the railway station, where the express train was about to depart (with) one carriage full of Russian revolutionaries. I also saw the Russian named Lenin, who was obviously travelling as the leader of the group. It seems that the departure should have taken place in secret, but present at the station were approximately another one hundred Russians of both sexes, who saw off those who were leaving with mixed feelings. Those in favour of pursuing war against Germany to the very end were cursing like cabmen, shouting that those who were travelling were German spies and provocateurs, or that 'You will all be hanged, Jewish instigators that you are!' Other cries were, 'Provocateurs, scoundrels, pigs,' etc. When the train started to move off, the travellers and many of their friends who had remained began to sing the Internationale, while the others began again to hurl at them, 'Provocateurs! Spies!' etc.[25]

Throughout the first leg of the journey, by rail, the conspirators were accommodated in a locked carriage, from which railway personnel were kept away by two escorting German officers, and in which Lenin, his wife Nadezhda Krupskaya and his mistress Inessa Armand grabbed the most comfortable compartment for themselves, leaving the second-class compartments for the women and children, while the other men slept on the floor in third class. As George Orwell wrote, 'All animals are equal, but some animals are more equal than others'.

Because they were going home, there was a certain amount of hilarity among the other passengers. This irritated the ever-irascible Lenin to the point of screaming at them to keep the noise down because he had important work to do. He also reprimanded anyone caught smoking and imposed his will also on use of the single toilet by imposing a system of tickets so that there could be no argument who had been waiting longest to relieve themselves.[26]

All that money may seem a colossal amount to hand over to a group of dissidents on the off-chance that they could stage a coup d'état in Russia but, given the escalating costs of the war and the millions of lives lost, it seemed a worthwhile gamble in Berlin. As so often, fixation on the short-term target completely blinded the planners to the long-term danger. That otherwise shrewd officer Max Hoffman afterwards wrote: 'We neither knew nor foresaw the danger to humanity from the consequences of this journey of the Bolsheviks to Russia.'[27]

NOTES

1. A comprehensive account is to be found in *Source Records of the Great War*, vol. 5, ed. C.F. Horne (National Alumni, 1923), pp. 87–8.
2. All these dates have been revised in accordance with the Gregorian calendar.
3. Neiberg and Jordan, p. 119.
4. Ibid, p. 122.
5. M. Wilson, *For Them the War Was Not Over: The Royal Navy in Russia 1918–1920*, (Stroud: The History Press, 2010), p. 15.
6. Ibid, p. 15 (abridged).
7. Point 4 of Order No. 1.
8. D. Boyd, *The Kremlin Conspiracy* (Hersham: Ian Allan, 2010), pp. 76, 78.
9. Neiberg and Jordan, p. 137.
10. Boyd, *Kremlin*, pp. 8–17.
11. Z.A.B. Zeman, *Germany and the Russian Revolution* (London: OUP, 1958), p. 6.
12. Moynahan, pp. 84–5.
13. Zeman, pp. 140–52.
14. Ibid, p. 3.
15. Ibid.
16. For greater detail, see Boyd, *Kremlin*, pp. 72–80.
17. Zeman, pp. 24, 92.
18. See also http://reformed-theology.org/html/books/bolshevik_revolution/ chapter_03.htm.
19. Occleshaw, p. 41.
20. Boyd, *Kremlin*, pp. 78–80.
21. Zeman, p. 26.
22. http://reformed-theology.org/html/books/bolshevik_revolution/chapter_ 03.htm.

23. Zeman, p. xi.
24. Ibid, p. 35, quoting text of telegram 603 from German Minister in Berne to Foreign Ministry.
25. M.S. Stănescu and C. Feneşan, *Lenin şi Trotski versus Ludendorff şi Hoffmann* (Bucharest: Editura Enciclopedică, 1999), p. 77, quoted in S. Tănase, *Auntie Varvara's Clients*, tr. A.I. Blyth (Plymouth: University of Plymouth Press, 2010), p. 38 (edited).
26. R. Service, *Spies and Commissars* (London: Macmillan, 2011), p. 19.
27. M. Hoffman, *War Diaries and Other Papers* (London: Secker, 1929), vol. 2, p. 117.

17

BLOOD IN THE STREETS, CARDS ON THE TABLE

The transparent device of paying a third-class fare for a journey impossible at that time without the active help of the German government did nothing to protect Lenin and co. from accusations by their revolutionary rivals and the provisional government that they were paid enemy agents when they returned to Petrograd in mid-April and Lenin published his Manifesto. Not one, but two official investigations into the Bolsheviks' finances and travels were launched, resulting in a public accusation of treason by the Minister of Justice in July. Leon Trotsky had arrived from Canada in spite of British attempts to prevent him until His Majesty's Ambassador in St Petersburg Sir George Buchanan feared that continuing to do so might provoke revolutionaries to attack British businessmen in Russia. Trotsky was a supporter of the Mensheviks but changed alliance after finding they were losing the struggle for power. Following the accusations that they were German agents, several of the Bolshevik leaders, including him, were arrested while others went underground. Prioritising his personal safety, Lenin fled Russian justice by returning clandestinely to Finland.

The anti-war *soviety* that sprang up in major towns and throughout the armed forces came together in the First All-Russian Congress of Soviets, which began on 16 June. At the congress, Socialist Revolutionaries were in the majority, followed by the Mensheviks and Bolsheviks, in that order. Without waiting for the term spin-doctor to be invented, Lenin took the small-circulation newssheet *Pravda,* which had been the party's mouthpiece since 1912, and used the laundered German subsidies to unleash a huge PR campaign, an important element in which was a daily printing of 300,000 copies of the paper under his personal editorial control. Meantime, he stayed safely in Finland, using the faithful Krupskaya as his courier to smuggle copy to the printers on the other side of the border. *Pravda* means 'truth', and it became an article of faith for party members that everything in it was true, which meant that disagreeing with anything in *Pravda* was heresy. As its headline proclaimed for the following seven and a half decades, it was to remain the 'organ of the Communist Party of the Soviet Union' until the USSR imploded in 1991.

Ludendorff rightly determined to exploit Russia's crippling internal problems by a bold drive towards Petrograd itself. By capturing Russian ports along the Baltic littoral, supplies to the advancing troops could be brought in by naval and merchant shipping, avoiding the problems of extended supply lines in difficult terrain further south. Continuing the offensive in Estonia, on 3 September 1917 German 8th Army under Ludendorff's cousin General Oskar von Hutier crossed the Daugava or Western Dvina River. Using what came to be called 'Hutier tactics', although they were not entirely original, he made liberal use of artillery firing 20,000 gas shells on the first day of the attack and followed up with special storm troops, who were volunteers attracted by better rations, more leave and no fatigue duties. Trained to 'think on their feet' without waiting for orders from the rear, they used flamethrowers, light mortars and light machine guns to exploit rapidly every opening while bypassing Russian strongpoints, which they left for the heavier troops to reduce with artillery.

Construction by the engineers of pontoon bridges over the Dvina – the modern border between Latvia and Belarus – allowed nine German divisions to cross in forty-eight hours. After offering them feeble resistance, the defenders withdrew, deserters being hanged on the spot, and left behind 250 artillery pieces, with the Germans in complete control of the important seaport of Riga, vital for the planned drive on Petrograd, by the end of the fourth day. From Riga to Petrograd as the crow files is less than 300 miles, and the news of this defeat shattered any public confidence in Kerensky's provisional government.

Supporters of General Kornilov, dismissed from the post of commander-in-chief at Stavka, now attempted a military coup, which was forestalled when pro-Bolshevik railway workers refused to transport them to Petrograd, forcing the rump army assembled by Kornilov to march there. Thus delayed, they found 20,000 Red Guards – mostly deserters and mutineers who had been armed by the *soviety* – facing them in defence of the capital, while more than 1 million workers were on strike in Russian cities. Declaring a Russian Republic under his leadership, Kerensky clung to a semblance of power a little longer. His father had been Lenin's headmaster, and the two families knew each other well. Possibly for this reason, Kerensky was allowed to escape in disguise after the Revolution. He died in New York in 1970 and was buried in Putney Vale cemetery, just a few miles from the Communist pilgrimage site of Karl Marx's tomb in Highgate.

The next step in the invasion and occupation of the western Estonian peninsula in Operation *Albion* was for German ships of the Kaiserliche Marine to drive all Russian warships out of the Gulf of Riga and capture the islands of

Oesel, Moon and Dagö (modern Saaremaa, Muhu and Hiumaa). Ludendorff and Admiral Henning von Holtzendorf planned a combined operation, integrating ground, naval and air forces to put some 24,000 officers and men of the reinforced 42nd Infantry Division ashore. The German fleet included ten battleships, one battle cruiser, nine light cruisers, a large number of destroyers and six submarines. Against them the Imperial Russian Navy had two outdated pre-dreadnoughts, three cruisers, an alleged total of twenty-one destroyers and three submersibles from the Royal Navy.[1]

The combined air forces assigned to *Albion* included the Baltic Airship Detachment of six Zeppelins, eight seaplanes with their own naval tender and land-based aircraft at Libau and Windau (modern Liepaja and Ventspils) within easy flying distance of the Gulf of Riga, totalling, according to some sources, more than 100 aircraft. Given the known degree of reliability of these, it can be estimated that about half might have been airworthy on any particular day, weather permitting – which it frequently was not. The huge bulk of the Zepps caused them to be grounded on 12 October, when only two spotter aircraft and a bomber could over-fly the landings. On the next day heavy rain and snow showers grounded the land-based fliers and one of three seaplane pilots paid with his life for defying the meteorological conditions.

The naval battle alone was an impressive clash, lasting from 16 October until 3 November 1917, when the Russian ships had suffered a total of 156 dead and 60 men wounded, against German naval losses of 54 dead and 141 wounded. However, by then German ground forces had captured territory, forty-seven heavy artillery pieces and 130 machine guns. Russian ground forces lost only 200 casualties against 500 casualties among the attackers. A number of ships were sunk and one went aground in the Gulf of Riga. For Ludendorff and Holtzendorf, the victory proved that OHL and the German navy could collaborate closely with careful planning. One mystery is why the defenders did not make more use of the aircraft they undoubtedly had. When a German air unit installed itself on the airfield outside the town of Arensburg on the island of Oesel, it found four Nieuports deliberately sabotaged by the retreating Russians. Although anti-aircraft fire was an occasional harassment to the German fliers, and especially feared by the Zeppelin crews, whose craft were highly flammable, the only recorded case of a Russian aircraft attacking German planes was on 14 October, when one was attacked by three Nieuports. The most probable explanation for the grounding of Russian aircraft after this is that the Russian pilots had all been condemned as 'bourgeois' by the revolutionary *soviet soldatov* and either arrested or forced to leave the island.

This permitted German aircraft to fly reconnaissance missions at will and drop orders to ground forces out of touch with their command centres – usually by the simple expedient of writing the message on a piece of cloth and wrapping it around a stone, to be lobbed onto the troops below. Failing this, they developed a drill of circling over ground troops and then flying off as aerial signposts indicating the direction to be taken. They also flew artillery correction missions when targets were out of sight of observers at deck level. An additional use of aircraft by the *Albion* forces was as repeater stations for weak radio transmissions otherwise blocked by topography. Wireless communication proved both a blessing and a complication: the communications hub aboard the battleship *Moltke* was overwhelmed by the volume of traffic from the 300 vessels of all sizes in the invasion force, let alone the additional traffic from ground forces once the landings had commenced. Bombing reports thus became out of date before being read, preventing ground forces swiftly taking advantage of, for example, a battery being knocked out. This on occasion drove the more daring German pilots to land near a command post so that they could deliver a message in person, in some cases leaving the aircraft unable to take off again after becoming bogged down on soggy ground.

German aircraft and Zeppelins also undertook bombing missions, although forbidden to 'soften up' the planned landing sites for fear of indicating their locations to the defenders. A particular problem for the Zepps was a shortage of hydrogen gas, so that the deficiency had to be made up from tanks of compressed air, which increased the risk of fire – as when L37 returned to base in a hurry after a mid-air conflagration.

An official German communiqué datelined Amsterdam 19 October 1917 announced the capture of Oesel, on which 10,000 Russian prisoners were taken, along with fifty heavy guns.[2] By then, panic had set in throughout Estonia. At Reval (modern Tallinn), residents who had hoped to avoid the unrest in Russian cities were hastily packing a few suitcases and leaving for Petrograd and points east by whatever means they could find. With the German vessels victorious, the Russian Fleet withdrew from the Gulf of Riga on 17 October 1917 through the Suur Strait separating Muhu from the Estonian mainland.

Thanks largely to Lenin's huge PR campaign, by now both the Petrograd and Moscow *soviety* were under Bolshevik control. After Kornilov's failed coup revealed the provisional government's feet of clay, the *soviet* arrested the members of the Duma on 25 October. News of this reached even Letuchka No. 2 in Romania when newspapers arrived with reports of rioting in Moscow and people starving in Kiev, where there was an outbreak of cholera. Soldiers were also falling ill with *chornaya ospa* – black smallpox, which was always fatal. A nurse returning from leave in the Caucasus recounted how food was scarce even in that traditional land of plenty, with tea and sugar already rationed. The only good news was that the nurses' salaries were raised from fifty roubles to seventy-five roubles a month – roughly £7.50 – but this was a time when a pair of boots, soon worn out in the damp and the mud, cost 100 roubles. Given permission to take some leave in Moscow, Florence Farmborough had literally to fight her way onto trains, insulted by crowds of men deserting en masse.

Nor dared she leave her seat on the long and tedious journeys, lest it be immediately taken by a soldier who would refuse to give it up on her return.

After waiting until Petrograd was safely under Bolshevik control, Lenin returned from Finland towards the end of October. The much reproduced iconic painting *At the Finland Station* showed him heroically clinging onto the outside of Finnish locomotive No. 293 as it pulled into the Finlyandski Vokzal, waving a footplate man's cap at the cheering crowd. Like most Communist icons, it was a fantasy. What was real was the PR campaign. At the first Congress of Soviets in June, only 105 of the 749 delegates had been Bolsheviks. At the second congress on 25–26 October according to the Julian calendar – or 6–7 November under the Gregorian calendar – out of 649 delegates, 390 were Bolsheviks, giving Lenin a workable majority over the other socialist revolutionary parties, many of whose elected representatives walked out in disgust or despair, increasing his majority still more.

While the congress delegates argued their way through the night inside the Smolny Institute, a former school for daughters of the nobility, armed revolutionaries stormed the Winter Palace. Actually, this was another myth. After Lenin proclaimed that the newly invented cinema film was the most important of the arts for propaganda, an heroic reconstruction, to be shown around the world, was filmed with soldiers firing volleys and brave workers falling dead. In the event, the Winter Palace garrison had dwindled, partly in mutinies but largely due to lack of rations, from its normal complement of 2,000 to three squadrons of Cossacks, some cadets and 137 women of 1st Battalion of the Petrograd Women's Brigade. They were swiftly overcome and locked up. By morning, the palace and virtually all places of strategic interest, like the main telegraph office, government ministries and power stations, were occupied by the Bolshevik activists but it was far from a bloodless coup. Conservatively estimated at 7,000, those killed included many innocent bystanders.[3] General Knox personally intervened to secure the release of the women soldiers, and succeeded after threatening to tell the world how the Bolsheviks were treating women.

It is almost pointless to attempt a comprehensive analysis of the many causes of the two revolutions in 1917. To do so would require more than one weighty tome. In any case, no two historians or economists have completely agreed on what was important and what subsidiary. Bruce Lockhart, who was neither historian nor economist, but who was in Petrograd and Moscow at the time as an accredited diplomat who knew Lenin, Trotsky and many other Bolshevik leaders, wrote with the benefit of hindsight in 1931:

The revolution took place because the patience of the Russian people broke down under a system of unparalleled inefficiency and corruption. No other nation would have stood the privations which Russia stood [*sic*], for anything like the same length of time. As instances of the inefficiency, I give the disgraceful mishandling of food supplies, the complete breakdown of transport, and the senseless mobilisation of millions of unwanted and unemployable troops. As an example of the corruption, I quote the shameless profiteering of nearly everyone engaged in the giving and taking of war contracts. Obviously, the Emperor himself, as a supreme autocrat, must bear the responsibility for a system which failed mainly because of the men he appointed to control it.

... the revolution was a revolution for land, bread and peace – but, above all, for peace. There was only one way to save Russia from going Bolshevik. That was to allow her to make peace. It was because he would not allow her to make peace that Kerensky went under. It was solely because he promised to stop the war that Lenin came to the top.[4]

If one deletes 'solely', because there was a complex of reasons why Lenin and his cohorts were able to grab power, that explanation is as good as any.

By the end of the second day at the Smolny Institute, the Congress of Soviets had elected a council of people's commissars to serve as an interim government, with Bolsheviks naturally holding the majority of seats. This, in turn formed a Central Committee, itself subordinated to an elite policy office, or Politburo, consisting of just seven members, of whom three held the power. Strangely in such a xenophobic country, they were the Tatar Ulyanov, the Jew Bronshtein and the Georgian Djugashvili – whose non-Russian origins were concealed by their aliases: Lenin, Trotsky and Stalin.

Lockhart described Lenin as looking like a provincial grocer, with his short stature, rather plump build, short thick neck, broad shoulders, round red face, high intellectual forehead, nose slightly turned up, brownish moustache and short stubbly beard.[5] From an equally comfortable middle-class family as Lenin, Trotsky was described by Lockhart as having a very quick brain and a rich, deep voice, excellent for public speaking. Tidily dressed with hands well-manicured and his huge forehead surmounted by a mass of waving black hair, he was considered by Lockhart the very incarnation of a revolutionary. Of Trotsky, he wrote: 'He strikes me as a man who would willingly die for Russia, provided there was a big enough audience to see him do it.'[6]

On 9 November R. Kühlmann, State Secretary at the Foreign Ministry in Berlin 'requested' a further 15 million marks from the 'extraordinary budget' for the Bolsheviks and indicated future need for further sums.[7] With the Party's financial stability assured by this transfer, there was for the Bolsheviks an urgent need to halt hostilities against the Central Powers, so that they could impose their rule on all the other revolutionary groups and use their armed supporters, now called the Red Guards, to eliminate the several 'armies' in areas of Russia still loyal to the Tsar. Lev Rosenfeld – who disguised his Jewish origins by taking the Russian name Kamenev – left a record of the initial contact at Brest-Litovsk, the border city where, in peacetime, the bogies of passenger trains were changed from European standard to Russian gauge and freight in both directions had to be re-loaded on wagons of the different gauge. He wrote:

We crossed the line, led by a bugler carrying a white flag. Three hundred yards from the German wire, we were met by German officers. At 5 o'clock, blindfolded, we were taken to the battalion staff, to present our credentials to two officers of the German General Staff, who had come for that purpose. Negotiations were conducted in French. Our proposal to negotiate an armistice on all the Russian fronts preparatory to concluding peace, was transmitted direct by telegraph to the commander of all German forces on the Russian fronts and to the German General Staff.

At 6.20pm we were driven to meet General von Hofmeister, who informed us that a reply would probably be received within twenty-four hours. Yet, just over an hour later a preliminary answer from the General Staff gave agreement to our proposals. By midnight, General von Hofmeister had given us a written reply. Since our communication had been in Russian, this was in German. It read:

'The German commander of the Ostfront is authorised by the German High Command to enter into negotiations with the Russian High Command, which is requested to appoint a commission with written authority to be sent to the commander of the German Ostfront, who will likewise name a commission with special authorisation.

'The day and time of the meeting are to be fixed by the Russian High Command and communicated to the German command in time to prepare a special train for the purpose. Notice must be given of where it is to cross the front.'[8]

The Russian delegates at this first meeting selected the junction of the Dvinsk-Vilna line as the crossing-point, from where the Russian negotiators would be conducted to the German HQ in Brest-Litovsk. The time selected for reconvening was noon on 2 December under the new calendar. After this, the Russian delegates were blindfolded anew and conducted back to their own lines.

A preliminary suspension of hostilities between the Central Powers and Russia was announced on 5 December. On 15 December an armistice was agreed, after which OHL began transferring troops to the Western Front and OAK began reinforcing the Isonzo front. On the following day OHL sent to Eastern Command a list of ten points to be included in the eventual peace agreement. Until then the German and Austro-Hungarian diplomats had been in favour of mild terms that could swiftly be agreed so that the mass of troops on the eastern front could be released for service in the West and the dual monarchy perhaps allowed to recover from the economic and political stresses of the war that seemed increasingly likely to fragment its pre-war empire. Indeed, Austrian Foreign Minister Ottokar von Czernin was a strong advocate of 'peace now', having convinced his emperor that the dual monarchy could not survive another winter of war. However, Hindenburg and Ludendorff took a strictly military view and were intent on a punitive peace treaty, annexing more than a half-million square miles of formerly Russian territory. Such was the power of the military in Germany that their view prevailed over the more enlightened approach of the Foreign Office in Berlin, leaving Vienna no choice but to go along with this.

On 22 December at Brest-Litovsk Bolshevik delegates led by Kamenev and Trotsky – now People's Commissar for Foreign Affairs – met representatives of Germany, Austria-Hungary, Bulgaria and Turkey to discuss the German peace terms. Point 5 was: 'Recognition of the right of peoples to self-determination. Russian evacuation of Finland, Estonia, Livonia, the Moldava, Eastern Galicia and Armenia.'[9] Although the 'right of peoples to self-determination' was originally included in Lenin's own programme, Trotsky refused to give up any 'Russian' territory.

To speed things along – Ludendorff urgently wanted to transfer more troops from the Russian fronts to the Western Front as soon as it was safe to do so – on the night of 28–29 December sixty German and Austrian diplomats arrived in Petrograd. They were accommodated in the Grand and Angleterre hotels, where Allied officers staying there had to pretend they did not see them.[10]

In the election of a new constituent assembly in November, the Bolsheviks had polled less than a quarter of the votes but, at the first session of the assembly their minority of elected members caused such uproar and confusion that any pretence of democracy was abandoned and the session ended after less than twenty-four hours. At Brest-Litovsk, negotiations dragged on into January because Trotsky and Lenin, brainwashed by their own propaganda, were certain that Germany would collapse in its own revolution because Karl Marx had prophesied that *the* Communist revolution would happen there. There were strikes in Berlin and other German cities. In Austria, beset by food shortages and the casualties at the fronts, strikes also flared up. Trotsky's blatant stalling tactics were based on an obsession that these strikes would rapidly spark revolution there, bringing down the governments and rendering the negotiations pointless. He amazed the Central Powers representatives by haranguing them like a mob in the street, calling for 'a democratic peace without annexations, reparations, respecting the right to national self-determination'.

Running out of patience with the Russian negotiators, the recently appointed German Foreign Minister Baron Richard von Kühlmann upped the pressure for a treaty to be signed. Leading the CP delegation, General Max Hoffmann then brushed aside all the rhetoric, and told Trotsky that, if the Soviet government really wanted peace, it would have to renounce all claims to the formerly Russian-occupied areas of Poland, plus the Baltic states and Ukraine.

Given the urgent need to resolve the internal chaos in Russia and Stalin's proclamation at the Third Congress of Soviets that same month of the right of 'all peoples to self-determination through to complete secession from Russia',[11] one might think that Trotsky would have agreed to any terms that left Russia itself intact. After all, the workers that he professed to represent had marched under the slogan 'Peace at any price'. Instead, since many meaningless slogans were being chanted in the streets of Russian cities, he invented a new one on his return to Petrograd, 'Neither war nor peace', i.e. a cease-fire without a formal treaty. Perhaps the saddest slogan of those times was 'All land to those who work it'. This was pure deceit, since Lenin already planned to seize all the peasants' land, not just the great estates, and collectivise it in a programme directed by party bureaucrats. The slogan and the great lie it contained were simply aimed at winning over the confused peasantry, which remained essentially loyal to the Tsar, whereas the revolutionaries' strongest following was among the organised urban workforce.

At the time, nothing was what it seemed to be. On the surface, the other socialist revolutionary parties were working in tandem with the Bolsheviks. Yet, as German ambassador Count von Mirbach, who was to be assassinated in July, reported to Berlin on 24 January 1918, of all the newspapers in Russia only the Bolsheviks' *Pravda* and *Izvestiya* remained free of a draconian censorship and 'politicians, (elected) deputies, editors and other such members of the opposition live under continual threat to their liberty, if not worse'.[12] In private, Lenin was already drawing up lists of former and present colleagues who would have to be eliminated in order to prevent them competing for power. Strangest of all was his list of socialist and other intellectuals who could not be imprisoned or killed because they were too well known and respected outside Russia. These were to be forcibly exiled in 1922, just before the Soviet Union was declared.[13]

The Finnish government declared independence on 6 December 1917, from which date the country that had been under the hegemony of Sweden and a Russian Grand Duchy since 1809 was at last to be governed by its own people. The Ukrainian provisional government also proclaimed its independence on 22 January and agreed a separate peace treaty with the Central Powers on 9 February at the price of a 6-month supply of grain and minerals. Despite the fine talk of national self-determination for the countries formerly forming part of the tsarist empire, and although still in a state of unresolved hostilities, the Bolsheviks invaded Ukraine to re-impose Russian rule, obliging OHL to keep more than half a million men there, to the great relief of the Western Allies. To force Trotsky back to the conference table the German Ostfront commander launched a new offensive against Russia. On 23 February Hoffmann gave him two days to get serious and three more to conclude a treaty. Realising that the

Bolsheviks could be brought down by public anger at home if the war continued, Lenin threatened to resign if the German terms were not agreed to.

So, on 3 March 1918 the deal was done, with Russia accepting the loss of Ukraine, the Polish and Baltic territories and Finland. Those territories have been estimated as representing 'half the human, industrial and agricultural resources' of the Russian Empire. Another way of evaluating the loss was that 90 per cent of Russian coal supplies at the time and much of its heavy industry was in this territory. Lenin called it 'an obscene peace'[14] but, as with France in 1918, most of the Russian population heaved a sigh of relief in the belief that their surviving menfolk could now return home and the killing would stop. At OHL and OAK there was more than a sigh of relief as train after train rumbled westwards transporting CP forces and vast numbers of rifles, artillery and ammunition of all calibres to the Western Front and the Isonzo, where fighting was to continue for another eight months. Other trains also headed west into Austro-Hungary with cargoes of grain, sugar, eggs, horses and pigs for slaughter.

For Russia, the war was over, but a new one was beginning.

NOTES

1. There is a blow-by-blow account of the battle on www.airpower.au.af.mil/chronicles/cc/dinardo.html.
2. Report quoted in Australian *Northern Times* of 27 October.
3. *Source Records of the Great War*, vol. 5, pp. 75–7.
4. Lockhart, *Memoirs*, pp. 171–2 (abridged).
5. Ibid, p. 237 (abridged).
6. Ibid, pp. 226–7 (abridged).
7. Zeman, p. 75.
8. *Source Records of the Great War*, vol. 5, pp. 396–7 (abridged).
9. Text of telegram 1895 reproduced in Zeman, p. 106.
10. R. Service, *Stalin – A Memoir* (London: Pan, 2005), p. 78.
11. Ibid, p. 154.
12. Telegram reproduced in Zeman, p. 117.
13. A full account may be found in L. Chamberlain, *Lenin's Private War* (New York: St Martin's Press, 2007).
14. Service, *Stalin*, p. 161.

PART 5

THE WARS AFTER THE WAR

18

NEITHER WAR NOR PEACE

Trotsky's deliberately confusing slogan 'Neither war, nor peace' was paradoxically an exact description of life in Russia after the Treaty of Brest-Litovsk. It is true that there was no *declared* war against an external enemy but, within the vast spread of the old empire, several armies of various sizes and differing politics were threatening the Bolsheviks.' precarious hold on power while Lenin and his associates were ruthlessly attempting to crush any opposition, of whatever political hue.

The Central Powers would have been stupid not to take advantage of this internal unrest and confusion. On 18 January 1918 their forces resumed advances against little opposition in the Baltic provinces and moved into Ukraine and the Crimea. Considering that the German advance in Estonia was threatening Petrograd, Lenin moved the capital 400 miles eastwards, reversing Peter the Great's decision of two centuries before, to open Russia to the West – and metaphorically pulled down the blinds that would become the Iron Curtain.

Moscow, the new capital, was in turn threatened by anarchists and White forces opposing the Reds in daily street fighting. Dated 30 April 1918, Minister Mirbach's report to his chancellor in Berlin gives a chilling picture of life in the new capital:

In every part of the city, and especially in the central commercial quarter, countless bullet-holes in walls and windows are evidence of the bitter battles that were fought for its possession. Even the Kremlin has suffered terribly. Various of its gates are badly damaged; the Iberian Gate has been partly destroyed and is now only boarded up. Hardly any better-dressed people are to be seen. It is as if the whole of the previously governing class and the bourgeoisie had disappeared off the face of the earth. Little can be bought in the shops except dusty remnants of past splendour, and these only at fantastic prices. It is unwise to go out towards evening. At that time of day one often hears rifle fire and more or less serious skirmishes seem to take place continually. The factories are at a standstill and the land is still, to all intents and purposes not being cultivated.[1]

Lenin's paranoia made it inevitable that he would sideline Marx and Engels as the founders of Communism and, by propounding an amended creed, dubbed Marxism-Leninism, achieve apotheosis as the Communist deity whose likenesses replaced all the previously ubiquitous icons in Russian homes and public buildings. In the resultant jargon-infested ideological confusion of the times, there was only one determinant of orthodoxy: the Communist Party itself. Indeed, the Party shortly became the sole arbiter of truth, while truth in Russia became whatever the Party decreed it to be. George Kennan, an American diplomat who served many years in Russia, later wrote:

A daring tour de force which the American mind must make, if it is to try to find Russian life comprehensible, (is) to understand that for Russia, at any rate, there are no objective criteria of right and wrong. There are not even any objective criteria of reality and unreality. What do we mean by this? We mean that right and wrong, reality and unreality, are determined in Russia not by any God, not by any innate nature of things, but simply by men themselves. Here men determine what is true and what is false. The reader should not smile. This is a serious fact.[2]

Lenin also initiated a programme of 'war communism'. The war in this case was class war, the enemy being everyone with aristocratic or bourgeois origins. The dialectic, or double-talk, was meant to justify the nationalisation of banks, shipping, railways, grain supplies, mining, oil, and all other businesses employing more than ten people. The promise to hand all land to those who worked it was rescinded, to the peasants' horror, when it was announced that all agricultural activities were to be collectivised under the strict control of town-dwellers whose credentials were their records as political activists, and who knew nothing about growing crops or raising animals. Ordinary peasants became effectively serfs again, tied to the land they worked and paid a starvation wage. The more successful peasants were branded *kulaki*, or fists, and found that they were class enemies too, millions being forcibly resettled on distant and unproductive land. With their going and the arrival of the all-powerful commissars to dictate all agricultural activities, several million people in some of the richest farmland of Europe were going to starve to death.

Not starving, but hungry were the crews of RN vessels in the Baltic ports. The customary method of purchasing supplies for British crews in foreign ports was with drafts on British Admiralty funds. These no longer being honoured in Helsingfors, Lieutenant Basil Downie showed initiative by bartering surplus clothing and tobacco on the black market for food and selling some to secure money to give his men some cash to spend.

Four socialist republics were established: the Russian and Transcaucasian soviet federated socialist republics and the Belorussian and Ukrainian soviet socialist republics. In Ukraine, despite the installation of a soviet regime, there was no wish to be 'south Russia' any longer. Ukrainians looked to Austria-Hungary for protection, which was forthcoming because of the importance to the Central Powers of the fertile black soil *chernozem* grain-growing area to compensate for the crippling effects of the Allied naval blockade. It was to regain the *chernozem* that the Red Army twice invaded to re-impose Russian rule.

The situation became even more complicated after the second Treaty of Brest-Litovsk, which caused a rift between the Bolsheviks and other revolutionary socialists who opposed Lenin's autocratic dissolution of the Duma. Lenin re-baptised his party the All-Russian Communist Party[3] to mark its opposition not only to capitalists and tsarists but also the foreign socialist parties who had supported their capitalist governments during the war as well as all the other Russian parties of the political left – former allies who had helped to bring down the tsarist regime, but were henceforth to be treated as dangerous enemies because any support for them diluted his power base.

Now Commissar for War, Trotsky employed tsarist career officers supervised by political commissars to turn his freshly christened Red Army into a professional force. Recruiting was not a problem; it was not that the men were politically motivated to enlist in its ranks, but rather that failure to do so resulted in denunciations that could prove fatal for foot-draggers. Of the several enemies it faced, Admiral Aleksandr Kolchak's White Army based at Omsk in Siberia was being trained with assistance from British and U.S. military advisers. In the Kuban steppes, the White Army commanded by General Anton Denikin was preparing to march on Moscow.

On 2 March 1918 Trotsky telegraphed the Murmansk *soviet*, ordering it to co-operate with the Allied troops in the Far North in order to block any incursion by Finnish White forces across the nearby border. On 6 March, in agreement with Aleksei Yuriev, chairman of the *soviet*, a company of Royal Marines was put ashore from HMS *Glory*. Later that month, another detachment of marines was landed and twenty-one Royal Engineers. Their tasks included the erection of quick-build huts as accommodation and the sabotage of rail links to the south to prevent more stores being transported to the Red Army.

In the Far East, Japanese forces landed at Vladivostok against local protests and were steadily reinforced. Czech and Slovak POWs and deserters from the Austro-Hungarian army had been permitted for linguistic reasons to serve in their own units, which stuck together as the tsarist armies disintegrated.

A substantial number were in Ukraine, where they had no wish to fight the Bolsheviks, but did want to join the struggle in the west in order to drive the Austrian and Hungarian occupiers out of their own countries. French officers who had landed in Ukraine in December arranged on 14 February for them to be allowed to leave Russia via Vladivostok after handing over all their heavy equipment – artillery and some aircraft – when crossing the Ukraine-Russia border at Kursk.[4] Mistrusting the Bolsheviks' promise that they would be given safe passage, the Czechs kept most of their personal weapons. That they were right to do so was proven when increasingly violent confrontations between them and Trotsky's Red Army ended with elements of the Czech Brigade seizing control of a critical stretch of the Trans-Siberian, along much of which armoured trains belonging to both sides thundered eastwards and westwards laying waste towns and villages suspected of harbouring the enemy.

On 3 April 1918 German forces landed in Finland to help General Mannerheim stamp out the Red Finns – by which time Commander Cromie had proven himself a man of some stature. Learning that the *soviet matrosov* or sailors' council in Helsingfors had decided to demonstrate solidarity with their 'comrades' in the German navy by sailing their ships to Kiel harbour, he prepared to prevent this by torpedoing the Russian ships, after which he and his crews would almost certainly have been killed. Fortunately, saner heads among the revolutionary sailors realised that they had no maps of the German minefields and were more likely to end up at the bottom of the Baltic than to reach Kiel, so the British submarine crews were stood down and their vessels scuttled at sea. Most of the crews returned to Britain via Murmansk in January 1918, leaving Downie in command of a skeleton maintenance unit.

Meanwhile, Locker Lampson's armoured cars had returned to Murmansk after at one stage holding 25 miles of the front lines for ten days when Russian troops simply walked away from their trenches. Some of the loneliest men in Russia were a party of his men left behind in Kursk, 1,000 miles south of Archangel – which would be the scene of the world's biggest tank battle in August 1943. They were guarding a dump of 500 tons of Allied materiel, stockpiled for operations in 1918 that were now never going to take place. After increasingly menacing confrontations with the local commissars, they prudently withdrew in January 1918, abandoning the stores.

Aleksandrovsk had been adopted as the second Allied base in northern Russia because Archangel, which did have a railway link to the capital, was ice-bound for half the year. Traffic to the two ports in 1916 peaked at 1,200 Allied ships carrying everything from coal to 4.5 million tons of ammunition.[5] Guarding these stores and securing the perimeter was a hard job for non-Russians. Sir Ernest Shackleton had been given a major's commission by the War Office so that he could design and procure cold weather clothing for the British Expeditionary

Force. The result was British soldiers with no visible sign of rank or regiment. Some were dressed in what were called Burberry suits: padded smocks with a parka hood, inside which a Balaklava helmet and snow goggles were worn. Hands had to be gloved at all times and were doubly insulated by enormous padded mittens taped to the jacket so they could not be lost. Trousers were lined – or two pairs were worn, with snow boots, or over-boots, to which were tied snowshoes or skis. Other men in less rigorous conditions wore canvas greatcoats lined with fur turned inside-out and Russian *shlyapy* – thick felt caps with fur ear flaps. Instead of riding grandly on horses, in winter officers were chauffeured around on sledges drawn by mules, reindeer and dog teams, which bravely displayed a Union Jack in the hope that this would prevent them being shot at by sentries who might mistake them for invading Germans!

Although the original reason to send the North Russian Expeditionary Force was to prevent a German breakthrough seeing the considerable stockpile of munitions and other materiel fall into enemy hands, at Christmas of 1918 there were still 30,000 men – half of them British – in the Far North under General Ironside. As the festive season drew near, men of the Royal Army Medical Corps at Archangel posed for a group photograph to send home as a Christmas card, wearing fur hats and foul weather overclothes that made them resemble a bunch of bandits. Two of them were on skis and the others shod with Shackleton boots.

The war diary of 2/7th Durham Light Infantry recorded quite a jolly Christmas, with a special dinner for the men paid for by a contribution of five roubles per head from the CO's fund and five roubles from War Office funds. Each man also received a parcel of comforts from Queen Alexandra's Fund. Also: 'the weather was not nearly cold as had been anticipated. Apparently, some snow fell almost daily but on level ground it was never more than two feet deep. For getting around the base, twenty-six pairs of skis were drawn by the battalion.'[6]

That sounds like civilisation compared compared with the Christmas recorded by Gunner H. F. Goodright:

We were opposite Archangel town when, two days before Christmas, orders arrived for two guns to proceed to the front. Two officers and fifty-eight Other Ranks set out for Obozerskaya (a nowhere consisting of three wooden huts). There in one small clearing, the forest dark and silent in the moonlight, were many nationalities: Frenchmen from 21st Colonial Infantry, American hospital orderlies, British and White Russian soldiers, men and women *drozhky* drivers. So Christmas was spent by Centre Section 421 Battery RFA.[7]

Far off in Siberia, operating along the Trans-Siberian mainline and supplied through the Pacific port of Vladivostok, was a multinational Allied force under General Alfred Knox. They had little fighting to do, the main enemy being the cold as temperatures plummeted to minus 28°C at midday and minus 47°C at night. The War Diary of 25th Middlesex recorded several men suffering from frostbite and the diarist 'anxiously awaiting further supplies of fur hats, mitts and boots, *repeatedly asked for*'.[8]

In the Far North, in addition to the severe weather, hazards afloat ranged from ice floes to German mines laid by U-boats and the U-boats themselves, which claimed many victims. The mines were theoretically cleared by eight Russian minesweepers and twelve armed British trawlers, fitted out for minesweeping. As General Knox had found, they were not always effective.

Trotsky was beginning to have second thoughts about the Allied presence in the Far North, in case it was taken by OHL as a breach of the Brest-Litovsk agreement. The Senior Naval Officer in Murmansk was Rear Admiral Thomas Kemp. It was not a position one would wish on one's friend. His pleas for reinforcement were grudgingly met by the Admiralty, but at first fell on deaf ears in Washington, where President Wilson had no wish to become embroiled in Russia's internal affairs. In mid-April a party of British marines and some French personnel who had been training the Romanian army set out by train for Kandalaksha aboard an improvised armoured train hauled by a wood-burning locomotive, the 'armour' being sandbags piled along the edges of several flatbed trucks to protect the crews manning 3-pounder guns and machine guns. The round trip totalled 260 miles, but the White Finns rumoured to have been there had vanished.

However, the Murmansk *soviet* ignored Trotsky's orders to cut off all contact with local Allied forces because it considered they were the best insurance against Finnish and German invasion. This led to the strange accord signed by representatives of Britain, France and the United States and of the *soviet* ensuring the status quo. At Archangel the situation was very different. There, the town *soviet* obeyed instructions from the Bolshevik government not to fraternise or co-operate in any way with the Allies. Initially, this caused less friction than might be imagined because access to the port was iced up until the end of April 1918, when HMS *Alexander* forced a passage through the thinning ice with two merchant ships. The idea was to unload the merchant ships' cargoes of food in return for the *soviet* turning a blind eye to the crews loading back on board some of the huge stock of Allied materiel lying ashore.[9]

Permission to do this being refused by Moscow, a *chrezvechainaya komissiya* or special commission arrived in Murmansk to conscript local labour to load the disputed supplies on trains for immediate transportation to the south. By this stage, nothing in Russia was functioning normally, so although much materiel was spirited away in this manner, a great deal was rendered useless by unwilling, unskilled labourers. The commission also drew up a plan to destroy the enormous dump of munitions, which came to nothing due to lack of military engineers – fortunately for the town, which would have suffered considerable damage and loss of life. On 22 June the commission attempted to comply with German demands by declaring that all Allied shipping must leave Russian waters but was stalled by a diplomatic device when informed that such a decision could not be made locally, but must be referred to London and the other Allied capitals concerned.

During the stand-off a number of lightly armed Russian vessels surrounded *Alexander*. Apart from ordering the engine room to make steam so that the gun turrets could be revolved to return fire, Captain Hurt ensured the crew kept a low profile to avoid an exchange of fire. He went ashore that evening to protest, with the Allied consuls in the town, to the *soviet* about this threatening behaviour. After a hint that an important British naval force was on its way and would exact terrible revenge for any attack on one of His Majesty's ships, the president of the *soviet* said there had been a misunderstanding and gave a not very credible alibi for the day's events. The Russian vessels withdrew and tension was de-fused by Hurt's diplomatic approach.

The next alarm came when the Murmansk *soviet* informed Kemp that a mixed Finnish White and German force had indeed occupied the Russian fishing village of Pechenga (modern Petsamo in Finland). Disembarking from HMS *Cochrane* there, a strange force of forty marines and forty Red Guards, afterwards reinforced by more marines and a naval 12-pounder landed from HMS *Glory*, drove off the invaders in a series of skirmishes. There was now also a British general present to command the increasing number of army personnel. Major General Frederick Poole arrived on board USS *Olympia* bearing the grand-sounding title Commander-in-Chief, British Land Forces in North Russia – another job one would not wish on a friend.

NOTES

1. Zeman, p. 120.
2. G. Kennan, *Memoirs* (New York: Bantam Books, 1967), pp. 562–3.
3. It was renamed the all-Union Communist Party in 1925 and finally the Communist Party of the Soviet Union in 1952.
4. Occleshaw, pp. 92–3.
5. Wilson, p. 26.
6. Ibid, pp. 189–90.
7. Ibid, p. 190 (abridged).
8. Ibid, p. 188–9.
9. Wilson, pp. 29–31.

19

WE'RE HERE BECAUSE
WE'RE HERE

In June Admiral Kemp's pleas for reinforcements were at last rewarded by the arrival of the 600-strong *Syren* force under Major General Charles Maynard, bringing British ground forces up to brigade strength on the Kola Peninsula. Early in July Kemp reported to the Admiralty that the Murmansk *soviet* was in trouble with Moscow for signing the treaty with the British, American and French commanding officers on 6 July, under which they undertook not to inter-fere in political matters and to supply food and training facilities for locally raised Russian troops. At Archangel, the situation was very different: an armed stand-off with the Red garrison of 800 men defying the expeditionary forces. After *Elope* force landed there on 2 August with a French colonial battalion from Africa and a battalion of British territorials, a small detachment of Royal Marines and sixty-four US infantrymen, they succeeded in taking over the town and total British strength rose to 8,000 men. Added to this, early in September several thousand more American personnel arrived, plus 1,300 Italians and a mixed force of 1,200 Czechs, Serbs and Poles.

As has often happened since, friction flared up between the British old hands and the Americans, who acted as though they had come to 'rescue the Limeys'. The American commanding officer in particular resented being placed under British orders and not being taken into Poole's confidence about the intended role of his men in this theatre of operations. A contributing factor was that many of the 'American' volunteers were recent European immigrants with an inad-equate command of English![1] If reasonable discipline was kept within these Allied commands, the chaos among the Russian personnel in the Far North was total. On one occasion, some British sailors met 400 disgruntled Russian sailors from *Askold* and *Chesma*, who were walking from Murmansk to Petrograd – a total dis-tance of well over 500 miles across difficult terrain – to join the fight against the

White forces. *Askold* was a five-funnel cruiser nicknamed 'the packet of wood-bines' by British servicemen because all those funnels reminded them of the thin, cheap cigarettes of the time. Named for a legendary Varangian hero, the ship had had a chequered war career, including an explosion in the powder magazine for which four crewmen were sentenced to death.

It was at this time that the success of a Czech column in advancing to within 30 miles of Ekaterinburg, where the royal family was under house arrest in a villa belonging to a wealthy industrialist named Ipatiev, who had had the good sense to remove himself earlier, was the indirect cause of the whole family's murder. In the night of 16–17 July, on the grounds that the Cheka had exposed a conspiracy to rescue 'citizen Nikolai Romanov and his family', they were awoken and made to go into a semi-basement room. There, they were clumsily gunned down with pistols by the local commissar and his acolytes. The ex-Tsar died first, from multiple bullet wounds. His daughters were carrying many jewels sewn into their clothing, which apparently deflected some bullets, so that they had to be finished off with *coups de grâce*. The bodies were stripped and dumped into a well – some sources say it was a shallow disused mine shaft – later to be retrieved and partially burned before reburial in an unmarked grave. There they remained until 1979 when amateur archaeologists unearthed the remains of two adults and three girls. Identified by Russian, British and American laboratories using mitochondrial DNA techniques, they were reinterred in the St Peter and St Paul Cathedral in St Petersburg. Twenty-nine years later in 2008, another amateur enthusiast discovered nearby the remains of a young boy and a girl, subsequently identified as the missing princess and the *tsarevich* Alexei.

At the beginning of August, with the aim of preventing the Archangel *soviet* sending any more materiel south for use by the Red forces in the civil war, but against the advice of the Allied diplomatic representatives in the area, General Poole embarked a miscellaneous force of 100 Royal Marines, some British ground forces, men of the recently arrived French 21st Colonial Infantry Regiment, American marines and some Poles who had got stuck in Murmansk – a total of 1,500 men – to capture the city of Archangel. Transport was by an even stranger collection of ships, including two Russian destroyers crewed by RN personnel. He also had HMS *Nairana*, a requisitioned merchant ship adapted to launch its deck cargo of five Fairey Campania seaplanes, lifted by crane into and out of the water, and two Sopwith Camels launched from a special ramp on the deck. The flying and servicing personnel all belonged to the newly created Royal Air Force, but most still wore their old uniforms. The first engagement of this shipborne air force was to bomb a small fort at the mouth of the Northern Dvina.

There was a brief exchange of fire before the garrison legged it ashore. Leaving the French cruiser *Amiral Aube* to guard the mouth of the Dvina, the remaining force proceeded to Archangel, Poole ordered the town to be bombarded by RN vessels under the nominal command of a loyalist Russian captain called Georgi Chaplin. The town was captured with only a brief exchange of fire. However, the operation changed irrevocably the nature of relations with Russia. When the Allied ground forces moved into the town, they found most of the Bolshevik officials had fled and some citizens greeted their arrival with enthusiasm. The weather by then was torrid, with clouds of mosquitoes emerging from the tundra and finding ample human flesh on which to gorge when seamen deployed 'ashore' wore blue shorts with boots and blue puttees – and straw hats with anti-mosquito veils instead of sailors' caps.

On the Kola Peninsula, although Allied forces controlled the town of Murmansk, a decision was taken to eliminate the menace of Russian crewmen on board several ships anchored in the estuary. The vessels themselves posed little threat to Allied shipping, but the guns could have been used to fire on the town. On 3 August 150 marines from HMS *Glory*, USS *Olympia* and the French ship *Amiral Aube* arrested the sailors on board, after which an anglophile named Nikolai Tchaikovsky formed a short-lived regional government. *Askold* was re-commissioned as HMS *Glory IV* and *Chesma*, which had run aground, was left there to act as a prison hulk if necessary. The local threat was removed but Moscow was under pressure from the Germans to remove all Allied forces from Russian soil. Georgi Tchicherin, son of a tsarist diplomat, had been locked up in Brixton prison for several months on account of his anti-war activities. His release obtained by Trotsky in a swap for some British hostages, Tchicherin replaced him as Commissar for Foreign Affairs, with an understandable bias against Britain, as Bruce Lockhart was to find at his regular meetings with him.

A month after these dramas, expeditionary forces from Archangel had 'liberated' territory for 170 miles southwards along the Northern Dvina, supported on the mile-wide reaches of the river by two shallow-draught RN monitors, each armed with one 7.5in gun, one 12-pounder and a 6-pounder, and several captured Russian vessels manned by RN personnel. After a number of confrontations with Bolshevik river craft, floating mines and irregulars sniping from the river banks, the drive south was halted at the regional capital of Dvinskoi Bereznik, to consolidate a position before the rapid approach of winter made both land and riverine travel difficult. A second column had advanced along the railway line but only reached half as far south, due to demolition of vital bridges by the retreating Bolsheviks.

On paper, the Allied position in the Far North looked good, with the arrival of the US contingent that included engineers and medical staff to man a hospital in Archangel. However, their orders from President Wilson restricted them to guarding the Allied material stockpiled and 'organising the Russians' self-defence'[2] – whatever that might mean. Probably less than half the new arrivals were fit for combat anyway, due to an outbreak of virulent influenza during the voyage. This was probably a manifestation of the 'Spanish flu' epidemic that killed – estimates vary wildly – between 30 and 100 million people worldwide in that year and 1919. At any rate, the new arrivals continued dying after disembarking.

In the rapidly cooling weather of mid-September the RN sailors were kitted out again in normal bell-bottom uniform for ratings and fore-and-aft rig for petty officers and chief petty officers. This too rapidly proved inadequate as temperatures plunged, apparently taking the clothing stores by surprise,[3] although that year the river froze late, a meteorological quirk taken advantage of by Admiral Vikorist commanding the Bolshevik flotilla on the Northern Dvina, whose naval guns easily outranged the field guns mounted on the improvised British gunboats. The weather too was an enemy with the rapid, although belated, freezing of the river threatening to immobilise any Alled craft that stayed too long before heading north. The geography favoured the Bolsheviks in this theatre of the war, the river freezing later as one went further south.

Even with the increased numbers of western forces, Bruce Lockhart wrote later:

We (the British) had committed the unbelievable folly of landing at Archangel with fewer than twelve hundred men [sic]. It was a blunder comparable with the worst mistakes of the Crimean War. The weakness of our landing force in the North resulted in the loss of the Volga line and in the temporary collapse of the anti-Bolshevik movement in European Russia. In the absence of a strong lead from the Allies, the various counter-revolutionary groups began to quarrel and bicker among themselves. The accuracy of my dictum that the support we would receive from the Russians would be in direct proportion to the number of troops we sent, was speedily proved. The broad masses of the Russian people remained completely unmoved.

The consequences of this ill-considered venture were to be disastrous both to our prestige and to the fortunes of those Russians who supported us. It raised hopes which could not be fulfilled. It intensified the civil war and sent thousands of Russians to their deaths. Indirectly, it was responsible for the Terror.[4]

If that is a brief rendering of Bruce Lockhart's personal analysis, few people were better placed to analyse the confusing events of the time. In Soviet history, the Red Terror was triggered by a mentally unstable Socialist Revolutionary calling herself Dora Kaplan,[5] who had been in an ultra-hard labour camp and a prison for attempted assassination under the tsarist regime, where abuse she suffered included being flogged naked. On 30 August 1918, she allegedly accosted Lenin as he emerged from a meeting and fired three shots from a Browning automatic pistol. One bullet missed him but the others lodged in his chest and neck.

The injuries are not disputed, but some historians believe that Kaplan, whose eyesight had been seriously harmed by her mistreatment in prison, could not have been the would-be assassin – and go on to name several other candidates for this honour! Be that as it may, Lenin was transported back to the Kremlin, where surgeons could not remove the bullets, for which he needed to be taken to a hospital. Having been robbed in the streets of even his automatic pistol, he refused to go there, convinced that he would be murdered if he did so. The bullet in his neck contributed to his subsequent health problems and early death in January 1924. Kaplan was long dead by then, having been executed by a Cheka firing squad four days after the attack with what one might call unseemly haste to prevent any investigation of her guilt or innocence. The attack – whoever organised it – gave Lenin the 'justification' for launching a purge on the Socialist Revolutionaries, deemed collectively guilty. More than 800 were executed in the next weeks and thousands more during the ensuing Terror.

One surprising victim of the Terror was Bruce Lockhart, who had diplomatic status and was personally known to all the Bolshevik leaders. To put pressure on him, his Russian mistress named Moura was arrested first and his apartment ransacked. Then he read in the Bolshevik press that he and other Westerners were accused of conspiring in the *zagovor Lokkarta* – the Lockhart plot – to murder Lenin, sabotage strategic targets and reduce the populations of Moscow and Petrograd to starvation. It was a classic case of the technique use by the Soviet authorities for the next seventy years. Lockhart had indeed had many meetings with a shady character from Odessa who was known to his British controllers as Sidney Reilly, but whose real name was Rosenblum. Whether he was a British spy or an *agent provocateur* secretly working for the Bolsheviks, or a double agent, was never established.

Lockhart presented himself at the Cheka headquarters at No. 11 Lubyanka – formerly the head office of the All-Russian Insurance Company – and demanded to see Yakov Peters, Dzherzhinsky's deputy. He asked for Moura to be released on the grounds that Peters knew there was no such plot and, if there had been, she would have known nothing of it. Peters made a noncommittal reply before saying that it was very convenient to have Lockhart in his office because he had a warrant for his arrest. The other French and British conspirators, he said, were already under lock and key.[6]

For five days, Lockhart was subjected to nightly interrogation by Peters, but no physical maltreatment, although his state of mind can be imagined when he saw groups of tsarist politicians and intellectuals being herded into vans taking them to their execution as 'reprisal' for the failed assassination. Lockhart was then sent to the Kremlin, from where no political prisoner had emerged alive, and there lodged in the small suite of one of the ladies-in-waiting. His cell-mate was a Lett who had 'revealed the Lockhart plot' to the Cheka, and was there as a stool pigeon. Lockhart refused to speak to him, but did learn from a copy of *Izvestiya* that the Allied governments had protested strongly at the way their diplomats were being treated.

Lockhart continued to badger Peters about the unfortunate Moura until she was released and allowed to send him food parcels, his personal effects and books to read. Although allowed exercise in the Kremlin grounds, he was informed that he and the other 'conspirators' would be tried by the Revolutionary Tribunal, chaired by Public Prosecutor Nikolai Krylenko. A Pole acting as sentry during an exercise period told Lockhart in a friendly way that the guards were betting two-to-one he would be shot because a French diplomat named René Marchand had converted to Bolshevism and furnished the Cheka with 'proof' that the diplomats had planned sabotage, which would be used in the show trial – after which they would all be executed. Marchand later returned to France as a Communist activist. Among the other VIP prisoners in the Kremlin was General Brusilov, who 'looked ill, haggard and very old' and walked with a cane because of a leg injury. Another VIP was Maria Spiridonova, a Socialist Revolutionary who had been condemned to death already once for her part in the 1905 revolution and was now locked up for daring to criticise Lenin's policies. Although only in her early thirties, she 'looked ill and nervous, with great dark lines under her eyes. She was clumsily and carelessly dressed'.[7]

A more cheerful note entered Lockhart's conversations with his *chekisti* interrogators as Lenin began to recover, with them taking soundings as to whether Lockhart could arrange a deal to get rid of the Czechs and other interventionists in return for the Cheka allowing the alleged conspirators to leave Russia. In the event, a different deal was arranged, under which the hostages were expelled in return for the repatriation of Maxim Litvinov and other Bolshevik sympathisers in British gaols. Leaving the Kremlin under house arrest a day before his scheduled expulsion from Russia, Lockhart bade farewell to Moura, politely declined a Cheka offer of compensation for his belongings that had been stolen when the apartment was searched – and waited. Even the train taking the 'conspirators' to the Finnish frontier was late and the diplomats had to stay in it within sight of the border for three days until Litvinov and the others arrived from Britain for simultaneous exchange.[8] Back in London, Lockhart found himself an embarrassment. Although Churchill continued to make bellicose speeches, the Hands Off Russia movement was growing in strength and few soldiers wished to prolong their time in uniform. Although Foreign Office officials were relieved to have procured his release, there was so little interest in his account of the situation in Russia that he feared he would never obtain another posting.

In the Far North, General Poole had grandiose ideas for his forces that eventually totalled 20,000 men, hoping to drive south and link up with the Czech Legion and facilitate its withdrawal through Murmansk to take up arms again on the Western Front. This caused cold feet in the War Office, worried by protests from Washington about Poole's patrician attitude to the US forces in his command. Ordered home – as he thought for a spell of leave – he was replaced by a giant of a man by any standards. Major General Edmund Ironside stood 6ft 4ins in his stockinged feet and weighed 20 stone. Although given to understand on leaving Britain that he would serve as Poole's chief of staff, he found himself on arrival the senior Allied officer in theatre and rose to the occasion. An accomplished linguist, he was able to swear fluently in Russian, which stood him in good stead, impressing the small numbers of local Russians who were volunteering to fight against the Reds. He also had diplomatic skills entirely lacking in his predecessor that swiftly reduced the animosity between the British and American contingents.

With winter approaching, he put in hand a crash programme of preparations for sub-zero weather with no sunlight for several months, which included stockpiling of food and materiel and the requisition of 900 sledges, to be drawn by mules, reindeer and dogs. That he was right to do so was borne out on 11 November – the very day that the guns on the Western Front fell silent at 1100hrs local time – when a concerted Bolshevik attack of riverine and ground forces came in along the line of the Dvina after the withdrawal of the Allied gunboats, to avoid them being frozen in for the winter. Although eventually beaten off, this attack was tantamount to a declaration of war by the Bolshevik leadership. The position of the Allied forces in the Far North was anomalous in that the Allies were not at war with Russia, yet occupying Russian territory by armed force. Nor were the rank-and-file, or even the officers, happy about spending another winter in temperatures far below zero, instead of being sent home and demobilised. Perhaps the more politically conscious officers realised that they had crossed a line in the sand: they had ostensibly been sent to Northern Russia to safeguard the stocks of materiel in Archangel and prevent it being handed over to the Germans. With Germany having surrendered, what were they doing there?

The American personnel were even more vociferous in criticising their orders. If the war was over, why were they still in uniform? They were not the only ones wondering that. On 29 October a mutiny occurred in the locally recruited 1st Archangel Regiment. Their officers having removed themselves, General Ironside persuaded two other Russian officers to talk the men round. The ploy succeeded but, when ordered to the front, the regiment again refused to obey orders. US troops attacked their barracks with light mortars, rifle and machine gun fire. The mutineers surrendered but thirteen ringleaders were executed by a firing squad made up of their comrades. Ironside, who was far from being a mindless martinet, saw this incident as a sea change in the relations with the Russian White forces he was supposed to be commanding.

On 19 January 1919 a determined attack by a force of about 1,000 Reds with supporting artillery was launched against Shenkursk, an American-held outpost on the railway line some 180 miles south of Archangel. After forty-eight hours of desperate fighting, the Americans withdrew to avoid being outflanked. Although not a strategic disaster, the local defeat did serve to discourage Ironside's Russian allies, understandably fearful of reprisals by the Reds after the eventual departure of the Allied forces. The situation was exacerbated by the poor relations between the loyalist officers and their troops. To cap Ironside's other problems, a newly arrived battalion of the Yorkshire Regiment mutinied at Onega, 50 miles west of Archangel.[9]

He ordered the execution of two ex-Pay Corps sergeants, thought to be the ringleaders, who had spent the war in 'a cushy billet' in Britain and could not believe the conditions under which they were now serving. But King George V had decreed that no further executions of British personnel were to be carried out, since the period of hostilities against the Central Powers had ended and thousands of organised workers in Britain vehemently disapproved of the British intervention. The sentences were commuted to life imprisonment but more and more of the officers and men – a good number of whom had been wounded on the Western Front or were otherwise not 100 per cent fit – were asking openly what they were supposed to be doing in Russia. At home there was increasing unrest at the undeclared war being fought against the forces of a former Allied country and several influential newspapers were printing hostile articles. Even Winston Churchill, the ebullient Minister for War and the Air, was unable to force his colleagues in Lloyd George's Cabinet to enthuse over his plans for a new war against Lenin's 'godless hordes'. The ironic song of the men in the trenches said it all: 'We're here because we're here, because we're here, because we're here.'

Rear Admiral John Green had replaced Kemp in November 1918 with a brief that left it unclear whether he was there to cover and assist in the evacuation of the Allied forces, or pursue an aggressive policy. On 5 February 1919, he was informed by the War Cabinet that his ships were 'for active defence, in cooperation with the army, and only as far as positions then occupied by the military forces on the rivers'.[10] That geographical limitation went all the way to Ironside's southernmost line, some 200 miles from Archangel. The heterogeneous force of which he was commander eventually included twenty-two vessels, not all of which could be sent up-river because they were not sufficiently shallow-draught to be risked in summer on the Northern Dvina, which dried up into a succession of pools and sandbanks, and would have left them sitting ducks for Bolshevik guns on the banks. A strange convoy left Rosyth bound for Archangel on 4 May 1919 to make up the numbers, but got stuck in the ice of the White Sea for six days and had to be rescued by two Russian ice-breakers in foul weather.

The War Cabinet at last clarified the role of the British North Russian Expeditionary Force. It was to be withdrawn, but Churchill was authorised to make the necessary arrangements to cover the evacuation and sent two more brigades strictly for this purpose and not for sustained operations in Russia. The shape of things to come was apparent at the end of April, when the Dvina was still frozen over at Archangel and the ships there immobilised. Inevitably rumours about the impending Allied withdrawal circulated among the local Russian troops. The grandly titled 3rd North Russian Rifle Regiment was holding back a Bolshevik advance 80 miles up-river from Archangel when 300 men understandably decided to change sides, rather than risk death or worse when taken prisoner by the Reds after the Allies had left. These mutineers shot their officers and turned their weapons on their comrades of yesterday, who fled north under cover of a bombardment from Canadian gunners across the river and the shallow-draught monitor M23, which was the first RN vessel to reach so far south that year. But the crews of the riverine flotilla were not all Jolly Jack Tars by far. Bad food, the heat, the uncertainty of engaging an enemy who was free to roam and keep under cover while they were exposed on the open water led to a mutiny on HMS *Cicala*, which was put down by the senior naval officer present ordering the other vessels to train their guns on *Cicala*. Mutiny over, the ringleaders were court-martialled locally and sent back to Britain for punishment.

Given all the disadvantages of service in North Russia and the possibility of being killed far from home in a war that did not exist, it is amazing that there were any volunteers. However, the worse things got for the German forces in the Second World War, the more volunteers from France, the Netherlands and Scandinavia opted to join the Waffen-SS. The romance of a lost cause, it is called. And if ever a cause was lost, the north Russian intervention certainly was. Yet, something like 300 Australian veterans of Gallipoli, plus some New Zealanders, Canadians and South Africans did volunteer on their own accounts, their governments refusing to be involved. Perhaps the alternative was queuing up for dole at home? Formed into two brigades named after the commanders, St George Grogan and Sadlier-Jackson, they arrived in theatre in early June, facilitating the withdrawal of the American Northern Russia Expeditionary Force, all of whom were gone by mid-June, as was the Canadian contingent.

About 140 miles south of Archangel, at the confluence of the Varga and Dvina rivers, a motley air force was assembled after tsarist aviator Major Aleksandr Kazakov discovered dismantled Sopwith Strutters and Nieuports still in crates dumped at Bakaritsa, where they had been overlooked by the retreating Bolsheviks. Kazakov's multinational air force eventually comprised four DH4 bombers, Camels, Snipes and the Sopwiths flown by Russian, British and Canadian pilots – who were advised to carry a pistol and shoot themselves if forced to land behind the Bolshevik lines, where they were likely otherwise to be killed more unpleasantly.[11]

Incredibly, since the intervention was supposed to be winding down, a new aircraft carrier HMS *Argus* arrived with seventeen float-planes and RAF ground crew. Towards the end of August, after the first rains the water level in the river began to rise and a new hazard became apparent. The Russian watchmen on an ammunition barge were cooking their supper on an open stove which overturned and set fire to the vessel. With more courage than sense, the CO of the river boat *Glowworm* went alongside with a firefighting team to extinguish the flames. The barge blew up, killing four officers and seventeen men, and injuring many more.

On 27 September forty-five ships crammed with personnel, 4,500 Russians at risk for having collaborated with the expeditionary forces and stores considered too important to leave behind sailed from Archangel in a half-gale, winter's way of announcing its approach. The role of rearguard was played by HMS *Fox*, stationed offshore with its guns trained on the town in case of any last-minute trouble. How right those Russians were to leave was demonstated in February 1920 when the Red Army walked into Archangel and Murmansk and the optimistic stay-behinds had to pay the price of optimism. Captain Georgi Chaplin was there almost to the last day. On 17 February 1920 General Yevgeny Miller tried to negotiate terms with the Reds. Their reply was *Nyet!* Miller, his staff, some Russian army and navy officers and a few local VIPs left on Chaplin's icebreaker, which dropped them off in Norway five days later. Miller, like so many other tsarist officers with fluent French, decided to live in Paris where he was kidnapped and murdered by an NKVD hit team in September 1937.

NOTES

1. Neiberg and Jordan, p. 174.
2. Wilson, pp. 33–4.
3. Ibid, pp. 35–6.
4. Lockhart, p. 311 (abridged).
5. Real name Feiga Haimovna Roytblat.
6. Lockhart, pp. 324–5.
7. Ibid, pp. 334–5.
8. Ibid, p. 330–46.
9. Neiberg and Jordan, p. 178.
10. Wilson, p. 42.
11. Ibid, p. 47.

20

THE BIGGEST BATTLEFIELD OF ALL - SIBERIA

In the West today, Siberia is remembered as a land of living death where post-Revolutionary Russian governments confined millions of 'counter-revolutionary elements', common law criminals and dissidents in the Gulag camps. Before the Trans-Siberian mainline was constructed in the nineteenth century to connect St Petersburg on the Gulf of Finland with the Pacific at Vladivostok – the name means 'lord of the East', implying Russian ownership of the East Asian littoral – long columns of convicts were marched into Siberia, many of them in chains. They stopped at the border for men and women both to kiss the earth of Mother Russia and wrap a handful of it in a piece of cloth or paper, to treasure during their exile. Few of them felt anything for Siberia except that it was immensely vast and about as hospitable as the far side of the moon; even fewer expected to return.

Its enormous climatic differences over a north–south extent of 2,000 miles include one of the coldest inhabited places on the planet: *recorded* temperatures at Verkhoyansk range from a low of minus 69°C in mid-winter, when there is no daylight for two whole months, to a midsummer high of 37°C. The construction of the Trans-Siberian railway, which cost thousands of lives and was largely financed by foreign loans that were never repaid, was for two reasons: to open up the territory's rich mineral and other resources to commercial exploitation with slave labour; and to move troops quickly from European Russia to the Pacific littoral, a train journey of 5,000-plus miles. It was indeed the perceived threat to Japan posed by the second purpose of the railway that triggered the 1904–5 Russo-Japanese war which ended so disastrously for Russia, the enormous number of casualties being a major cause of the 1905 revolution.

How many diners in a Chinese restaurant realise that the Tsingtao beer which washes down their *dim sum* is made from a recipe first brewed at the

Germania brewery established in Tsingtao (modern Quangdao) after the German annexation of the port in 1898? What had originally been a poor Chinese fishing village became the home port of the Kaiserliche Marine's Ostasiatische Kreuzergeschwader or Far Eastern Squadron. On 7 November 1914 a joint British and Japanese force captured the port from the German navy, making passage to Vladivostok safe for supply ships that transported millions of tons of materiel, to be dumped there for forwarding along the Trans-Siberian to the tsarist forces fighting 5,000 miles to the west. Some supplies, including Japanese rifles and ammunition, were transported, but despite the French and British governments urging their Japanese allies to take responsibility for security in eastern Siberia, where geography favoured them, Tokyo was playing a different game, in which the real prize was the hoped-for seizure of Manchuria and a large slice of north-eastern China.

By December 1917 no less than 600,000 tons of undistributed supplies had accumulated at Vladivostok, although the Bolsheviks had taken command of the harbour area and were sending shipments to the Red forces. To discourage them, the Admiralty tried the technique that had worked so well against 'the lesser breeds without the law' through the nineteenth century, and sent a gunboat: the British Monmouth Class cruiser HMS *Suffolk* was despatched from Hong Kong. In a game of nautical chess, Tokyo moved two rather ancient battleships – *Asahi* and *Iwami* – to outbid the single cruiser flying the White Ensign in Vladivostok harbour, but Japanese ground forces made no move, even when it was again suggested that they would fulfil a useful function by taking over security of the Trans-Siberian.

The railway still functioned, after a fashion. Florence Farmborough had been given permission in Moscow to travel with a group of other foreigners on the longer, northern route to Vladivostok for repatriation. After leaving behind the Urals in March 1918 in the dirt and discomfort of what was termed 'a fourth-class

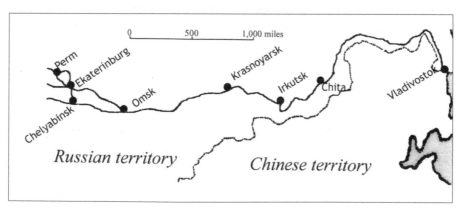

Simplified schematic of the eastern stretch of the Trans-Siberian railway.

carriage' attached to a freight train, their journey was described as 'twenty-seven days of hunger and fear'. From Perm to Ekaterinburg and on to Chelyabinsk they progressed slowly, their train making only 10 or 12 miles on some days after being repeatedly shunted into sidings as more important traffic thundered past. At Omsk, Red Guards stormed the foreigners' carriage, pushed aside the screen of male passengers and insisted on searching every compartment in the hope of finding fleeing tsarist officers to execute by firing squad. Finding women and children instead, they ignored the protests, the properly authorised Soviet travel papers and the British passports to search the baggage for arms or contraband. From Omsk, the train slowly continued to Irkutsk and skirted *svyatoe morye* – the holy sea of Lake Baikal – on the last stretch of the line to be completed, which had required forty tunnels to be blasted and hacked through mountains that came right down to the water.

The people in the virgin forests and tundra of Transbaikalia were Asiatics: Kalmuk and Buryat. Soon Chinese faces became more common. After Chita, the Manchurian border being closed, the train followed the mighty Amur River, where mutinying troops had killed the governor, but allowed his two teenage daughters to *walk* away. One of them, called Anna Nikolaevna, later taught the author at the Joint Services School for Linguists in Crail. That she was somewhat odd is understandable after living through that and having to beg her way with her sister on foot for 600 miles from Blagoveshchensk to Vladivostok, where they hoped to find a ship to take them to Europe. On the way, they soon learned that poor peasants would normally share food with them while richer people turned them away.

At least Florence Farmborough did not have to walk. After arrival at Vladivostok, the passengers on her train were immensely cheered to see His Majesty's ships *Suffolk* and *Kent* moored in the harbour. British, American, French, Belgian, Italian and Japanese soldiers patrolled the streets, thronged with thousands of civilian refugees of many nationalities. Whilst Red Guards were still a nuisance, their worst excesses were restrained by the Allied presence. She was told this was because a White general named Semyonov – but who behaved more like the Baikal Cossack *ataman* or warlord that he also was – was expected shortly to drive the Bolsheviks out of the port-city altogether. At night none of the passengers left the train, which was parked in a coal siding, because shots were frequently heard. The greatest joy for the weary, and very hungry, travellers was to find that food could freely be purchased in the Chinese street market, at a price. Spirits fell somewhat when a Chinese ship sailed into harbour flying a yellow fever flag and they learned that there was an epidemic of typhoid and smallpox among the undernourished coolies working as dockers.

After three weeks in the coal siding, guarded at night by a shore patrol from HMS *Suffolk*, great was their excitement at the arrival of a passenger ship to take them to San Francisco. Embarking themselves and their luggage under the protection of American sailors who beat off any interference from the locals and from other refugees who did not have the right papers, Florence and her exhausted companions settled into their overcrowded cabins, revelling in clean bed linen, clean towels and even clean curtains at the portholes. They went on deck to be played out of harbour by Royal Navy, US Navy and Japanese bands on the decks of the ships moored there.[1]

Among the passengers on board was the indomitable Maria Bochkaryova, who had narrowly escaped execution by Red Guards on two occasions since being invalided back from the front. Early in 1918 she had been asked by loyalists in Petrograd to take a message to White Army commander General Lavr Kornilov. After fulfilling that mission, she was again detained by the Bolsheviks and sentenced to be executed until a soldier who had served with her in 1915 convinced his comrades to stay her execution. Thanks to him, she was granted an external passport instead, allowing her to leave for Vladivostok, en route to the USA. There, she dictated her memoirs to an émigré Russian journalist and met President Woodrow Wilson – and later King George V in London – to plead for Western intervention forces to crush the Bolsheviks.

Although she could certainly have requested political asylum in the West, she begged the War Office to let her return to Russia and continue the fight. In August 1918 she landed in Archangel, where she attempted to form another women's combat unit without success. In April of the following year, she returned to her home town of Tomsk, hoping to recruit a women's medical unit to serve under Admiral Kolchak. Captured by Bolsheviks, she was interrogated in Krasnoyarsk and sentenced again to death as *vrag naroda* – an enemy of the people. Sentence was carried out by firing squad on 16 May 1920. So ended the life of one of the bravest people to fight on the Russian fronts.[2]

It has to be admitted that both sides in the civil war committed atrocities. The Whites justified this by regarding the enemy as traitors to Russia. The Reds regarded them as traitors to the Revolution. General Semyonov had one of the worst records, frequently holding hostages for ransom and holding up trains belonging to both sides like a bandit. However, he had his uses, so the British decided in February 1918 to pay him £10,000 a month. Two months later, the subsidy was cancelled, since his 'army' was more interested in looting than fighting. With smaller handouts from the French, he stayed in the region. To stop the large-scale pilfering of stores from the widely separated dumps of Allied stores, the captain of *Suffolk* proposed landing Allied ground forces, meanwhile deploying fifty Royal Marines in a cordon around the British Consulate. The Japanese took off the velvet gloves and landed 500 troops to restore order, but by 25 April these troops were withdrawn and the Bolsheviks were again masters of the port, the city and the stores.

A Belgian armoured car corps arrived – *sans* armoured cars or guns, which they had sabotaged after being given permission to withdraw via Vladivostok. Next came some of the Czech Legion, now several thousand men strong – and all impatient to get out of Russia and participate in the liberation of their homeland. The war on the Western Front was, of course, still ongoing at this point. Suffering some casualties, they kicked the Bolsheviks out of Vladivostok after just fifty-eight days of skirmishes and demanded stores from the Allied dumps so they could travel back along the railway to rescue the large number of their comrades far in the rear, who had taken control of the major Siberian city of Irkutsk after fighting with the Bolsheviks there. These were men who, forcibly conscripted by the Central Powers, had been taken prisoner and then volunteered to go back into action until Trotsky signed the second Treaty of Brest-Litovsk. It says something about their *esprit de corps* that the slogan painted on the cattle wagons in which they lived on the railway was 'Each of us is a brick, together we are a rock'.

The original intention had been to withdraw the Czech Legion through Archangel but, to delay the Legion's arrival on the Western Front, the Germans had pressured Trotsky into changing the exit route to the far longer and more difficult journey via Vladivostok. Deliberate obstruction from the Bolshevik authorities played a part in further delays, but the Trans-Siberian was genuinely over-loaded with trainloads of Central Powers POWs who had been released from the camps in Siberia and were required under the Treaty of Brest-Litovsk to be repatriated speedily, so the Czechs had a low priority on the line. Their progress stopped entirely at Chelyabinsk on 14 May 1918, when a released POW being repatriated westwards threw a stone or piece of metal that killed a legionnaire. Tensions between the legionnaires and their westbound compatriots, whom they regarded as traitors, were high. Hauling the stone-thrower off his train, the legionnaires lynched him on the spot. After local Bolsheviks arrested several Czechs for this, other legionnaires occupied the whole city with some bloodshed and released their comrades, proceeding to take over Petropoavlovsk, Kurgan, Novo-Nikolayevsk and several other towns along the railway until they were masters of the whole stretch of the Trans-Siberian from the Urals to Lake Baikal.

Some sources, however, disagree as to exactly why and how the Czechs became masters of the strategic railway line. As so often after Brest-Litovsk, when Russian history was completely re-written in accordance with the party line and Allied accounts conflict, confusion rules. Some historians believe that the take-over of thousands of miles of track could not have been accomplished spontaneously, which would indicate that British and/or French money was made available to a body calling itself the Czech National Council, which enabled the extended coordination called for by such an exercise in hostile, Bolshevik, territory.

In early July 1918, after Japan had landed some 70,000 troops in eastern Siberia and Manchuria to seize control of the Chinese stretch of the Trans-Siberian as far as Chita, President Woodrow Wilson seemed suddenly to realise that the billion dollars-worth of US materiel sitting in warehouses at Vladivostok and in the Far North was being filched away to the Red Army, fighting not the Central Powers as planned but the interventionist forces. On 2 August General William Graves was ordered to meet Secretary for War Newton Baker in Kansas, where he was instructed not to proceed to France with US 8th Division, but to take command of an American Expeditionary Force of 8,000 US servicemen being shipped to Vladivostok to protect the stores and assist the Czechs to extricate themselves from Russian territory – but not to fight Russian troops! It was like ordering a man to save a child from a crocodile without hurting the crocodile.

France also sent a battalion of colonial soldiers from Vietnam. A battalion of the 25th Middlesex Regiment arrived fom Hong Kong for garrison duty, the men being almost all medically unfit for active service. General Knox returned to the scene, arriving at the head of a British Military Mission with responsibility for setting up a training school for the White forces 4,000 miles to the west at Ekaterinburg – and organising the rear area, including all those stores. There were even some Canadians for a while, conscripted in fraught conditions by a coalition government that was unsure whether to back Britain's intervention or not, but agreed to send a Canadian Siberian Expeditionary Force (CSEF) on condition that it was not to be sent into action! A number of men mutinied before even embarking at Vancouver, which resulted in a dozen courts martial.

After arrival at Vladivostok, pressure from General Knox and others to support Kolchak's troops against the Bolsheviks was resisted by Canadian Brigadier General James Elmsley, although he did contribute guards to escort supply trains and despatched a token force of one lieutenant colonel and fifty-five men to Omsk, where they were to act as headquarters staff for the British battalions there – in other words, standing sentry to free British soldiers for more active service. By February 1919 questions were being asked in the Canadian parliament as to why, the war being over, Canadian citizens were still deployed in Russia. One Party leader said explicitly: 'The question of how Russia shall settle her internal affairs is her concern – not ours.'[3] Fortuitously, a few Canadians just missed seeing action in April 1919 after American troops refused to get involved in a rescue column tasked with driving off some Bolsheviks attempting to liberate comrades taken prisoner by Kolchak's forces, but by the time they arrived on the scene, the Bolsheviks had fled. Between late April and early June all the CSEF was withdrawn.

By September 1918 the Czechs had control of the Trans-Siberian from the Pacific to Samara (modern Kyubyshev) and Kazan, only 400 miles east of Moscow. Admiral Kolchak held the title Supreme Ruler of Russia after a murky deal that was attributed to Knox and the British Secret Service – and also because he had managed to secure a significant part of the Russian gold reserves, which travelled everywhere with him on his armoured train. However, this did not go down well with the other White generals, who regarded him as an amateur in ground war-fare – which he was. Kolchak's increasingly large staff became too top-heavy for him to exercise command efficiently, and included for a time General Maurice Janin, head of the French military mission, as well as a gung-ho officer from *Suffolk* by the name of Commander Wolfe-Murray. By a combination of circumstances, on 13 October 1918 Kolchak reached Omsk and set up a provisional White government there. In July it had seemed briefly possible that the Czechs might unseat the whole Bolshevik regime as their columns advanced towards Saratova and Kazan, only 400 miles from Moscow, but news of the General Armistice on 11 November caused considerable unrest in their ranks. Why, the Czech and Slovak legionnaires asked, are we still fighting in Russia when our homelands have been freed from German and Austro-Hungarian domination under the terms of the Armistice? At the end of the year, all the Czech columns were pulling back eastwards, so that, when Kolchak's forces looked likely to reach Moscow and link up with a British force from Archangel in the spring of 1919, the game was lost after the Czechs failed to support his initiative.

The resilient Joseph Bumby described the chaos of being stuck in Petropavlovsk with 30,000 other European ex-POWs:

> There was no accommodation for so many men, so we had to sleep on the pavements. Then we found an apartment in the house of a trader in Tatar goods and 250 men lived on the first floor above his shop and in the next house. For food, we had to walk about one hour to the central kitchen, where you could eat from 9 a.m. to 3 p.m. For a lunch there, we had soup with a piece of meat the size of a sparrow's head and *kasha* or buckwheat gruel. It was already snowing in early October, so they were building a wooden camp of huge sheds, each with two stoves to warm 500 men. We had very little cash left. Even water had to be paid for. When some mail arrived, everything quietened down, especially when we got the Czech-language newspaper from Kiev.[4]

Shore patrols from *Suffolk* and *Kent* were not confined to Vladivostok city and port. The most distant mission the RN personnel undertook was executed by a mixed bag of thirty-three British volunteers from *Kent* under Royal Marine Captain Thomas Jameson which departed in April 1919 to join the Kama River Flotilla after *Suffolk*'s artificers fitted out an armoured train with a 6in naval gun and four 12-pounders. This headed west to support White and Czech forces. The medically unfit men from Middlesex found themselves in action after all, along the line of the Ussuri River, north of Vladivostok. Others were posted to Knox's training school at Ekaterinburg, along with – believe it or not – a battalion of cycle troops from the Hampshire Regiment. Both battalions were withdrawn from the theatre in November 1919.

Patrolling the immense Kama, a major tributary of the Volga some 600 miles east of Moscow and 3,000 miles inland from Vladivostok, was no sinecure. The flotilla was composed of eighteen craft under the command of Rear Admiral Nikolai Smirnov. Allotted a supernumerary paddle-wheel tug and a river barge, on which to mount the naval guns they had brought with them, the RN personnel named these two craft *Kent* and *Suffolk*. Flying the White Ensign, they distinguished themselves by being the only British forces under Russian command.[5] Placed on the ration strength of Smirnov's flotilla, they lived on a diet of stale or mouldy black bread and bear meat with whatever locally grown vegetables they could purchase.

With the advent of winter, poor food and inadequate clothing would have caused problems, but the guns they had brought were already suffering excessive wear from sustained use long before then. The 6in gun fired 356 rounds in two days of engagements. At the end of June, Smirnov decided that the Reds were getting too close for comfort and relocated eastwards to Omsk. The RN team stripped all the armament off the two boats and loaded it onto a train with the help of conscripted women labourers. Some muscle, those ladies! A total of 225 tons had to be transported and loaded, the 6in gun alone weighing nearly seven tons. The two vessels were then scuttled to deny them to the enemy. With the city of Perm crowded by thousands of refugees fleeing the advancing Reds and all trying to find transport to the east, Captain Jameson took an armed squad to the marshalling yards, commandeered a locomotive at gunpoint and had it coupled up to the British train on 29 June. That he was right to do this was abundantly clear when the Reds marched into the city just three hours after the train pulled out – next stop Omsk, 1,000 miles to the east. There, Jameson handed over much of the equipment to the Whites, although it was already obvious that time was running out for Kolchak. Bidding farewell to the other naval personnel, Wolfe-Murray stuck it out alone as an adviser to the admiral while Jameson took command of the train, travelling through a vast zone suffering an epidemic of cholera and typhus, where he kept railway staff at a distance with loaded rifles, to avoid infection.[6]

By mid-September, Kolchak's bolt had been shot. His last reserves having been beaten, he withdrew his HQ to Irkutsk on the Angara River, which runs into Lake Baikal – from where there was no retreat. In January 1920 he 'resigned' as Commander-in-Chief White forces, passing command to General Anton Denikin in southern Russia. Having alienated the Czech Legion and the Japanese with typically Russian xenophobia, Kolchak was now abandoned also by the British, and 'traded' by General Janin to the Reds, together with the gold, in order to buy free passage along the railway for the 50,000 Czechs, Poles, Yugoslavs and other Europeans stuck at Irkutsk, so that they could travel through to Vladivostok. General Janin became known as 'the general without honour' for having betrayed the Russian leader. Whether he was right to do so or not, one would have to ask the 50,000 men who might otherwise have been lost forever in the vastness of Siberia that swallowed up 100 times more people than that with no difficulty in the Gulag years.

By the end of December 1919 men of the Czech Legion were already being shipped back to Europe from Vladivostok, the evacuation being completed a few months later. Fortunately for history, Tomek, Filacek and Bumby were among them. Inevitably, Kolchak was executed by firing squad on 7 February 1920. As to what became of the Russian gold bullion known to be kept on his armoured train, there is a mystery.

Tourists visiting Prague who look for the McDonald's fast food outlet on Boulevard Wilsonova may stray down the nearby street named Na Poříčí. There, they will find an extraordinary Cubist building that was obviously very expensive to build. Commissioned as the offices of Legionářská Banka – the bank of the legionnaires – it is the work of the famous architect Josef Gočár, whose services did not come cheaply, and incorporates the work of several well-known sculptors. The idea of a bank to help out legionnaires who would be in financial straits when they got home was mooted by a number of senior officers in the Legion before they left Russia. Some say that the funds to build the bank came out of savings the legionnaires had put by from their meagre pay in Siberia, but unconfirmed reports infer that some at least of the gold bullion on Kolchak's train was brought back to Prague and financed the construction of Legionářská Banka. Next to the famous Charles Bridge in Prague is a bridge ceremonially opened in 1904 by Emperor Franz Josef I and named in his honour. In a microcosm of Czech history, it was renamed Most Legii – the Bridge of the Legions – twenty years later and, twenty years after that, under the German occupation, Smetana Bridge. The Communists who took over after 1948 renamed it again as 1st May Bridge. With them too consigned to history, it is again called Bridge of the Legions.

The American ground troops were evacuated from Vladivostok in April 1920. In October of that year some 70,000 Eastern European soldiers who had survived the Russian front hostilities, the POW camps in Siberia and the civil war embarked on eight British troopships, sent to bring them back to Europe. After their departure some kind of law and order was kept by the Japanese ground forces because the government in Tokyo had it in mind to exploit the chaos in Russia to regain the territory Japan had occupied and then lost under the terms of the peace conference after the war of 1904–5. They too were withdrawn in the autumn, when a variety of vessels embarked the last thousands of desperate refugees, destination the international concessions in Shanghai. These included the author's teacher Anna Nikolaevna. Last to leave was HMS Carlisle, which cleared the port one week after the Reds occupied Vladivostok on 23 October 1922.[7]

NOTES

1. Farmborough, pp. 393–408.
2. Ibid.
3. J.E. Skuce, *CSEF 1918–1919* (Ottawa: Access to History Publications, 1990), p. 9.
4. Bumby account.
5. Wilson, pp. 60–1.
6. Ibid, pp. 62–4.
7. Ibid, p. 65–5.

21

THE RAINBOW OF DEATH

Of all the Allied nations Italy played least part in the interventions, but 2,000 French troops landed at the Black Sea port of Odessa – then the largest city in Ukraine – on 18 December 1918, a few days after the Germans had evacuated the city. In addition to French and French colonial troops from North and West Africa, there were also Greek and Romanian contingents.

The most important White general in the region was General Anton Denikin. He was a career soldier who first distinguished himself in the Brusilov offensive, and afterwards became chief of staff to three successive commanders-in-chief: Alekseyev, Brusilov and Kornilov. Imprisoned for supporting Kornilov's failed coup, he escaped in the chaos of the October Revolution. After Kornilov's death in April 1918, command of the so-called White Volunteer Army passed to Denikin, who had to retreat to the Don in terrible weather conditions. Regrouping, he led what looked like being a successful drive on Moscow in summer 1919, but was foiled by Trotsky forming a temporary alliance with Nestor Makhno's Black Army of Ukrainian anarchists. Makhno attacked Denikin's extended lines of supply and defeated him at Orel, 400 miles south of Moscow, in October 1919. Having weakened the Ukrainians, Trotsky then attacked and defeated Makhno's force before driving Denikin's Whites south, where they enforced a White Terror, targeting particularly the Jews with the logic that they were an evil force epitomised by the large percentage of Jewish activists in the Bolshevik movement.

Why the men in the French contingent thought they were there is a mystery. Except during the Crimean war, their country had no connection with this territory and the morale of France's troops was already low after the massive mutinies in 1917 caused by the appalling slaughter due to bad generalship on the Western Front that had claimed the lives of so many of their comrades.

With the arrival of the other contingents, a total of 90,000 Allied soldiers occupied a 120-mile swathe of territory 50 miles deep along the northern littoral of the Black Sea from the Romanian border to Kherson. In addition to Denikin and the Reds, also active in the area were Ukrainian separatist forces and a motley army of Cossacks under their leader, a former gendarme who had taken the name and style of Ataman Nikifor Grigoriev. Having served as a staff captain in the tsarist army, after Brest-Litovsk he fought at different times and with different ranks both for and against the Reds, Denikin's Whites, the Green Army and the Black Army, indulging his rabid anti-Semitism in pogroms that claimed more than 6,000 victims.

The Romanians were there to ensure the security of formerly Russian-occupied Moldavia, which bounded the Ukraine on the west. The city of Kherson had been founded as a Greek trading port on the River Dnepr 2,500 years earlier. Whether for historical reasons or not, the Greek force had been allocated the right of the line, based on Kherson, where their main enemies were Grigoriev's Cossacks. Once the decision to abandon the whole enterprise was taken early in 1919 and the Greeks started to withdraw to the coast, they apparently massacred 500 civilians. In retaliation, Grigoriev decreed that all Greeks taken prisoner should be shot – and they were. By mid-April 1919 Odessa had fallen to the Reds and the Allied forces were busily destroying all their stores and materiel – except for a few tanks that were re-commissioned by the Reds – and embarked the surviving Greeks, some Poles, 10,000 men of Denikin's army and 30,000 Russian civilians who had reason to fear the Bolshevik take-over.[1]

Various other evacuations were in train. On 23 April a mixed force of 3,500 French and Greek troops found themselves in a pocket around Sevastopol, facing the advancing Reds with no hope except evacuation by sea. The situation was complicated by a mutiny on board the French destroyer *Protêt* on 20 April, led by André Marty, an engineer whose name would become infamous when he was the chief commissar of the International Brigades during the civil war in Spain, and was responsible for many executions of loyal Communist comrades whose sole offence was not to toe the Moscow line. His plan in the Crimea was to take over *Protêt* and hand it over to the Bolshevik navy. Although he was clapped in irons and transferred to another vessel to await trial, a wave of mutinies in the French Black Sea Fleet saw the French flag hauled down on six other ships. The battleship *France* even displayed the Red Flag, which earned its crew a swift return to Toulon, where twenty-three mutineers were given varying sentences. Marty emerged from prison in 1923 and went on to be elected a Communist *député* before finding his lethal niche as a murderer in Spain.

During the mutinies, disaffected sailors came ashore looking for trouble. Some were shot by Greek troops using live ammunition to disperse a pro-Bolshevik demonstration in Sevastopol. The crews of the other French ships returned to duty after being promised that they would not be involved in active operations, and would very shortly be repatriated in any case. The final decision of Admiral Jean-François Amet was further complicated by the accidental grounding of a French battleship which needed considerable repairs and could not be abandoned. He spun out negotiations with the Bolshevik commanders to gain time for the ship to be made seaworthy. Meanwhile Vice Admiral Somerset Calthorpe, the Royal Navy Commander-in-Chief Mediterranean and High Commissioner in Constantinople, arrived in the battleship HMS *Iron Duke*.

Uncompromised by Amet's negotiations, RN ships and the Greek battleship *Lemnos* shelled Bolshevik positions on the peninsula and RN personnel set about sabotaging the entire fleet of Russian battleships, cruisers and destroyers in the harbour, scuttling fifteen submersibles at sea. At one point relations between the French sailors and the Greeks deteriorated to the point where they were only prevented from opening fire on *Lemnos* at point-blank range by their officers removing the firing mechanism from the French ships' guns. Admiral Amet finally agreed a cease-fire on 26 April, gaining two more days, so that the last Allied troops in Sevastopol were evacuated on 28 April, together with 33,000 Russian civilians.

In June, Denikin's forces broke through the Red positions hemming them in on the Kerch peninsula, which separates the the north-eastern corner of the Black Sea from the Sea of Azov. This local success was largely due to Trotsky withdrawing forces to fight off Kolchak's advance that had reached within 400 miles of Moscow. With some help from RAF aircraft and fliers, Denikin reached Sevastopol and pressed on to Kiev and Odessa, pressing further north to Orel – at which moment they were only 250 miles south of Moscow – in mid-October. Had it been possible to concert this advance with Kolchak's, and squeeze the Red Army from two directions, the whole course of the civil war might have been different.

Instead, the turn of the year saw Denikin routed and pushed back into the Ukraine. By early February it was obvious that another major evacuation by sea was the only way to save lives. Royal Navy, British merchant ships and other vessels headed for Odessa, to find scenes of panic as thousands of civilians and soldiers fought to gain access to the jetties, severely encumbered by the abandoned cars, carriages and baggage of the fortunate ones already embarked. The SS *Rio Negro* under a British captain could normally accommodate 750 passengers, but took on board 1,500 hungry and sick refugees, many of them suffering from the bitter winter weather, but grabbing literally their last chance of escape. The RN sentries enforcing discipline at the gangway had to run for their lives as Bolshevik machine guns opened up on them after *Rio Negro* cast off.

Denikin, meanwhile, was being pushed further and further east. In abandoning Novorossisk – which had been his army's main port of entry for arms, ammunition and even a half-million British uniforms – at the end of March, the panic evacuation by sea was accompanied by wholesale destruction ashore of stores before the British Military Mission was withdrawn. In addition to Royal Navy and British military presence, USS *Biddle* of the American Black Sea Squadron landed Rear Admiral Newton McCully for a fact-finding tour to advise President Wilson what should be done. After meeting both Denikin and one of the Red Army commanders, he decided the situation was too fraught to get involved in, even had domestic American opinion favoured another intervention. His brief from the White House was merely to protect the lives of American dependents but, to McCully's eternal credit, appreciating what was going to happen after the Bolshevik take-over, he disregarded his orders and used the cruiser USS *Galveston*, three destroyers and a merchant vessel to evacuate 70,000 civilian refugees on the night of 26–27 March as the Bolsheviks took the city and port. On 1 April a less spectacular American and British naval evacuation saved more civilians and White soldiers by evacuation from the nearby port of Tuapse.

In April 1920 General Denikin handed command of what was left of his army to General Pyotr Wrangel, leaving Russia to settle in France and write his memoirs, which spread over five volumes. As his name implies, Wrangel was a Balt of German origin. He had had severe differences of opinion over strategy with Denikin, who forced his resignation in February 1920. A month later, Denikin was forced to resign and Wrangel was begged by the other White commanders to return from his brief exile in Constantinople. After succeeding Denikin, Wrangel had a stroke of luck in the shape of the simultaneous three-way war between Poland, Ukraine and the Bolsheviks, which obliged Trotsky once again to take the pressure off the Crimean front. Wrangel's strict but fair rule in the White-occupied territory made it briefly seem that he was there to stay, but the Reds eventually drove his rump army into a pocket on the Crimean peninsula.

There Wrangel held out long enough for 150,000 soldiers, family members and civilian sympathisers to be evacuated in French, American and Russian warships and merchant vessels from Sevastopol across the Black Sea to Turkey and onward to Yugoslavia, Bulgaria and elsewhere. As historian Michael Wilson comments: 'Forbidden by their government to help (in this evacuation), it was a distressing time for the men of the Royal Navy, especially as the British government had on many occasions been the strongest supporter of the White cause of all the Allied governments.'[2] London was here exploiting the technicality that it had not formally recognised Wrangel's regime, but it was a distasteful episode.

The last military and civilian evacuees left with Wrangel on board the *General Kornilov* on 14 November. Wrangel then retired to live on his yacht moored at Constantinople. This was rammed and sunk by an Italian steamer that had sailed from Soviet-held Batum. Being ashore at the time of the sinking, Wrangel was unharmed by what was regarded as a Bolshevik assassination plot. In the Russian diaspora he was regarded by many as the most likely figurehead for any revanchist adventure – which never took place. In 1928 his sudden death in Brussels led to rumours that he had been poisoned by an agent of Smersh, the Soviet assassination network.[3] Other politically or militarily important émigrés were definitely assassinated in this way, an exception being Anton Denikin, who lived through the Second World War in German-occupied France. For the last two years of his life, he moved to New York City, dying in 1947 at the age of seventy-four.

Several hundred of the White officers and NCOs stranded without money or even food in Constantinople accepted free passage on French ships that took them to Tunisia, where the experienced Cossack, Polish and Russian cavalrymen were recruited to form the 1st Cavalry Regiment of the French Foreign Legion. Because so many of these men had titles of nobility, it was dubbed 'le Royal Etranger'. A joke of the time has Lt Col Frédéric Rollet – later to be the Legion's commanding general – inspecting a new intake and asking a new recruit the usual question about what he had done before enlisting. The reply was: 'I was a general, colonel.'[4]

During the First World War the Baltic had been a no-go area for the Royal Navy, except for the small number of submersibles that were able to sneak in. However, two days after the cease-fire on the Western Front, Foreign Secretary Arthur Balfour chaired a meeting to discuss an oblique way of possibly weakening Lenin's Bolshevik government – by preventing it from recovering all the territory of the imperial Russian empire. It was no secret that the Baltic states had long been yearning for independence from Russian hegemony, and they were now easily accessible from Britain, so the meeting explored whether the three states could use some of the now surplus materiel stockpiled for use against the Central Powers. With much of the eastern Baltic territory still occupied by German forces – whose arrival had been welcomed by the large German-speaking population there – and in considerable disarray, it was decided not to make a military intervention with ground forces.

The better option seemed to be to detach to the Baltic 6th Light Cruiser Squadron commanded by Rear Admiral Edwin Alexander-Sinclair together with a destroyer screen, both to land supplies and support by naval bombardment, if necessary, action by the Baltic states to secure their independence. Since the sea was dotted with German and Russian mines, many of which had broken loose from their moorings and drifted far from the charted minefields, minesweepers were included as part of this force. The complications were twofold: there was a problem supplying coal for them, which did not apply to the larger, oil-fired ships; secondly they had to turn back early as the northern Baltic iced over, leaving the larger ships vulnerable to this menace.

Under the terms of the Armistice, Germany agreed to evacuate its troops and had done so in Estonia, after which the Red Army invaded. Prime Minister

Konstantin Pats requested British help. The first form this took was the delivery of arms and ammunition to the Latvian and Estonian governments, but with the warning that no British ground troops would be sent. The RN vessels then continued north to blockade the Soviet naval base on Kronstadt Island and prevent the fleet there from sailing to bombard targets in Estonia and Latvia. Although it was debatable whether the unrest in the Russian fleet would permit ships to be readied for sea, this was a prudent measure in any case.

An astonishing 'battle' that earned a VC for Lieutenant Augustus Agar took place there. Several 60ft high-speed coastal motor boats (CMBs) were based just inside Finnish territory and used in agent-landing-and-recovery missions of considerable danger. Lieutenant Agar also led a two-boat attack on the Bolshevik cruiser *Oleg* inside the Kronstadt anchorage and sank it with a torpedo. When one realises that the torpedo had to be dropped into the water stern-first so that a tug on the control wire could activate the engine – after which the CMB had to get out of the way fast! – it becomes clear that his courage, let alone his achievement, merited the award. A warrior with writing talent, Agar left a very readable account of his operations in the Baltic.[5]

The first casualty of Alexander-Sinclair's force was the cruiser HMS *Cassandra*, sunk by a drifting mine on 5 December. The weather was also against the navy. The cruiser HMS *Calypso* grounded on a sunken wreck in Libau and two of the destroyers also had to return for repairs after colliding in fog. Naval commanders seemed to be particularly good at interpreting positively the sometimes Delphic instructions from their political masters. Alexander-Sinclair took on board in the metaphorical sense the real risk of a pro-Bolshevik rising in Estonia in concert with the Russian incursions that had already reached within 40 miles of the capital. With two cruisers and five destroyers, he therefore bombarded targets in the rear of the Bolshevik advance, destroying their lines of communication before leaving two cruisers off the coast of Estonia and departing with the rest to Libau in Latvia, also threatened by a Red advance.

On Boxing Day many of the British officers and men were being feted ashore in Reval when they found themselves the target of shells from a Russian destroyer standing offshore, which ran aground due to incompetent seamanship and was taken as prize by the destroyer HMS *Wakeful*. Another Soviet ship standing offshore was also captured and handed over to Estonia, which re-commissioned both vessels under Estonian names in its own navy.

Alexander-Sinclair faced an even more knotty problem in Latvia, where the strongest support for anti-Bolshevik Prime Minister Karlis Ulmanis was in the hinterland and therefore could not be supported from the sea. The coastal regions were pro-Bolshevik and in some areas where Baltic Germans predominated the population wanted the German troops to remain. Two cruisers and two destroyers were despatched to Riga, where HMS *Princess Margaret* took on board 350 very relieved Allied and neutral refugees before her captain put on a diplomatic hat and attempted to persuade the German Commander-in-Chief and the High Commissioner to comply with the terms of the armistice and withdraw their occupation forces to the west. They retorted that they had an obligation to remain and impede the arrival of Bolshevik forces but also, para-doxically, that their officers and men – like the Allied officers and men still in uniform – wanted simply to return home. The captain then showed the spirit of the White Ensign when two Lettish regiments mutinied in barracks at Riga. He opened fire on the barracks, ending the mutiny in minutes, although it was plain that the Reds would very shortly take the capital.[6]

With RN shore patrols policing the harbour area, Alexander-Sinclair arrived and embarked Ulmanis and the ministers of his provisional government, convey-ing them to Libau, where they hoped to continue the struggle for independence. The British cruisers and destroyers then set course for home ports as winter was closing down the north Baltic but in London the First Sea Lord was pressing the Cabinet for a more positive stance in the following year. Before the British gov-ernment had come down firmly on one side or the other, a new element entered the equation with the posting to the German Baltic Command of General Gustav Graf Rüdiger von der Golz. Far from a stranger to the Baltic and its tangled ethnic and political scene, he had commanded a German Expeditionary Force in 1918 that supported the Finnish White troops and drove the Reds out of Helsingfors. Since the Inter-Allied Control Commission overseeing the implementation of the Armistice by Germany had originally required German occupation troops in the Baltic states to remain there and prevent the Red Army taking over, Golz decided to exceed his brief and turn the three states with their different roots and languages into German satellites.

Although unsuccessful in this grand design, in 1919 he was to play an important part in defeating the Reds in Latvia and installing a German-biased provisional government that found itself enlisting Estonian occupation forces in northern Latvia to fight both German and Red forces. Instead of fulfilling his mandate to halt the Reds, Golz then attacked the Estonian-Latvian forces, who drove the Germans back. After the peace treaty was signed at Versailles in June 1919, Golz finally ordered a formal withdrawal of all his forces that wished to return home and handed nominal control of the others over to the White Cossack General Pavel Bermont-Avalov, commanding the so-called West Russian Volunteer Army. Despite the name, it was a German cover for a stay-behind force to continue Golz's policy of Germanising the Baltic. The Latvians drove the Volunteer Army into Lithuania, where it was defeated, after which the survivors finally staggered home to Germany.

NOTES

1.   Wilson, pp. 80–1.
2.   In his book *For Them the War Was Not Over: The Royal Navy in Russia 1918–1920*.
3.   The name is a contraction of *schmert shpionam*, meaning 'death to spies'.
4.   D. Boyd, *The French Foreign Legion* (Hersham: Ian Allan, 2010), pp. 313–4.
5.   A.W.S. Agar, *Baltic Episode* (London: Hodder & Stoughton, 1963).
6.   Wilson, pp. 93–5.

22

WHO WON?

Towards the end of 1917 another interventionist force of 1,000 British, Australian, Canadian and New Zealand troops was assembled in western Iran – then called Mesopotamia – under Col Lionel Dunsterville. Dubbed 'Dunsterforce', it had a fleet of 750 vehicles to carry not only the officers and men but also all the supplies they would need to cross more than 300 miles of desert and mountainous terrain between their base at Hamadan and the shores of the Caspian Sea. The objective was not to support a White army, but to seize control of the oilfield there before a Turkish column could arrive or, failing that, destroy it. Riding shotgun were vehicles of the Armoured Car Brigade, some of whose crews had come from Archangel after being transferred from the Admiralty to the Army especially for this mission. At Enzeli (modern Bandar-e Anzali) on the south-western coast of the Caspian, Dunsterforce was intercepted by some 3,000 Reds and driven off. Ignominiously, it retreated back to base, losing men to typhus, cholera and sandfly fever.

In Tiflis, the capital of Georgia, a lonely British consul named Stevens was doing his best to implement the instructions of his government in distant London with the small funds normally available to a consul in a minor post. Suddenly presented with 2.8 million roubles in notes by a King's Messenger from Mesopotamia, he was then supposed, in concert with the commander of the British Military Mission in Tiflis, to distribute this among the Cossack and Armenian forces fighting the Bolsheviks in the Caucasus. This being a rather lawless area, he must have anxiously been awaiting a more positive British presence.[1]

It came when Dunsterville made a second foray with forty armoured cars, leaving Hamadan in June 1918, after being given the temporary rank of major general. In a complete volte-face, this time the British troops were *invited* by the Bolsheviks in Baku to help the garrison of 10,000 Reds and Armenians to hold off a large

Turkish-Azeri force that threatened the town. However, whilst they were still on their way in July there was a *coup d'état* against the Bolshevik commissars, setting up the Diktatura Tsentrokaspia or Central Caspian Dictatorship. The dictators who thus replaced the Bolshevik commissars were Socialist Revolutionaries who disagreed with Lenin's increasingly extreme policies. Something of the confusion surrounding this mission from then on may be gleaned from these extracts from Dunsterville's diary. The first was written in Baku while under siege by the Turks:[2]

September 1st 1918

The five dictators Yermakov, Lemlin, Verluntz and two others are as weak as water. They are all young, about 25 to 30 and I do not believe in councils without grey-beards. There is no order, discipline or organisation among the troops. They retire whenever the enemy attack, and my troops are annihilated owing to failure of support. I told some Armenian troops to occupy a position already prepared and they refused to go, because the enemy were about to attack it. Yesterday a regiment was ordered to the front. They held a meeting to decide whether to go or not. The votes were 30 per cent for and 70 per cent against. The 30 per cent were real stout fellows, and opened fire on the 70 per cent to punish them or compel them to go. The bullets whizzed near one of our armoured cars whose driver telephoned their Commander, saying, 'If they don't stop I shall open fire on the lot of them.' The Commander replied, 'Please do!'

Baku town and port are shelled a good deal by day and night, but the inhabitants are getting accustomed to it. I did not like the risk of having (our HQ steamer) moored beside the big ammunition dump on the wharf so I wrote an urgent note (requesting) its removal. While writing, a shell exploded absolutely in the middle of it, smashing open a case of shells and wounding slightly two sentries but nothing more.

Today the Turks captured Diga without much difficulty, though Diga was a strong point that should have put up a stout defence. The Turks go from success to success and God only knows why they do not walk straight into the town. If only I had troops for a counter-attack I could destroy the whole lot of them. Unless they have the bad luck to come against a detachment of my brave 900 (Warwicks, Worcesters, North Staffords, Gloucesters) they just come through without casualties. Casualties in the town from their artillery are so far almost nil. The question is how to save the wretched population from the impending massacre – all these women and children (some 80,000 of them, I suppose). I called a meeting in the Hotel d'Europe, of the dictators, the Fleet, the Army, and the Armenian National Council and I exploded on them the following bomb: 'The facts are as follows. My troops are the only ones fighting. They are only 900 and no more reinforcements are coming. The Turks can enter the town whenever they have the pluck to come straight in. The (Russian and Armenian) troops go from bad to worse. I was present at a War Council last night when the general's plans were overridden by a common sailor. This morning when Binagardi Hill was taken, a small counter-attack could have retaken it, but I found the entire citizen army loafing back in Baku with their hands in their pockets and their backs to the enemy. I will no longer throw away in vain the lives of my brave soldiers. So I am about to withdraw my troops entirely and leave Baku to its fate. I will hold on till tomorrow to give you a chance of negotiations. Send at once, under a flag of truce, an offer to surrender the town to the enemy intact, asking for 48 hours to remove all the women and children and our British forces from Baku first. Tell them, if terms are refused, their losses will be heavy and we shall destroy the power stations and the machinery that pumps the oil to Batum – which is the only thing here worth capturing. So all their efforts will have been in vain.'

They knew that what I said was true, yet none had dared to put it in words. After rather bitter remarks were thrown at my head, I left them to talk among themselves and went off to see the C-in-C and the War Minister who agreed with me. They went on talking all night and eventually decided to continue the defence. I am glad, because every day we hold out is of great value to the Allies, but I fear for the civil population in the dreadful sauve-qui-peut which I foresee.[3]

Two weeks later, Dunsterville did pull out to save more pointless casualties:

September 15th
Here we are, on the *Kruger*, steaming back to Enzeli with the remnant of the brave 39th Brigade. The final assault of the Turks began at 4 a.m. yesterday, by 11 a.m. they were holding the heights above the town and soon after were driving in our right. Our troops fought magnificently and their 800 rifles coupled with our artillery and the local artillery under our control – about forty guns – bore the whole brunt of the battle against, perhaps, 7,000 Turks. The armoured cars too, did splendid work. At 4 p.m. I learnt that the Baku troops were as usual retiring, instead of fighting, and leaving my troops exposed. I, accordingly, sent Bray with a note to the dictators informing them that now the situation was definitely lost, I proposed to embark my troops as soon as it was dark and sail for Enzeli. Bray found the commissars in a state of bewilderment and they practically said, 'Do what you please.'

At 10 p.m. we were just ready to sail, when dictators Lemlin and Sadovsky came on board with orders for me to send my troops back to their positions and not to sail till I got their permission. I decided to risk it, and ordered each ship to move off independently for Enzeli, showing no lights. If pulled up by a gun-boat for instance, they were to halt and parley. So far, I do not know the fate of the other vessels. At 1 a.m. I was on the bridge with the Captain and the Commodore as we tried to creep by the guardship, but she twigged us and gave three whistles to stop. We answered three whistles which meant compliance; and then went full speed ahead.

She was at anchor so unable to chase, but she opened fire as long as we were in range, to no effect. And here we are in this beautiful scenery, moving merrily with a light breeze over a rippling sea as if there were never any wars in the world. I sent a very strong wire to Baghdad and the War Office, pointing out that their policy (in the Middle East) was a bad one. They object to my impertinent criticisms, and state they would remove me from my command if they could do so, but they cannot.

I think the intention of the Baku dictators was for us to do all the fighting and then use us as a pawn (with the Turks): 'We will surrender to you the British General Staff, etc, etc.'

I was very anxious indeed about the other boats and thanked God when I found all in the harbour at Enzeli, except the little Armenian one, which Col. Rawlinson had left loaded up with ammunition from the Arsenal.

September 16th

Received a wire telling me to return to Baghdad. I am not offended. I have done excellent work under trying conditions, and produced very good results out of nothing in spite of apathy and misunderstanding of War Office and Baghdad. But after my telegrams they had no course but to relieve me and to try me, I suppose by Court Martial. Thank God Rawlinson and his little steamer arrived safely after having run a heavy gauntlet of fire. Armenian refugees a great problem.[4]

The last sentence is a reference to the thousands of Armenian refugees who had escaped the genocide in Turkey and followed Dunsterforce back to Hamadan, rather than face the Islamic Turks and Azeris at the fall of Baku. There were other British ventures in the Caspian area, including a Royal Navy flotilla of requisitioned ships backed by RAF aircraft that totalled more than 1,000 officers and men – all of which proved pointless when, less than two months later, the Turks withdrew after the General Armistice. Arguments were then raised at the Admiralty that men should be sent back to the Caspian to seize the ships which had been handed over to General Denikin's army in order to prevent Russian penetration into India. The part of Churchill in this scheme was played by the First Sea Lord, Admiral Sir David Beatty. Happily, the British Cabinet vetoed the idea.

Inside Russia, one of a number of spontaneous rebellions against the Bolsheviks came in the Tambov region, 300 miles south-east of Moscow, where

Lenin's *prodrazvyorstka* programme of forcible requisitions of grain and other foodstuffs was increased by 50 per cent in 1920. This meant death by starvation for many of the peasants who had produced the grain. On 19 August, after a Red Army unit applying the new regulations used exceptional violence against the population of a small town in the region, a political group calling itself Soyuz Trudovovo Krestyanstva, or Union of Working Peasants, set up a local constituent assembly that abolished Bolshevik power, restored civil liberties and, most critically of all, returned the land and crops to the peasants. To fight off the Red Army, by October it had assembled 50,000 peasants, many of whom had fought on the Russian fronts, aided by many deserters from the Reds. This force was designated the Tambov Blue Army, to distinguish it at various times from Red and White forces, the Polish Blue Army, the Green Army of Ukrainian nationalists and the Black Army of Russian and Ukrainian anarchists that made a rainbow of death hovering over their blighted land. In January 1921 similar peasant revolts broke out in Samara, Saratov, Tsaritsyn and elsewhere. By then the Tambov army numbered 70,000 men and had successfully kept the Reds at bay for some months.

Since the Polish-Soviet war had ended and General Wrangel was defeated, Trotsky unleashed 100,000 Reds on the Tambov rebels, using heavy artillery and armoured trains against men armed only with personal weapons. Frequent executions of civilians launched a reign of terror and special Cheka detachments used poison gas to kill the guerrillas hiding in the forests. This chemical warfare continued for at least three months. Some 50,000 civilian 'enemies of the people' were interned in seven concentration camps with a very high mortality rate from malnutrition, but total losses among the population of the area were estimated to be four or five times higher than this. The following month Moscow announced the end of the *prodrazvyorstka*, replacing it with a new policy of *prodnalog*, which taxed the peasants, rather than the punitive requisitions. So the Tambov peasants could be said to have won their war. The facts were subsequently repressed in the Soviet Union until brought to light again by a local historian in 1982.

More alarming to the Bolshevik leadership was a rebellion by soldiers and sailors who had been among their most faithful supporters during the October Revolution. In sympathy with widespread strikes and demonstrations against the famine and epidemics caused by the government's failure to provide basic food for the civilian population, and for the Bolsheviks restricting political freedom and placing all workers under military law, the garrison of the island fortress of Kronstadt in the Gulf of Finland formed a Provisional Revolutionary Committee in March 1921.

The 10,000 sailors and 4,000 soldiers on the island demanded an end to the Bolsheviks' monopoly of power, the release from prison of other socialists, and the establishment of political freedom and civil rights. The Bolsheviks responded by accusing the rebels of being in foreign pay. Had this been true, the revolt would have taken place a few weeks later after the thaw when Kronstadt was a defensible island that could have been re-supplied from abroad by sea. With the island joined to the mainland by thick ice, Trotsky despatched 60,000 Red troops to put down the rebellion, with political commissars manning machine guns in the rear to force them onto the ice, which was swept continually by the garrison's machine guns. On 17 March, when the Bolshevik forces finally entered Kronstadt citadel, a few rebels managed to escape across the ice to Finland, causing a major problem for the newly independent Finnish state, whose government had to decide what to do with asylum-seekers. For those who did not get away, casualties were heavy, with captured rebels summarily executed or sent to prison camps set up by Dzherzhinsky.[5]

As the Tambov rebels and the Kronstadt garrison learned too late, the Bolsheviks occupying all seats in the Soviet of People's Commissars and key posts at every level of government made the Russian Soviet Federated Socialist Republic a dictatorship. Trotsky's eventual victory over all the other elements in the civil war had nothing to do with popular support and was mainly due to the Red Army's brutally established control of European Russia, in which it could be deployed and coordinated far more easily than the several White armies on the periphery of the old empire, separated from each another by thousands of miles. It was nevertheless an amazing military achievement for a civilian – and ultimately the cause of Trotsky's assassination. He knew too much about Stalin and was too important to be allowed to live and possibly return to Russia one day.

The uprising at Kronstadt by men who had been the Bolsheviks' strongest supporters made Lenin realise that his rigid adherence to the doctrine of war Communism had not only brought the national economy to the brink of meltdown, but also provoked a real danger of a concerted counter-revolution, kept at bay only by a perpetual reign of terror. Accordingly, at the Tenth Party congress in March 1921 he unveiled the New Economic Policy (NEP), under which most agriculture, retail trade, and small-scale light industry was returned to private hands, with the state retaining control of heavy industry, transport, banking, and foreign trade. Entrepreneurs who took advantage of this to start up small businesses and farms were known as *nepmen*. Money, which had been abolished under war Communism, was also re-introduced. The peasants were again allowed to own and cultivate land – and pay taxes for the privilege. What the public was not told, was that Lenin only intended it as a temporary expedient to re-boot the economy and give the Party time to consolidate its power.

Lenin and Trotsky had assumed that the success of their revolution would light a powder train, igniting fires of rebellion worldwide. On the night of 7–8 November 1918 King Ludwig III of Bavaria was deposed by a Red coup. Its leader, Kurt Eisner was assassinated three months later, after which the Bavarian revolutionary committees carried out a Red Terror purge of enemies and imposed a short-lived soviet republic, which was repressed by federal German troops in May 1919, following which a backlash White Terror was unleashed against the defeated Communists.

Just five days after the Bavarian coup, with Serbian, Czech and Romanian troops occupying two-thirds of Hungary, the rump was declared a soviet republic on 21 March 1919, under a government led by Béla Kun. Born Béla Kohen, he had been captured in Hungarian uniform in 1916 and stayed in Russia after the Revolution to become an agent of the Cheka, sharing with his sadistic mistress Razalia Zemlyachka the distinction of personally killing 50,000 White officers who had surrendered. Many were burned alive or drowned in barges deliberately sunk with them battened down below decks while Kun and Zemlyachka watched.[6]

Kun created a Hungarian Red Army that reconquered much of the territory lost to the neighbouring states, at the same time eliminating all political opposition in his own Red Terror. He alienated the peasantry by confiscating private estates for the state instead of distributing the land to those who lived and worked on it. That same month of March, Lenin inaugurated the Communist International or Comintern to control the Communist parties outside Russia, and Kun pushed his way into a position of eminence there, despite Lenin's mistrust of him. Lenin rarely demonstrated humour, but in this case he referred to the pushy Hungarian's 'kuneries' – a pun on the French word *connerie*, meaning 'crass stupidity'.[7] When Soviet reinforcements that Kun had been promised for a revenge invasion of Czechoslovakia failed to arrive, the Hungarian economy came to a standstill and food distribution ceased. Having lost any vestige of popular support, Kun's brief but bloody regime ended on the second day of August. To save his life, he fled to Vienna and led other unsuccessful coups in Germany and Austria during the 1920s before fleeing to the Soviet Union, where he was accused of Trotskyist deviation and eliminated in Stalin's purges before the Second World War.

Although in Ukraine guerrilla bands continued for years to harass Bolshevik occupation forces, once Russia itself was secured Trotsky cast his net wider. After the Turkish surrender to the Entente in 1918, the three Transcaucasian republics of Azerbaijan, Armenia and Georgia enjoyed temporary freedom, but this did not suit Bolshevik plans. In April 1920 the Azerbaijan government surrendered to the Red Army. In December 1920 the former Caucasian *oblast* of eastern Armenia was incorporated into Soviet Russia, and the short-lived Republic of Western Armenia handed back to Turkey. During February to April 1921 the Red Army invaded and reconquered Georgia, Stalin's homeland.

In Central Asia, the October Revolution had prompted Uzbek Muslim nationalists to declare autonomy, terminated by the Red Army in February 1918. This sparked a prolonged anti-Russian resistance movement, despite which the emir of Bukhara and the khan of Khiva were deposed in 1920, so that by the end of 1921 Communist puppets controlled the region under Moscow's firm hand. In neighbouring Turkmenistan, too, Soviet rule was imposed by force. In Kazakhstan, the Red Army drove out White forces and easily overcame a provisional government established after the demise of the tsarist regime. Here also, a Communist puppet government was imposed in August 1920 – after which, as in other Central Asian republics, a Moscow-imposed influx of Russian settlers changed the demography for ever.

A mere five years after the October Revolution, the Russian empire existed again – at the cost of millions of lives and the loss of ethnic and political identity for millions more that would last three generations. On 30 December 1922, the four soviet republics united in the Union of Soviet Socialist Republics. The carefully chosen word *union*, which implied a voluntary association of equals, stopped three generations of Western liberals seeing that the expanding USSR ruled from Moscow was the old tsarist empire re-created in five years of bloodshed, starvation and chaos. Looked at another way, it was the only empire to be amassed in the twentieth century.

What is the historian to make of the sacrifices and suffering of the quarter-million men who fought in the interventionist contingents after the Brest-Litovsk armistice? Few of the rank-and-file or even the officers had any clear idea of why they were there. Those who had enlisted or been conscripted 'for hostilities only' desperately wanted to get back to their homes and families, and pick up the pieces of their interrupted lives. Even the interventionist politicians cannot have sincerely wanted to re-establish autocratic rule over the former Russian Empire by a royal successor to Nicholas II. Yet, under Lenin's deliberately confusing title 'dictatorship of the proletariat', autocratic rule is exactly what the surviving inhabitants of the former tsarist empire lived through under the Bolshevik and Communist governments. From a historical point of view, all the fine speeches of the interventionist politicians and all the suffering their ventures imposed on millions of inhabitants of the huge territory over which this bloodshed was spread achieved one thing only: to drag out the pointless killing for longer.

Bruce Lockhart said it as well as anybody:

The consequences of this ill-considered venture were to be disastrous both to our prestige and to the fortunes of those Russians who supported us. It raised hopes which could not be fulfilled. It intensified the civil war and sent thousands of Russians to their deaths.[8]

So who did win the *other* First World War? The real winners – as in all wars – were the arms manufacturers, for whom the protracted civil war came as a bonus.

Militarily, the Central Powers, Bulgaria and Turkey won, but their victory only lasted eight months.

The long-term winners were the Bolshevik leaders. The war enabled them to seize power in a country devoid of authority, so that no armed uprising was necessary against a strong government. Thanks to the Germans' deniable dirty trick, they were able to eliminate political opposition, after which the Allied interventions furnished them with the 'justification' ruthlessly to root out every vestige of real or imagined resistance to their reign of terror and brutally extinguish any spark of democracy for seven miserable decades.

So, did the western and Japanese interventions in Russia achieve *anything*? No intelligent military mind would have launched what amounted to a war on several discrete fronts separated by thousands of miles. The spurious justification was that the Allied interventions were 'to protect the billion dollarsworth of materiel' and prevent it being handed over to the Germans. Yet that alibi was overtaken by events in March 1918. In any case, would not a better way of achieving the same ends have been to send in small fast-moving task forces to sabotage and/or blow it all up and get out fast afterwards? So why get involved in a slugging match that could not be won?

The only incontrovertible result of the Allied interventions 1918–22 was to earn the participants seventy years of justified Russian hostility. During the Second World War, when officially the Moscow regime was the ally of London and Washington, Stalin took especial pleasure in alienating President Franklin Roosevelt from Churchill, whom he regarded as the arch interventionist. This split between the two main Western Allies had the direst results for the peoples of Eastern Europe and the Balkans.

Interventions by foreign powers rarely do seem to achieve the professed aims of those who launch them. Despite millions of combatant and civilian deaths, the American intervention in Vietnam did not prevent the country going Communist. The Soviet intervention in Afghanistan 1979–89 only set the scene for the equally unsuccessful UK–USA intervention launched in 2001. The massive Allied intervention in Iraq of 2003 destabilised the entire Gulf region, which was surely not the intention. It is almost as though von Clausewitz's dictum that no campaign plan survives first contact with the enemy's main force has a corollary: that any military intervention by foreign powers has an at least equal chance of achieving the opposite of their professed intentions.

NOTES

1. Occleshaw, p. 45.
2. Major General L. Dunsterville, *The Adventures of Dunsterforce* (London: Edward Arnold, 1920), pp. 277–81.
3. Ibid.
4. Ibid.
5. J. Carmichael, *Russia, An Illustrated History* (New York: Hippocrene Books, 1991), pp. 204–5.
6. D. Rayfield, *Stalin and His Hangmen* (London: Penguin, 2007), p. 80.
7. Service, *Stalin*, p. 175.
8. Lockhart, p. 311.

ACKNOWLEDGEMENTS

So many people have contributed over the years to this book that it would be impossible to name them all, even if they were all alive.

Just to pick out the more recent, I should like to thank Stella Dvořákova, William Sirben and the resources of Český Rozhlas 7 – Radio Praha for the Czech memoirs; that doyen of Portuguese translators Miguel Mata was, as ever, a fund of information on matters military; my artist friend Jennifer Weller once again emerged from her stained glass studio to undertake the mundane task of drawing maps for me; and Atarah Ben-Tovim lived through another year with a historian – which might be defined as a person who is always somewhere and sometime else.

At The History Press, I should like to thank: Mark Beynon, who first talked this book out of me; my publisher Jo De Vries, who commissioned the work; project editor Rebecca Newton; editor Peter Stafford; proofreader Tony Williams; designer Jemma Cox.

ABOUT NOTES AND SOURCES

1. All translations are by the author, unless otherwise attributed.
2. Place names are transliterated to give the closest approximation to actual pronunciation.
3. Personal names are transliterated from Cyrillic script, but where a person is widely known by an English form of his name, that is used instead, e.g. Tsar Nicholas II, but Grand Duke Nikolai, his uncle. Patronymics and their initials have been ignored.
4. All illustrations are from the author's collection.
5. Every effort has been made to trace copyright owners. In the event of any infringement, please communicate with the author, care of the publisher.

INDEX

Visit our website and discover thousands of other History Press books.

www.thehistorypress.co.uk